Situational Awareness at Home and Personal

Mark LeClair

Mark LeClair

CONTENTS

Situational Awareness at Home and Personal

1

WHAT IS AWARENESS?

Awareness...the Merriam-Webster dictionary defines it as: "the quality or state of being aware: knowledge and understanding that something is happening or exists"(i) (2022). This is important to grasp because most, that's correct: MOST people exist within a false sense of awareness. Unfortunately, it is because of this fact, that if/when those people experience a traumatic environment, they quickly become victims.

I've taught many thousands of people, from all walks of life and in many different subjects, and the experience has highlighted a severe problem in our society: being too comfortable. An example of a negative end result is as follows: If you were to go home and your front door was wide open and your entire house was emptied, you would forever be paranoid (maybe a little, maybe a lot) that it would/could happen again to you. If you gain the education on awareness and preparation and you came home to a ransacked home, you would be angry that your planning and efforts for security were breached, thus rethinking and executing a better plan (and lessen the possibility/chances you would become paranoid).

What does that mean?

The second scenario means you would rethink your security protocols, then find the weak points and fix it so it doesn't occur again. In the first scenario, the victimization and assault on your personal space is something that makes you fearful it will occur again. The second scenario helps you take ownership that your security was breached because you missed something in your efforts to safeguard your home. The second scenario doesn't increase the paranoia of the person, it motivates them to find the weakness/deficiency and fix it.

Now, I'm sure many would respond negatively to that assessment because they feel they are well prepared and super-aware! Sadly, they are wrong. Very, very wrong. So why would people walk around with such a lack of awareness? Why is awareness important? Why should someone make an effort to safeguard their home? All valid questions, but so many avoid asking them. Is it fear of hearing the truth, because it may counter their reality? Is it ego? Is it ignorance? Is it a combination of everything mentioned? Again, all good questions.

Awareness, to put it in the most simplistic way possible, is: opening your eyes to what is around you, taking in the people, smells, sounds, and self-identifying where you are in the location you currently exist. This means your vision is up and about, not buried inside your phone. That, simply put, is awareness.

HEAD IN THE SAND SYNDROME

The head in the sand syndrome is a very real thing. I've experienced it in many locations and each time I did, I was blown away at the level of commitment those people had with that concept. Head in the sand syndrome means people believe that nothing bad is currently happening on their front stoop, so why should they have to worry about something bad possibly happening to them, ever? It's hasn't happened to me, so it will never happen to me! That's another whopper of a concept. One that will quickly create victims.

Awareness in your home does begin with you. It doesn't matter if your home is a house, a condo or an apartment. Security and awareness could save your life and the lives of your loved ones. If that's not an important aspect to your life, then I suppose nothing that is said will actually reach you. Sadly, some refuse to embrace safety and awareness

in their home, and it is those people who will scream the loudest if/
when bad things arrive on their doorstep, or worse, hiding inside their
home.

Awareness doesn't mean investing money you don't have. Awareness
does not have to cost a lot of money. In many cases, it takes minimal
finances (some solutions are free) to safeguard a home against intruders.
There may be some investment needed, because some items should not
be skimped on, and depending on where you live, it could decrease the
chances that your house becomes a target. Some have to learn the hard
way, that going the cheaper route will not complete the job as they had
hoped, and the impact ends up much worse than it has to be.

Alas, I have always embraced the thought that I cannot reach everyone. I want to. I try to. I hope to, but there is no chance that everyone
would suddenly see and acknowledge the personal benefit of becoming
more aware. Again, I have taught for a long time and have done so with
the intention of helping others avoid becoming the victim. My goal has
always been to help others avoid a traumatic experience that can be
avoided. These attempts were to also attempt to reduce needless deaths.
Can lead a horse to water, but cannot make them drink.

COLOR CODES OF AWARENESS

What is awareness? You've read the definition and the simplified
explanation, but what does it actually mean to the average person? It
means paying more attention to your environment and not your phone.
It means walking with your head up and paying attention to oddities
around you, which could become possible threats. There is a color code
chart that exists, which outlines different levels of awareness. There are
a couple variations online, but the importance lies with knowing what
the colors mean and where you are amidst the colored parameters.

The color code of awareness broken down, is as follows:

WHITE: This level is the lowest level of awareness in existence. This
level means zero awareness of your surroundings. An example of the

White Level of Awareness, is when you are consumed with something on your phone and no attention to what's occurring around you. Being at home, for some, means being at this level of awareness. Why? It's that false sense of safety and security of being inside your own home and knowing no one else has a right to be there uninvited. Not a level you want to remain in.

When would it be okay? When in a secure location, such as your home, that has had safety protocols and equipment installed, that are actually implemented. That, in itself, relaxes the person and allows them to comfortably reside in that location under condition white. Even at home, though, it is only appropriate to 'live in White' if you have created your safety protocol and conduct the practices mentioned within this book.

After you read this book, you will have a much better understanding of what will keep you safe and secure in your home. It also prompts you to create your own Standard Operating Procedures (SOP) for 'what-if' scenarios. Once those protocols are put in place, being in the White stage of awareness has a different meaning, because if something were to occur, you would then have a plan that works, to counter the situation(s) presented.

YELLOW: The yellow level of awareness is when you are in a location you are familiar with, know the people with you and are alert to the things around you. This can be while you're at home because you are paying attention to your environment. This is the level of awareness I impress others to remain. This level grooms you to carry that awareness to every/any location you travel. Being alert increases the chances of you being safer (and prepared) if something unexpected were to occur.

ORANGE: The Orange level of awareness is: when you are in a location you are unfamiliar with and unsure of the possible hazards. You pay closer attention to possible threats, and your environment. At this level, the person is more alert and may identify possible threats, or a threatening environment unfolding. A possible threat could just be something, or someone, out of place for that location. It could also be a suspicious vehicle parked two houses down in your neighborhood, and no one seems to address it. Being in the Orange level of awareness also means preparing to act on a threatening scenario because it cannot be avoided.

Condition Orange is where you solidify the possible plans in your mind, if things begin to get dangerous. At home will be different than outside your home (such as at the mall, coffee shop, or restaurant) because you (should) know your home well enough to have your 'Plan B' executed, if needed. An example of this could be: you're at home and notice someone walking slowly by your home. The unknown person stares at your home as they walk by. They disappear for a moment and slowly walk by the other way, but this time they are on your lawn as they walk slowly across your property. This is where you would consider your options for action, before it is needed. This moves us into:

RED: The Red level of awareness means action is needed because the threat is imminent. Imminent means something is going to happen (versus 'might' happen). This is where being aware and having a plan could save you. Consciously, those without a plan may freeze in such situations. Why? They freeze because they do not have a plan, and it is 'data overload' for their brain when a traumatic event occurs. Those who practice awareness and gain the understanding of each level have a much better chance at survival, because they have (or create) a plan everywhere they go. These same people are also more prepared to act out their plan when they are in condition orange, anticipating the situation to turn Red. Red is action. Red is activating your plan for survival.

An example, piggy-backing on the Orange level example, (the strange person pacing in front of your house, last time he was walking closer to your home, on your property as he walked by): Again, that person disappears, only to reappear and sprint straight to your front door. He violently shakes your doorknob, trying to gain access to your home and you. This situation has escalated, this is when you enact your plan. If you were not aware, this is where fear could freeze you in place, due to the situation.

BLACK: Jeff Cooper had come up with the color codes of awareness and did not include Black as a level. The Black level of awareness is when you are in the actual fight, and trying to save your life. Condition Black can be achieved with training and practice, but practice and training are necessary (please reread that again).

In the event you have to defend yourself, how are you going to do it? What training do you have in such situations? What training do you perform on an ongoing basis? Why is this important? If you don't have any training in you, if you were to encounter a life-threatening situation, what are the chances you will figure it out at that very moment? If you are honest with yourself, you shouldn't say that you'd be prepared without the education, or defensive training investment. If you are honest, that is. Condition Black is embedded actions, which you have practiced often enough to create what some call: 'muscle-memory'.

There have been numerous arguments/discussions regarding the term 'muscle-memory', because some do not believe actions can be trained into muscles. If you were to shut down consciously due to a traumatic event occurring in front of you, you would have nothing to rely on to save you from the occurrence. I suppose an easy way to relate this concept to each reader could be with driving. If you never learned how to drive and you decided to get into a vehicle that was running and drive off with it, if a car were to pull out in front of you, what would be the result? If you were a seasoned/experienced driver, you would probably swerve while either braking or accelerating. If you were never taught how to drive and do not have any practical experience with a motorized vehicle, you would probably freeze and slam into the car.

RUN / HIDE / FIGHT

Each person needs to make decisions in their life, each day, multiple times each day. The same is true for personal safety and defense. You MUST make the decision to run, if you think you need to escape the situation. You MUST make the decision to hide from a violent encounter, if you want to survive. You MUST (and this is an important one to embrace) make the decision to fight, if you desire to live through a violent encounter. This is why training, and gaining the education on personal safety is important.

The term: 'Hesitation kills' is appropriate here. If you hesitate when a threat is sprinting towards you, if you cannot make the decision to run, hide or fight, that threat will not take it easy on you when they arrive at your location. The threat doesn't know you, they don't care about you, they don't know/care about your story, they only want to fulfil their objective, and allowing you to stop them is not part of their success plan. You have to make that decision. This is why the Color Codes of Awareness are important to implement.

MAKE THE CHOICE

Most of the us try to do right by others, to not deliberately hurt anyone, and we try to follow the laws. With how we were/are raised, mentorship and guidance from others, most of us try to be peaceful and not cause problems with anyone else. We especially avoid being violent with anyone. This is where you need to give yourself permission to defend yourself by any means necessary. You must embrace the fact that you may need to be violent against an attacker, to survive the encounter. True, we do not try to harm others because we know it is not the right thing to do, but what happens when someone tries to assault us?

If you do not give yourself permission to apply needed aggression against an attacker(s), you are setting yourself up to be the victim (and possibly the dead victim). There are numerous soft spots, opportunity locations for you to target when under duress. The goal is to be able to break contact with an attacker, so you can run away to get help (but survive the attack). You have tools at your disposal: cell phone, fist, flashlight, keys, etc. and you can easily jab those tools into opportunity locations, to escape the situation.

If you can give yourself permission to defend yourself by any means possible against another human being, then you have a chance at survival. Opportunity locations include: eyes, nose, underneath the jaw, behind the ears, ribs, knees, armpits, the throat and the groin. The attacker has obviously made the conscious decision to harm you, now it's your turn to defend yourself by any means necessary, but only to escape contact from your attacker. This means if the attacker is down, you cannot/should not continue kicking or hitting (or anything else) the attacker, because the attacker is no longer a threat to you.

There have been too many stories that have surfaced, of females who willingly entered a vehicle because her attacker had a knife on her, or a gun in her side, and the female figured if she got into the car and did what her attacker said, she would survive. The statistics are gruesome, on those who got into the vehicles. Outside the vehicle is your last attempt at survival. If you get into the car, statistically you are never going to be seen alive again.

STATISTICS

Below are some statistics take from the FBI's Crime Data Reporter (ii) portal:

Property Crimes in the U.S.: In 2016 7.9 million; in 2017 7.7 million; in 2018 7.2 million; 2019 7 million; and 2020 6.5 million crimes.

Robberies: 2020 over 31% of robberies occurred on streets and/or highways. 17% occurred at homes; 17.5 at residences; 7.5% convenience stores; 3.75 at gas stations; 1.1% at banks; and 22% at misc. locations.

Violent Crimes: 2016 1.3 million; 2017 1.2 million; 2018 1.21 million; 2019 1.21 million; and 2020 1.3 million violent crimes.

Home Invasion Statistics (iii):

An average of 12% are planned in advance; approximately 2.5 million burglaries annually (with over 65% being break-ins of the home); 65% of the criminals are familiar with those they rob; every minute in the

U.S. approximately 3 burglaries take place; 85% of home invasions are NOT conducted by professional criminals; 62% occur during daylight hours; approximately 17% of home in the U.S. have a security system installed; approximately 7% of home burglaries are violent; a home without a security system in place is 3 times more likely to be targeted and burglarized; more than a third of the burglars questioned admitted a barking dog would deter them from breaking into a home; burglaries are most commonly committed during the summer; over a third of burglars entered the property using the front door; approximately half of the burglars admitted they would not progress with burglarizing a home if they heard a noise inside; over 36% of all burglaries happen with unlawful entry; only approximately 13% of burglaries end in arrest of the criminal.

'I'M PREPARED'

I have met entirely too many people who carry with them a false sense of security and truly believe, if and when the time arrives to defend against a violent attacker, they would be successful because they carry a [insert defensive tool here]. I have met entirely too many people who carry concealed, who believe they don't need defensive training and actually think they would be accurate and efficient (on target) during a violent encounter. This mindset only creates victims (if they survive) and/or customers for funeral homes.

Carrying a [again, insert defensive tool here] does not solidify your ability to adequately defend against an intruder, or multiple attackers. If anything, with some of these people, this mindset makes them a danger to those in the vicinity of this person if they have to use their defensive tool. This is definitely a hard pill for these people to swallow because it dents their egos a bit. Yes, I have hurt some feelings, but ignorance is not a defense. Not realizing you don't have the training, or skills to be confident and completely accurate against an attacker, can never be a valid defense for anyone.

Yet they exist all around us. I have tried to educate some of these people and it was quickly met with a defensive, almost arrogant, retort. I have heard:

-I was military
-I was a security guard
-I've hunted my whole life
-My dad was SWAT
-My uncle was a SEAL
-I've carried a gun since I was 18
-I've always hit the target when I shoot
-My dad was military
-I was a police officer
-My dad was a police officer
-I have a lot of guns
-I shoot competitively

First, let me dispel the rumor that many people have thought: Just because someone was in the military, doesn't mean they are a decent shot. It doesn't mean they know how to use a firearm. It doesn't mean they can effectively neutralize a situation, or a threat, if the moment arrived. It doesn't mean they are uber-safe with a firearm. It doesn't mean they can defend themselves on a minor level. For some in the military, they shoot once to get their ribbons and that's the extent of their capabilities.

Now, same thing goes for most of the others on the above list. I have trained military, law enforcement: local, state and federal, as well as many other organizations. A lot of training. Does that mean that I'm a perfect shot? Not at all, which is why I train, train, train, and then train some more. I was military. I was in Special Warfare. I was a certified instructor for many disciplines AND I was certified to certify instructors. So what? That's all accomplishments, but without ongoing training and practice, that skill depletes over time.

I know what you're thinking: but my uncle was a [insert some cool title here] and he taught me how to shoot and I hit the target. That's awesome! Good for you...but...was the target attacking you? Was the target advancing on you? Were there multiple targets? Were they moving? Were you enclosed in an area with innocent, frantic people around you? Did you have to draw from a concealed location? Were people yelling and screaming around you? Were frantic people scrambling around you to get away from the threat(s)? All important questions.

I have seen many types: good and bad, those who were convinced they were prepared to defend themselves, but couldn't hit their target accurately (or at all), and those who were prepared adequately. Being realistic is important for self-preservation and security of your loved ones. Without being realistic, innocent people can and will get hurt. Training equals being better prepared when bad things happen. Why do you need to know this in your home? Why is this important when you feel completely safe inside your home (plus no one has a right to enter your home without permission, right)? Right?

It is because of the copious amount of information that exists under the subject of situational awareness, that it would be entirely too much information for one person, at one time. Another book will be in the works for safety and awareness outside of the home, which will also have an abundance of information in it, but will focus on outside the home topics. I'm not doing this to make more money, I'm doing this to benefit the reader.

Awareness and capability at home increases your odds at successful defensive action, be it with or without a firearm. Being prepared means training for contingencies. Those who have sat in on my classes and seminars have heard me say many times: if there is one bad person present, there are three. This means that I don't/won't let my guard down until the situation is completely neutralized. I will assume there is always more than one attacker, because that will allow me to not drop my guard, and not celebrate early. Celebrating early makes you vulnerable.

Most people do not carry a firearm while they are inside their own home (but some do). One shouldn't have to carry while inside their home, but should be prepared to defend themselves if an attack is initiated. How does one do that? First, it is important to set yourself up for success, which is the purpose of this book. Being aware and being prepared are two separate line items, but taking the steps towards being prepared and increasing your awareness are not hard to achieve, but does take effort.

It does not matter what someone has done in the military or as a career choice, without proper training and ongoing practice, the skill needed to defend oneself against multiple attackers is of vital importance. It should be important to everyone. What shouldn't be a concern, is getting shot by someone who wasn't trained, wasn't prepared but thought they were, who frantically shot at an attacker with zero control. Can we fix those around us who may have that mindset? Probably not, but we can train ourselves and practice what we need to, to remain safer and more protected and most-importantly: remain aware that these people exist around us.

Why is it important to have awareness in your home? Look out your window right now. That's right, stop reading this, set the book down, stand up and look out your window. Any window. Is there a police officer parked outside your home? Are they standing guard for you? Are they remaining on station to ensure no one breaks into your home and/or hurts you and your family? I'm quite confident in saying the answer would be a resounding no. Am I right? You don't have to actually answer, I know that I am correct in my statement.

Being aware and prepared does not mean you will survive an encounter, but it greatly increases the odds in your favor. Nothing is for sure, especially when it comes to safety, security and awareness. This is something that you must embrace if you want to keep you, and your family, secure and prepared for possibly-deadly scenarios. The main point in looking out your window to see if an officer was parked there, was to drive the point home that if a threat or threats were to invade your home, chances are you are on your own to defend yourself against such an attack.

To leave you with a last little bit of encouragement that you didn't waste your time or money on this book, let me leave you with this: my friend and his wife were murdered in their home by a teenager who was trying to steal his video gaming system. My friend and his wife were at work when the home was broken into, and the alarm company called them. My friend was an Army soldier with combat experience, defensive skills better than most, and always had a defensive mindset. His wife was skilled, but not at his level.

They both arrived at the house and decided to go in, despite seeing the front door wide open. The police had not arrived yet, but they went in instead of waiting for the police. The teenager was armed and hiding inside the home. My friend and his pregnant wife were executed by this teenager, who shot them both in the back of the head. The teenager escaped, but was caught soon after. Regardless of his apprehension, my friend and his wife are dead.

My friend knew better. My friend knew he should wait for the police, but he went in anyway. Was it because the front door was open and he assumed the burglar had left? Was it because the alarm was screeching and he assumed it scared the burglar away? No one will ever know the why, which is a hard pill for many of us to swallow. He was better than that and knew better, yet he went into his home and did not survive that encounter.

My friend is you. My friend is the everyday person who blindly goes through life without realizing their home is being cased-out by burglars. What you do inside/ outside your home matters. What you do for defensive preparation matters. What you do for training matters (and who you choose to train with). How you make your standard operating procedures (SOP) matters. Again, it is all up to you. My goal is to provide you with information that works for your situation (and if it doesn't, it may give you ideas on what would work for your home).

You may think that information changes, and some writers will give a little bit of information so they can sell different volumes of books to the needy readers. I believe in keeping it ethically and morally simple:

Awareness in the home. Awareness outside the home. To add a caveat, I am leaving the possibility of a third book for traveling situations, but that is dependent on how much information I can put into the other book. My pursuit is to provide information without fluff or fillers, while keeping the costs low for the reader.

I will admit that I am guilty of purchasing something because it was the next volume in a series. I was quickly disappointed to see that the writer only changed one portion and regurgitated most of the same information from the previous volumes. This made me angry to think I was duped into thinking it was evolving information, which it was not. It was because the writer is 'famous' in defensive circles, that this person pushed out more volumes and gets readers to invest. To me, that's ethically wrong because it takes advantage of those motivated to continue learning.

This book is for awareness and preparation inside the home. I hope it reaches you, and hope you are not disappointed with the results. I hope it doesn't bore you or cause you to question the information, but if it does, please research what I wrote to verify the information is valid. I would say that to each student I've had, and there's been more than 100k. Enjoy and learn!

I wanted to include my background so the reader can understand my motivation. I joined the Navy at 19 and pursued becoming a Special Warfare Combatant Craft operator (SWCC). This was accomplished in 1996. I loved my job, the people I worked with, the countries I've been to, and the experience/knowledge I gained. I had a couple life threatening parachuting situations, which left me very damaged. I was honorably discharged in 2006.

In my last few years in the Navy, I was responsible for the Armory at my Team in Virginia, and the training on weapons. I created information for our secure website, to be accessed across the globe, on all weapon systems we had, but also information for our Team's page, on the secure net. I conducted training almost daily and loved every moment of it. I left my Team, sadly, in 2006 and had over 2,000 hours of training I had conducted for my teammates.

I then worked for a company that contracted with the U.S. Army on Fort Eustis, in Virginia. The contract was for simulation training with a weapons simulator, which had fantastic technology to train on real weapons, but with laser 'bullets'. There I trained law enforcement (state, local, federal), all branches and other entities. I was able to create the courses that would benefit the group, which was over 1,200 different courses of fire.

At the same time, I had started my own business where I was teaching civilians firearm safety courses, personal safety and awareness seminars and certifying instructors for a national organization. I was a certified instructor and training counselor, and I was teaching almost every day. I began to create personal safety and awareness seminars because the news was reporting attacks, murders and home invasions every night. I thought that someone should do something, to better educate the public and save them from those situations. That someone was me.

Why the book now?

My memory and brain-ability has greatly diminished due to the traumatic brain injuries (TBI) that I incurred during those parachuting situations. I wanted to get information to the masses before my brain-ability got any worse. As much as I would like to think my mind would remain sharp, I have to be realistic about things and embrace the possibilities that lie ahead. This is not a pity-party by any stretch, just an explanation on why I would not string subjects along to make more money. It has never been about the money for me.

I use writing to keep my brain healthy, such as a weightlifter would push weights to get stronger/bigger. Writing is my mental weightlifting. Once I am finished writing my last bit for publishing, I will continue to write screenplays to keep my brain active. These books are to ensure the information I had learned, had taught so many people, does not get lost with my digressing memory. That's the only reason and as much as I hope people buy and learn from my book(s), I know I did my part to offer a valid solution that could save lives. The choice is yours and if you learned something from this book, please spread the word.

I hope you never need any of the information that is contained in this, or any of my books.

Sources:

i: Merriam-Webster. (n.d.). Awareness. In *Merriam-Webster.com dictionary*. Retrieved March 4, 2022, from https://www.merriam-webster.com/dictionary/awareness

ii: Federal Bureau of Investigation (n.d.). Crime Data Explorer. Retrieved March 5th, 2022 from CDE Https://crime-data-explorer.app.cloud.gov/pages/downloads

iii: Policy Advice (Smijanic Stasha, 24 September 2021) 27 Alarming Burglary Statistics for 2021. Retrieved March 5th, 2022, from Https://policyadvice.net/insurance/insights/burglary-statistics/

2

EXTERIOR OF THE HOME

Does it matter if you live in an apartment, a condominium or a house, when it comes to safety and awareness? Depending on where you reside, your options can be limited due to ownership rights. Things change depending on location: security devices, exterior lighting and camera options change, and egress options change for the occupants. Yes, it does matter where you live.

There are many topics that have crossover, where the information works for a house and an apartment, or a house and a condominium. It's important to grasp the information and then apply it to your specific location. For those that live in a house they own, they could do alterations because they own the home, whereas the person(s) that rents an apartment, they do not have that luxury. Grasp the information and apply it to your situation/location. Solutions that are the most cost effective and/or provide the best chance of security success and safety, will present themselves.

The exterior of the home is the beginning for security options, because threats approach from the exterior (it's doubtful a threat will invest the time, money and risk to tunnel their way into your home from underground). This is the area we begin to assess our home's security and vulnerability. Threats evolve, and a key aspect to their plans to initiate illegal actions are: they don't want to get caught! This section begins the discussion on how to make your exterior uninviting to a possible threat and suggestions to make it more secure.

SECURITY CAMERAS

Are you able to install security cameras if you live in an apartment complex? Probably not on the exterior of the apartment, but you can on the inside. Security cameras have evolved nicely and provides the homeowner with a peace of mind and inner strength that their home is more protected. Security cameras and accessibility has increased exponentially, while the pricing remains competitive. It doesn't have to break the bank to be safe and secure.

Many security cameras today have IR capabilities and internal DVRs. Some, if not most at this point, are WIFI accessible and come with an application for your phone, computer and tablets. This allows the user to access any camera at any time from those devices. Some systems have microphones/speakers attached where the homeowner can speak through their camera system and hear the response through their phone or computer system. Technology is incredible.

That being said, it's important to think about the system you need before investing in a security system. As with everything: just because it is expensive, it doesn't mean it is good and just because it's cheap, doesn't mean you should buy it. Do your research, read the reviews and check prices, but make your list first. What goes on the list? Internal or external camera needs, Bluetooth/WIFI information, internal DVR, number of cameras, location of cameras, and so forth. Each person should create a customize list (to include requirements of the home), to then do an accurate search for the appropriate system.

Cameras will need to be wired to a power source, so it would be a good idea to have a licensed electrician install the system's power. If the cameras have Bluetooth/WIFI capability, which most do, it's important that you have a secure WIFI avenue with an unbreakable/un-hackable password. If you do not secure a pathway for your cameras, a hacker could have access to your cameras at any time. Research the security options of each camera to ensure you have added safeguards, to restrict any hacking situation.

Camera systems have DVR boxes that the video records and stores. These systems have options that allow files to be saved onto the DVR, which protects those files from overwrite if the system records on a loop. This means you can check your recordings and if the recordings show no threats or odd visitations, the files will be re-recorded over. These systems work on a loop to save space. If there's a file you want to save, you have the option to save that specific file and protect it while it remains in the system. Recordings will not 'swallow up' that file once it is protected.

Walking around your residence to figure out the best possible location(s) is important. You shouldn't purchase 40 cameras when 4 cameras provide adequate coverage. Look at your home like a burglar or home invader would look at it. This action allows you to conduct an assessment to identify weak areas, or areas of interest for entry. Criminals have something in common with each other...they don't want to get caught. This means: to deter a threat, burglar, and/or invader, you must first think like one.

HOUSES:

For those that live in a house, mounting options are available on the exterior of the home. Now, before I go any further, please read this paragraph multiple times: FAKE CAMERAS may deter a threat for a short time, but eventually it can/will be tested! This means: if you decide to pursue the cheapest route, by installing fake cameras on the exterior of your home, then eventually a motivated burglar will test your security to see how valid your system is. In addition, installing yard signs and window stickers advertising a security alarm or a monitoring company without actually having a system, could end horribly for you, eventually! Read that again and again and then again.

Now that you have read that paragraph enough times to absorb the core message, let us continue.

When thinking like a criminal and assessing your home, where would you assess your home from? Some people ignore the sides of the home because of the location of the neighbor's house, the tree-line is far/close to the house, or no one ever goes to the sides of the home. All bad reasons to avoid thinking about the sides of the house, because I can assure you that criminals are thinking about all aspects of your home. Remember, they don't want to be seen and they don't want to be caught.

Usually, and this depends on the actual layout of the home (design), the corners of the home provide the best vantage point for a camera to capture. Angles are important and depth of recordings are topics to think about. Overlap protection is another topic that should be considered. Does it seem like there's a lot to think about before you even purchase a system? Indeed, there are, but if you put in the time and effort now, you can save yourself some time and money in the future...and possibly your life.

ANGLE OF CAMERA:

The angle of the camera is important because you do not want to restrict the areas to be recorded/watched. If your angle is too low, you give the burglar (from here on out referred to as threat/criminal) the opportunity to get closer to your home and could be increasing their probability of success in the invasion. You want to avoid providing threats with an opportunity to get closer to your home. The closer they can get, the more data they can collect.

If the angle you choose is too high, you run the chance of recording the average traffic that may occur on your roadway. This can fill up your DVR faster, and possibly cause an overwrite of previously-recorded video of a threat walking up your driveway. If you are at work, or didn't have time to review/save files you felt were important and the DVR is full, the loop of recording will overwrite previous data. This is why the appropriate angle is important.

What is the 'perfect angle'? Good question, and the layout of your home determines what would be considered appropriate. The angle you should consider is one that can capture any trespasser that breaches inside your property line. Restricting the angle could allow a threat to block the camera with a vehicle, (or by using other tactics) and allow them to get closer to your home. Threats will make it their goal to avoid being caught on camera, while trying to get as close as possible to your home. There are steps you can take before you lock in an installation point and angle. For example:

-Draw a rough sketch of your home, looking down from above.

-Draw the property line around the home.

-Add the road to your drawing, with the distance from your house.

-Include obstructions within your property line (such as trees and bushes).

Once your sketch is drawn, you can take a step back and look at the specifics of your home. It will allow you to draw in camera locations and identify possible hiding spots for a threat. It will also allow you to note the distances that you should identify, which in turn allows you to identify locations that would benefit from a second camera. This is the legwork that will help you out in the long run.

When you draw your cameras, you can then draw their field of view. This is the angle of coverage for that camera (some cameras have greater views, such as 360-degree capture, while other cameras have 90- or 45-degree restrictions). Drawing the angles will show the overlap protection, and/or any areas that may not get coverage due to the distance from corner to corner. All important aspects. Overlap is desired to eliminate opportunity points for a threat to capitalize on.

Many systems today will allow you to set the recording distance on your cameras. This means you can mount your cameras, open the application on your phone (or tablet) and set the distance you want to the camera to begin recording. Depending on your property line and location, the distance will vary. As an example, I set my distance to twenty-five feet. If anyone were to breach that line, my cameras would begin to record. Motion activated cameras are a great thing to have and most systems today also include IR cameras.

IR (infrared) allows the camera to see in no light/low light conditions. The camera clarity today is amazing and even with IR video, one can clearly make out specifics upon replay. IR cameras are used inside and outside, specifically for low/no light conditions. Usually, IR cameras have a row of tiny light bulbs surrounding the camera lens. IR is not viewed/seen with the naked eye. Think of IR as a camera's flashlight that only it can see.

For those that live inside apartments, it's not advisable to install anything on the exterior since you do not own the location. This goes for those renting a home, be it an apartment or a house (or condo). If you do not own it, do not take it upon yourself to install an exterior security system or cameras. This could get you into financial trouble. If you are in this predicament, contact the complex owner/manager and ask them to install an exterior security camera system. If you do a little research and gather some data to provide the complex owner/manager, there is a better chance they will go for it.

If you do live in an apartment, you could install a camera system with a DVR within the home. I will discuss this further down the line.

DOORBELL CAMERAS:

Technology improves by leaps and bounds almost daily. More and more companies are producing high resolution cameras for doorbells and security cameras, greater than ever before. Another security option is a doorbell camera. There are companies that have these doorbells outfitted with cameras, which also have IR lights. This is a great asset to have to increase the security of your home, and is relatively inexpensive. One brand name is RING, which is what I have installed on my house.

The doorbell camera is battery powered, so you would have to charge it when the storage battery is low. It has an application that you download to your phone or tablet, allows for live conversations and viewing, and saves the videos it records. It's easy to install, easy to download the application and easy to set up. Ring started to expand their services and product line, to offer more items to connect together. As long as I have phone service, I can speak through my doorbell, can check the recordings, and receive alerts of any crimes within a five mile radius of my house.

With this specific doorbell, I set the recording-distance so it would not record anything on the road. The IR camera works great at night and has great clarity. If I am curious about what is in front of my house at this moment, I access the application and click on the live view icon and I get a live view of everything. I personally like having this device, but know that there are multiple options that exist. Do your research to determine which is the best option for you before you invest. Anyone that breaches the distance line I set, is captured on video.

There are residents in my area that post their doorbell camera video to the site and to community social media sites, to warn others of someone breaking into vehicles/homes etc. They explain where they are and sometimes post screen captures (still photographs from the video) also, to get more people aware of who may be breaking into things and what they look like. This helps law enforcement find the culprits and allows for information dissemination throughout the world in seconds. Technology is incredible, not for the threats out there, but for those who obey the laws and have security in place.

Bottom line: it doesn't matter which product you go with, as there are many, what matters is you have taken the steps needed to secure the safety of you and your family. I do not recommend any name brand, but will give my opinion of what I use, good or bad, to provide an honest assessment to the readers. It is up to you to do your own research and come to the right decision.

MOTION ACTIVATED LIGHTS:

Having motion activated lights in key locations around your home can greatly increase the chances that threats will avoid your home. Having motion sensitive/activated lights can create immediate hesitation (once they pop on), which allows the camera(s) to record the threat longer, thus producing a much better image on DVR. These lights, in combination with the cameras, increases the security of the home and reduces the chance that a threat will choose your home to break into. Threats want easy marks and not a location that could identify them.

During the day, if someone were casing out your home, they may see the security cameras on the corners of your home. They may see the lights on the front of the house. The combination of the two together means a threat will likely avoid your house, especially at night, because they don't want to take the chance of getting caught, or spotted by those lights. Threats that identify your house as a target will notice the lights and cameras. Threats may try to test your security to see if the lights and cameras are real. What then? This is why you avoid purchasing/installing fake cameras and lights.

Assume your house is watched, not all of the time, but just for the moment. What should you look for? What should you look out for around your home? This may be something you say to yourself: "That's common sense", but if you dig deep and truly be honest with yourself, you would admit that it wasn't common sense. Nothing is common sense until someone tells/educates you about it. After that point, it is common sense and you cannot use the excuse of not knowing. Back to your house being watched:

If you have your security cameras and motion activated lights installed, then you have a daily review that you need to do. Why? If your house is marked for break in, or worse, then someone has walked down the road next to your home and glanced at it, perhaps a couple of times. This someone also drove by your house, (probably multiple times) and even slowed down as they reached a mid-point in front of your home, then sped up and drove off. There may have been someone in the passenger seat taking pictures as the slow car passed by. That car could have driven up your drive way (and perhaps tried to ring your doorbell, to act like they were looking for someone).

How would you know?

You would know if you check your DVR when you arrive home from work. You would know by being aware of the things that occur around your home. Such as: the slow-moving car that has a passenger taking pictures of your home; the figure in the woods, next to your home, who was taking pictures of your home; and/or the person that walked by and looked at your home while speaking on their cell phone. All suspicious actions that you should take note of. By checking your DVR, you can spot these actions and save those files (if you set your distance to record that far). With a DVR system, you could save those files onto a thumb drive, if you are concerned with filling up your DVR storage.

Most DVRs today have great storage and it's doubtful it will ever truly fill up. However, if you are concerned about that becoming a problem, then go out and purchase an external drive with a terabyte of storage capability. That is plenty of space to save files...lots and lots of files. Main point of the DVR is to have the luxury of checking footage at any time and saving what you deem to be important.

At this point, I want to include this tidbit of advice: take the time to install a hidden location that supplies power to the DVR, where you can keep the location of the DVR private. If someone were to break into your home, they should not know where your DVR is, nor should they have cables to trace, to find the DVR. Some create a secret space in a closet, others get more creative in their hiding spot. Use your imagination, but make it a location you can easily get to, but a threat would have a very hard time trying to locate. If the threat gets the DVR, they get all of the captured-data and there would be nothing you could do about it. Be creative.

ALARM COMPANY STICKERS

Some people believe that having stickers on their windows and yard signs placed on their property facing the street, will deter criminals from targeting their home. Eventually, these people find out the hard way that their thought process only gave them a false sense of security. Having stickers on the windows and a yard sign displayed on your front lawn does/will not deter motivated threats. Eventually, if the threat truly wants into your home, they will test your property to see if you actually have an alarm system (and if it is usually armed).

It is the same thing as purchasing/installing fake cameras around the exterior of your home. It makes you feel good that a criminal will see those cameras and avoid breaking into your home, but it's not the full reality. Criminals evolve but maintain the same mindset: Don't get caught! Will your fake cameras and alarm company yard sign/window sticker deter a criminal? Possibly...but then again, maybe not. Are you willing to gamble the safety and wellbeing of you and your family on that chance?

Criminals look for weak points in a home they have targeted. This means, if they are motivated to access your home, they will case it for some time (and at different times). They will note when someone comes and goes. They will make note of alarm company stickers on the windows and any yard signs, but they will eventually test that theory. Threats will try to identify locations where there are no sensors or alarm devices, then they will test that location.

What does that mean?

If your house is the target, they will do the above homework prior to attempting a break-in. Then, they will locate the weak point on the house and test the alarm system. The threat may test the system by breaking a window they think is in an area less-likely to be identified. Once broken, they will run away and hide, while remaining close enough to watch for police to arrive. It is possible the threat(s) that attempt this 'test' of the alarm system, are close enough to watch for police to pass by, which could confirm an active alarm system. No police equals no active alarms. Keep in mind that many people who have alarm systems, never arm their system!

What?

That's right. I mention this elsewhere, that people will have a system, pay the monthly fees and never set it. Just having the system is good enough for them.

Now, if a threat were to break the glass and take off, they are checking to see if there are any broken glass sensors within the area. These sensors are activated upon identifying a specific decibel that glass makes when it shatters/breaks. These sensors work really well, but can also activate if someone were to drop/ break a glass or plate. This is what the criminals are looking for. No police presence equals no activated sensor(s) in that area, and they can move onto another test.

Criminals will return to the location to see if the window they targeted/broke has any repairs. No repairs could mean occupants have not spotted it yet. To the criminal, that confirms the area is not checked (or not checked often) and could be a viable option for entry. Another test would be to lift the window fully. This is to identify if it's wired on the inside. They open it fully and rush away, again, to see if the police show up. Next visit to the location would be to see if the window was fixed or closed.

If you walk around your home and spot a window not fully closed, be concerned that it was checked by a threat who wanted entry. A threat may not open it fully and keep it open, instead they would open it fully and then close it fully (or leave a small gap) and then take off. They do this just in case an occupant was to walk outside, around the area of the window. Threats don't want the occupants to know they were there and want to avoid the occupants of the home spotting the slightly-opened window, because then they will go inside and secure it. A determined criminal who is motivated to get inside your home will do their homework. This means repeat visits to your home.

Why is this relevant?

Here is a great example of why it is important to avoid just having stickers and yard signs on your property:

One day, while working from home, I received a knock on the door. My neighborhood was a good, quiet neighborhood with mostly elderly residents. I opened my door and there was a young, well-dressed, college-aged young man standing at my door. I stepped outside. This young man had on a laminated identification badge hanging from his neck, he was clean shaven and had a fresh haircut. He looked the part of someone who expects to be taken seriously and respected. Our conversation went as follows:

Me: Hi! Can I help you?

Him: Yes sir, I wanted to speak with you about alarm systems.

Me: Alarm systems?

Him: Yes sir.

Me: I have an alarm system.

Him: Yes sir, but you probably don't activate it while you're home.

Me: What?

Him: You probably don't arm it when you are at home.

Me: Why would you say that? If I'm paying for a system, I am surely going to use it.

Him: That makes sense, sir. But your wife probably doesn't set it when she is home alone.

Me: Again, why have a system if we don't use it? Plus, my wife is a great shot with her pistol.

Him: But your windows are not armed.

Me: Let me stop you there...there is not an access point in my home, nowhere, where someone could gain entry and us not know about it AND waiting on the inside for them to gain entry.

Him: (very nervous now) Oh, that's great to hear. You have a great day, sir.

Me: (points to my vehicle at the door magnet for my business) Do you see that, there?

Him: Yes sir.

Me: That's me. That's my business. You may want to check out that website, specifically the bio page, and read the biography's of myself and my people.

Him: Thank you sir, I will check it out.

Me: Great. Have a great day.

Him: Thank you sir.

He quickly walks away. Now, initially I warmed up to this kid because he looked the part, but asking those questions is not normal and were probing questions that divulge specific security information about our security protocols. That information was not going to be divulged by myself, nor my wife. Ever. He walked away and I stepped to my neighbor's backyard and asked him to call his police officer-son and request a drive-through of the neighborhood, to speak with this young man. His son drove through, the young man was nowhere to be seen.

Odd, right?

Fast forward a week. Just seven days later, there's another knock on the door. Again, I open the door and step outside. There was a male and female standing in my yard, dressed in normal, everyday clothing (nothing professional-looking) and spaced apart by about twenty feet. The woman remained partially in my yard as the man spoke with me. At first glance, it looked like a husband/wife or boyfriend/girlfriend couple. I greeted them as I had the young man, the week prior.

Our conversation went as follows:

Me: Good morning, what can I do for you?

Him: Good morning, sir. I wanted to speak with you about an alarm system for the home.

Me: (smiling now) I already have an alarm system, thanks.

Him: You don't have any signs.

Me: Why do I need to advertise that I have an alarm system on my house?

Him: Well you (interrupted by his wife/girlfriend)

Her: He has a sign.

Him: What? Where?

Her: (points) On his window, there.

Him: Oh.

Me: Oh look at that, I do have a window sticker.

Him: Well, you probably don't set your alarm while you're at home, alone.

Me: Let me stop you right there...I'm not going to have a service that I pay a monthly fee for, and not use that service. I'm also not going to advertise that I have an alarm system, or where the sensors are.

Him: I'm sure your wife... (I interrupt him)

Me: Let me stop you again. Look at that door magnet. Go ahead, look at it. Read the name of the business.

Him: Okay.

Me: Notice it matches my shirt? That's because it's my business. Write down the website and look specifically at the bio page and read what you see there. Pay close attention to the first bio and the picture. He may look familiar.

Him: You own the business?

Me: I do. My house is armed with sensors and lots of cool things that you would never spot, even if you were right on top of it, and my wife and I practice defensive options often.

Him: So you teach classes?

Me: A bit more than that. Again, read the bio page, then, if you are interested, perhaps sign up for a class.

At this point, the female was very nervous and was trying to pry her husband/boyfriend away from our conversation, but I was deliberately making it uncomfortable for them by keeping the conversation going. I finally took a little pity on them and let them leave. Again, I stepped to my neighbor's house and asked him to have his son drive through the neighborhood. His son did and again the people vanished into thin air. What are the odds that the same questions would pop up within the same time period? Pretty slim.

People easily divulge information that can harm them in the long run. The business-looking young man was a smooth talker and I am sure people would have no problem giving him information. He seemed nice, he wasn't nervous, was well spoken and confident. The other two that showed up were not. Alarm signals went off immediately when they began speaking and got worse as time progressed. The young man didn't stress about anything, nor did he stumble in his speech patterns.

The moral of the story is: purchasing window stickers and yard signs with the thought that it will deter/stop criminals from testing your home to see if you truly have said-systems in place, may save you for a short amount of time, but eventually your luck can/will run out. Are you willing to take that chance in the off chance that a criminal will never check your residence? Think about that question real hard before you commit to an answer. Then think about it again.

BUSHES:

Look at your shrubbery around your house. Are there any bushes located next to your entry way? Your main access into your home? Around your back door? Lining your house? Next to where you park your vehicles? If you are going to have shrubbery around your home, please consider using shrubbery that has thorns (or remove them completely). Why? To deter anyone from hiding within your bushes, who could ambush you when you least expect it. Action will always beat reaction, regardless who you are or how 'bad' you think you are. That is a fact.

Now, I am not telling you to not have shrubs or bushes around your home, nor am I saying you should avoid flowers or trees in your yard. Set your home up as you see fit, it is your home after all. However, I am saying that if you provide a hiding place for a threat, they will figure it out and could ambush you (or your family) when you least expect it. Is that a situation you ever want to be in? Being surprised means the threat has the upper hand (their action), which also means you MUST create an immediate defense to that surprise (reaction). The sum of that problem equals you losing.

Keep an eye out for any location(s) that provides an adequate hiding spot and/or ambush point. This includes staging trash bins (or recycle bins) in a location that won't provide an ambush point for a threat. If you could hide behind something to surprise someone, so could they. If you think you have nothing to worry about, you're setting yourself up for a lifetime of stress and paranoia. Taking the time and being proactive now increases your safety and security, while empowering you with the confidence that your awareness is primed.

IDENTIFY WEAK POINTS

Walk around the perimeter of your house. As you walk around your home, ask yourself where would you attempt entry. Where are the weak spots? Where are the probable locations where you, the threat who doesn't want to get caught, would likely try and access as an entry point? Is there a ladder leaning against your house? Is there a shed attached to the house, where someone could climb on top, walk up your roof and break into a 2nd story window? Is there a window (or windows) that remain open/unlocked? Are there old windows that can be opened with a credit card? Is there an egress window?

Identifying these locations early on allows you to remedy the problem. What's the problem? By leaving items outside, it creates a possibility for a threat to use, to gain access into your home. It doesn't take much time/effort to lock up the ladder you keep in the back yard. It doesn't take but a minute to lock up your shed. Especially since it contains all of your yard tools, which could be used to gain access into your home (or stolen for the threat to sell).

Walking around the exterior of the house allows you to pinpoint weaknesses, but can also help identify possible hiding spots. The closer a threat can get to your home, the more information they can gather about you and your family. It's easier than you might think. You may say you won't, but if you found out someone had been standing outside your window each day for hours and taking pictures, you would feel violated, at least on some level. That creates the victim mentality, where you will always feel or fear that someone was hiding outside your home. That's not a good feeling and does not make for a happy, relaxing life.

OUTSIDE TOOLS AND EQUIPMENT

If you have a shed attached to your home or located on your property, you should consider keeping it locked when not in use. Storing items in your shed is normal, however, it could provide a criminal with tools to break into your home (or use against you). I am not suggesting you lock up every tool you have in your shed, but I am recommending you devise a secure-system that can retain your tools and make it harder for any criminal to access or retrieve them. It doesn't have to be expensive, nor time consuming.

To give up an example: if I had a shed in the backyard, I could attach a bracket on the ends of the wall and run a cable through the handles of my tools. This would allow me to lock the cable on one end of the shed, onto the end bracket. If I want the tool, I can unlock the cable and remove it from the tool. Something as simple as this, could deter or stop a criminal from accessing something from your shed.

If you usually store a ladder in your shed, or outside and along your house, you may consider locking the ladder to something, or using a cable/lock system. By removing the ladder as a possible access-tool for the threat, it becomes more difficult to access the ladder from a location that homeowners usually keep unlocked (such as 2nd floor windows). These are common mistakes that many make because they do not consider their second floor a viable access-point. This can end up being a deadly mistake.

It's complacency that can cause problems. Most do not consider anything above their first-floor level as a possible access point for threats. I don't know if that's because homeowners only look at their first-floor windows as a possible access point for themselves (if they lock their keys inside the house), or if they somehow believe the threat(s) can/should only access from the ground level (or front door only). This can be a very deadly mistake. Threats want easy/quick access so they can get in and get out, and just because they use a ladder to access an upstairs window, it doesn't mean that will be their exit strategy. The threat(s) will choose an exit that allows them to escape quickly and reduces their chance of getting caught.

A ladder can be locked up in many different ways and however your home is laid out, you can easily figure out a way to keep your ladder secure. Some examples to lock up a ladder:

-Use a bicycle lock to wrap around the rungs of the ladder, thus impeding the extension of that ladder.

-Attach mounting brackets onto the side of your house or shed, and drill a hole into one of the brackets. Use a cable and lock system, using the hole to run the cable through or the lock itself (into the bracket's hole). The ladder will remain on the brackets until the homeowner unlocks it.

These are simple examples. For some homes, I've seen some people lock their ladders to their gas or electric meter, which I do not recommend ever doing. If, and this is a stretch, anyone tried to pry the ladder and cable from whatever it is wrapped around, there is a chance it could damage the object. If that's a gas line and it breaks, it can cause greater problems for the homeowner and the home itself, more than just a busted pipe. Think logically and safely, and above all...don't give a criminal an open invitation to anything that gives them easy-access into your home.

HIDE-A-KEY

I know many people may believe their hide-a-key location is better than the average person, but let me assure you: it is not. Take a moment to identify locations you believe to be a great place to hide a spare key. Next, look at those locations as a criminal would. Would they also believe those places were a good place to hide a spare key to your home? If the answer is yes, then it is NOT a good place to hide a spare key. Be creative and think about the perfect place to store a spare house key, and possibly a spare vehicle key.

Using a fake rock, which some people still use, is not as clever as you think it is. Using a fake rock to hide a key and placing that rock amongst your other rocks could expose the fake rock quicker. Now, the fake rock hide-a-key gimmick has gotten creative by using a fake stone frog holding a sign, or a fake rock gnome holding whatever, but that is (read that again: that IS) one of the first places someone who intends on breaking into your home, will check.

Hiding a key underneath the planter on the porch, or underneath the front door mat are locations I would keep clear from. Those locations will be checked for sure, by someone who is motivated to break into your home easier. This is where having a doorbell camera pays off! Criminals don't want to be caught by police OR by video cameras. If a criminal was tooling around your 'rocks' (or gnome statue) and you received an alert from your doorbell, one click of a button and you can speak through your doorbell. Make sure to save the image of surprise when the criminal looks at the camera, before they run away.

There are creative ways to hide a key and many of those options do not involve using a fake rock or garden gnome. When thinking about a location to hide a key, also keep in mind that you want to retrieve said-key without looking like you are retrieving a hidden key. If you step into your front garden and pick up a rock, turn it over and play with the bottom, then anyone watching you will immediately know what it is you are retrieving. They will also know where you place that 'rock'. The purpose is to keep a hidden spare key, hidden.

Options that are cheap or free, include:

-Altering underneath your mailbox, where you could install a small, flat locket to store the key.

-Outside light enclosures, depending on the design, has multiple locations to hide something. It is wise to check the location during the darkness hours when the light is turned on, to see if the key is showing on the outside panels. Other lights have a frame with ledges, which could easily house a key.

-Shed door: A groove can be 'tunneled' at the top of a wooded door, where a key can be placed and not seen. The homeowner could reach up and pull it out. Since it would be exposed to the elements, a small piece of wax could be used to cover the groove.

Solution: Many department stores that sell sports gear, toys, clothes, arts and crafts, etc. have swimmers wax in their sports section. This is the wax that swimmers place in their ears, to stop water from entering their ear canal. It's low cost and easy to use.

Important: If you decide to tunnel a groove into the top of a wooden door, it is recommended to tie a piece of string, a twist-tie, a piece of thread, something onto the key, and allow that to come out of the tunnel before the wax is installed. This allows the homeowner to pull the key out of its hiding spot.

Your motivation is to keep your home safe from an intruder by not being lazy, and finding the best possible location to store a spare key. Assume you will be watched when you have to retrieve the key, is it still a good hiding place? Some people use existing objects, which I commend them for being very creative with this idea: Some homeowners will use an abandoned wasp nest. Wasps make nests and wasps are nasty, stinging creatures which can make any day horrible. This is why, if you use this idea, make sure you spray the nest with wasp spray first. This ensures the occupants are no longer living, or have left the nest for good.

Next, wait a couple of days before taking a stick and smacking it against the siding next to the nest, to see if anything comes out. If all is quiet, great! Take the nest down and bring it to your shed or garage (wherever you can do some work on it in private). Spray the nest with a protectant (anything that will coat the outside so it doesn't deteriorate with wind or rain) and let it dry. Now you can glue a piece of cardboard to the back of the nest and let that dry.

Since the occupants of the nest are now gone, it is safe to cut a groove into the back of the nest and through the cardboard. This is where you could place the key. Add Velcro to the back of the nest and to the corner of the house where it had previously been and you have a way to secure the nest again, and the wind won't blow it away. If you don't want to use Velcro, then double-sided tape works just as well, but know this: if you have to remove the nest often, you will have to replace the tape. Over time and use, the glue will not work too well.

Using the wasp nest idea is great because most people (that is: most people who have common sense or have been stung by a bee or a wasp) will move far away from a wasp nest to avoid being stung. This makes it an ideal location to hide a spare key, but make sure it's in a location where you can easily retrieve it. The better you plan now, the easier it will be for you in the long run.

Lastly, a mounted lockbox could be installed onto a porch railing, or siding of a house. Lockboxes are used by realtors and by homeowners for spare keys. Lockboxes come in different variations, with combination lockboxes being quite popular. With a combination lockbox, you would need to program the combination into the lockbox. The important aspect to a lockbox is: you are going to have to remember the combination of the lockbox to retrieve the key. Make the combination something you won't forget, but harder than sequential numbers (i.e. 1, 2, 3, 4).

DRIVING UP TO THE HOUSE

Most, if not all people, are guilty of not paying close attention to their surroundings, especially when approaching their home. Why? I believe the reason we're not hyper-aware when we approach our home is because it's our safe haven. It's the one place that we can be alone and not worry about the pressures of work or traffic. It's a place we don't have to interact with anyone we don't want to, and we can walk around in our underwear if that's our thing. It's the one location we know the best. We gain a false sense of security, just by getting close to our home.

DAYTIME

During the day, when approaching your home, it is recommended that you pay attention to the vehicles in the area and anyone who may be loitering about. Most people ignore what is happening outside of their home, once they are inside. Ignoring a parked vehicle that has remained parked and doesn't belong to the neighbors, is a sure sign that a house is being watched. Pay attention to vehicles that remain on station and always vacant, or if someone drives it periodically.

Approaching your home in the daytime allows you to see more around your home as you get closer. This is the time to pay attention to what's around your home. As you slow your approach, look at the side of the house (a view you may not have as you pull straight into your driveway). Is there anything suspicious? Are your garbage cans side by side instead of aligned in a row? Is there anything out of the ordinary or out of place? This is the time to capture that data and decide if you should exit the vehicle or not.

Glance at the bushes and the trees as you approach. If someone were to hide behind a tree or bush, could they reach you before you were prepared to defend? Could they remain hidden as you approach? Do you have safeguards in place if someone were to attack by rushing out from behind the trees or bushes? This is the time to think about what sort of bushes to have around your home, if you choose to have bushes. Make no illusion about it, a threat/criminal wants the advantage and an ambush is the best advantage for them. A pre-thought-out plan is an advantage for you.

As you pull up into your driveway, glance around the surrounding bushes/shrubbery and trees as you move. Doing so as you move can break up the static scene and allow you to spot something or someone who may be trying to hide from sight. This is the area of concern before you enter your home, because this is where most people try to shed the stress of the day, or are mentally consumed with the rest of their day. That could make for a perfect ambush opportunity. This is not the time to become a victim.

WINDOWS

I want to first plant the seed that it's your home and no one would/should know it better than you should/would. That being said, the windows are an important location to watch as you approach your home.

Think like a criminal when you are assessing your home. A criminal would use a location or two inside, to peek out from behind if/when a vehicle was to approach, to ensure they have a chance of escaping the area and avoid capture. That would be the windows of your home. If you set yourself up for success, you can be warned ahead of time that someone is inside your home.

This subject is best expounded on when discussing the awareness and safety protocols inside your home, but it is just as important to include this information here. Setting your curtains in a manner that can alert you that someone inside your home has disrupted them, could save your life. Think to yourself: "If I was a criminal, where would I look out from to see if a police officer was pulling up?" and understand that the answer should be in multiple locations throughout your home, depending on the design of your home.

If you have pets inside your home, that's something that you need to take into consideration. Pets can disrupt how you stage your curtains and make it appear as if someone was inside your home and waiting for you. In that situation, if there's a window area that you feel is pristine as a lookout spot and you don't want your pets to disrupt that curtain, you could put up blockades to deter the pets from that area. Animal pens, pillows, boxes, child gates and many more options exist to impede pets from messing with your set up.

You set up the curtains to look normal, but if they were moved, it would be impossible for an 'outsider' to replicate their exact original location. This allows only you to know how you set them up and also gives you the ability to spot a location that was breached after you left the home. This setup costs you nothing but time and imagination. I set up the configuration in a manner that looks normal, but if anything moves one section of the curtain, it would forever disrupt the original positioning, and can be identified from the road. This works for day and night approaches.

NIGHTIME

Once the sun sets, it becomes harder to identify someone hiding out in your yard, especially if they are wearing dark clothing. If they are smart criminals, they would ensure they are not wearing anything reflective or bright. The things you have to your advantage are head-lights. As you pull into your driveway, your headlights will sweep the area. This is the time to be extra aware of what that light is showing you. Criminals will try to remain hidden as the lights sweep by, but some may peek out, and if the light happens to catch their eyes, you can spot them by the glow.

The evening brings cooler temperatures, which can cause dew to form on the grass. If someone were to step across your grass once the dew has begun, the footprints can be seen. This can give you an indicator of which direction the person traveled and approximately how many sets of footprints may accompany. These are the things to pay attention to.

GARAGE

If you have or use a garage to park your vehicle, it's important to think about the vulnerabilities involved. Once you pull into a garage, you no longer have the ability to see anything to the left and right, beyond the walls. You have limited views forward (as the car enters the garage) and have to use the rearview mirror to see behind you. Any-thing/anyone lower than your back window can remain hidden from your view. Think about that!

A threat could wait for you to pull into the garage far enough for them to rush to the opening, hunker down to avoid being seen as you are looking forward (trying to not hit your snow blower or Rubbermaid containers), and successfully infiltrate that space as you engage the auto-matic door remote. The door may close but the criminal could be inside the garage with you, and that is a surprise that I am sure nobody wants to experience at the end of their day.

What are your options? If you like to park in your garage, what can you do to increase your safety? Here are a couple of suggestions:

-Time yourself from the closest, possible location a criminal/threat could hide if/when trying to ambush you. This will give you an idea on what changes you need to implement to increase your probability of success, while reducing the criminals probability.

-Make it your protocol to (making sure you're aware as you get close to your home) enter the driveway and immediately close your garage door. If someone were to try and sneak into your garage as the door is closing, the sensor beam will break and cause the door to immediately stop. This is a safeguard for automatic garage doors, to ensure it doesn't injure the homeowner if they accidentally step inside as the door is descending. If the door stops, you could remain in your locked vehicle, safe from the threat.

-Set up obstructions to slow any criminal down as they sprint towards the garage to ambush you. Small fencing (which can be great trip-hazards for those you don't want wandering into your yard) works well and is inexpensive. Large stones can be pricey, but effective. Children's toys strategically placed work well also, as it creates a slalom situation for anyone to navigate to get to you.

-Perimeter fencing works well, but is going to be a cost-investment for anyone.

-Cameras are also a good deterrent and something I recommend in this section. Motion activated lights are another option (and another thing I recommend) for the evening.

-Have defensive tools in the same location as you would exit your vehicle. This would level the field if an ambush were to occur, but you must practice retrieving this item, in order to identify possible problems with the tool you choose (and its location).

FRONT OF HOUSE

Another effective deterrent is if you set large food dishes out, on your front stoop/porch. A large food dish and large water dish could mean you have a large dog somewhere on the property. If you add a large, chewed-up bone next to the dishes, to a criminal casing out your house, you're solidifying there's a large dog that occupies that home.

"But I don't have a dog?"

If you do not have a dog, find someone who has a large dog and buy that dog a really large bone to chew on. Let that dog chew on that bone for a couple of days so it looks chewed on. Having dog dishes (beat up dishes) and a large bone can be a great detractor for anyone looking to break into your home. Criminals prefer easy marks and NO BIG DOGS!

FLASHLIGHT

Something that I will mention many times is to have a flashlight on your person, day and night, inside your home, outside in the yard, out shopping, it doesn't matter. Have a flashlight on your person at all times. For those that stop reading to mockingly sneer: "What about when I'm sleeping, dummy?", I say back: "Sleep with it in your hand, dummy!" no, I'm only kidding, my flashlight sits on my dresser, at arm's length, each night when I go to bed.

A flashlight is a great neutralizer, especially for those who do not desire to carry a firearm. A flashlight is a tool that can be used to illuminate, to stop a threat from seeing well (by flashing it into their eyes as they try to ambush you), to jab into the face of an attacker, to disengage from the threat, and to strengthen your punch, if necessary. I will expound further but know this: a flashlight is not expensive but could save your life in an instance...and brighten up the dark areas!

BUSY MOMENTS

Regardless if you're driving up to your home during the day or evening, it's important to remain aware of your surroundings, regardless of what you have to do. What this means is: if you arrive at home (and are satisfied that your curtains are as you left them) and need to bring groceries into your home, you may lower your awareness level by focusing on the many trips you'll need to bring it all inside. Most (if not all) will also leave their door unlocked the entire time they are bringing their groceries inside.

Should you lock the door each time you enter with an armload of groceries? Depends on if you feel threatened. Would you lock the door behind you after entering your home? Probably not. What are your options, then? Many men (I don't want to say all) and some women will try to grab every bag at once, to get everything into the home in one trip (I admit that this is me most of the time). Most, if not all, will not lock their door behind them after each trip and why would you? For safety? It's an inconvenience and everyone (yes, I said everyone) wants everything to be as convenient as possible.

So, I am not strongly suggesting that you should lock the door behind you on each trip inside. I am, however, strongly suggesting that you do SHUT the door behind you each time. If you shut the door behind you, a threat/intruder still has to get over that hurdle to get inside. That small amount of time could make the difference between you being prepared adequately and you being ambushed. Shut the door fully behind you on each trip, it can add a level of safety for you and your family inside the home.

CHILDRENS TOYS

Many people have children and those children play outdoors. This means there may be children's toys outside, lying around the yard. This could give a criminal an indication that small children reside at that home. That could make it dangerous for your child(ren). Multiple toys: wagon, tricycle, dolls, action figures, etc. can give someone a quick indication on an approximate number of children in the home and their sex. A unicorn hobby horse and a child's punching bag is a good indication that a male and female child are at that home.

Note: The same warning applies to those who have the family window stickers plastered onto their back window. You're telling a possible threat that you are a single parent with 3 small kids and a dog in that house. Not the information you want exposed, especially if you're a single parent.

Teach your children to put their toys behind the house when they are done playing with them. Have them bring their toys inside once they are done playing. It teaches responsibility and obligation to maintain the health of their toys. As a child, I remember being told: "if you break your toy, you won't be getting a new one! You need to take good care of your property!". I played with my toys and after some time those toys would break, sure, but that's to be expected. The moral of the story here: Move the toys inside or around the back of the house to avoid projecting information that a threat could use against you.

Why is this important? I mean, other than it's the safety and security of your children I'm talking about here. You are the parent or relative of the small child and it is because of that, that you should feel obligated to protect them at all cost. It is because of the children, that your safety and ability to act defensively or adequately lessens. You can't just run into the house and leave the children outside in the car if/when a threat tries to ambush you.

Having a plan and implementing that plan is important, plus it's a way to train the response-action into your children. As I will speak about in other areas of this book, practicing is important, but you'll have to make it fun so you maintain the investment from the children. No one likes homework, so don't try to make it homework. Practice should be inventive and realistic, but not scary. It's of the utmost importance that the child(ren) immediately respond to your commands without pause and without question (I know what you're thinking...a child who doesn't question EVERYTHING the parent says?)!

ARRIVING HOME PRACTICE

The first thing to consider, when trying to train your children, are their ages. Creating a game that they can contribute to will increase their investment. The goal is to not frighten them. This means to avoid saying: "Okay kids, there's a murderer behind that tree with a bloody knife and he wants to kill us all...okay...get out of the car!". That could scar/scare them too much and then you'd have to deal with the nightmares.

Involve your children in the planning. Let them know that you created a neat game, where each time it is played (this would be the ongoing practice), a different person gets to state the scenario (investment). Be playful with the scenarios at first by stating something along the lines of: a stray dog is in the yard and everyone needs to get into the house before the dog gets closer. Use specific commands and inform them of those commands and what they mean. This will help get the 'action' you need from them without confusion. A good word for moving action: GO.

Make sure you scan the area as you approach your home (as discussed) before stating the practice scenario. This way you're not focusing on just the scenario and end up ignoring the person hiding behind your trash cans. Remember, you have to make a decision when you face a situation. If you see a person hiding, or something is off, you don't have to get out of your vehicle. If you spot something, avoid pulling into your driveway. Keep driving past your house, and if you pull into your driveway and spot something/someone, back out immediately.

There have been scenarios where a bad guy was poorly hidden behind a tree and was spotted by the driver of the car, but the driver remained focused on that person and didn't see the other two people rush up to the car and ambush the occupants. This brings us to a great point: Always keep your doors locked! Always! The action of a threat will always (ALWAYS) beat the reaction of the occupants (ALWAYS)! Remember that: action beats reaction every time.

Train your children to lock the doors upon entering the vehicle, no matter what. Inside the vehicle, it's easy to unlock the door just by opening it again. I state this because if you are doing a training session (practice) with the children, you would want them to have their hand on the handle, but not to open it until you command it. Practicing this often will help when it comes to training on the inside of your home.

The way the scenario/training would work is: once you ensure your awareness was top-notch and you didn't see/sense any danger, you inform the children of the scenario and ask them each of their plan. The main goal for each is to successfully get to a safe space, so options are needed and they need to know what those are. In the scenario with the stray dog, if you say the dog was sitting in front of the main access door with a foaming mouth and growling like an angry pooch, the children shouldn't be directed in that direction. Where else could they go?

If you trust your neighbors, and this is only if you absolutely trust your neighbors, it's wise to ask them if it would be okay for your children to run to their home if they are ever in danger, or needed help. That becomes another option for the children (and yourself) in the event something bad were to occur (such as a house fire). Alternative locations provide options that they won't have to think up themselves, because in a traumatic/dangerous situation, their brains are not going to work well when they feel their life is in danger.

At this point, you made sure there is no danger about, you've shut the car off and given the scenario. You give the command and the children quickly exit the vehicle. You follow, as the rear security of this egress, until you get to the door. Once inside (and door is locked) give a positive debrief and be prepared to give each child a treat of some sort. It doesn't have to be a new toy, or even a sugary treat (although those work REALLY well, but can get expensive if you practice as you should). A hug and giving them praise is a great reward.

The main point is: practice is necessary for success and safety. If you empower the children to create a scenario, even if it involves dragons or unicorns, they will feel as they have contributed to the mission and that will go a long way. Don't forget to use the same 'activation' word for the scenario, regardless who's turn it is to create the scenario. Ask for the children's feedback (i.e. "How did mommy do?" and "What other ways could we have done this?") to make them feel they had the overall power to call the action.

It's important to not get complacent in your actions of awareness, because it will be that one time that you get comfortable that nothing is going to happen, that something actually happens. We are creatures of habit and pursue the easiest solutions to our everyday repetitions, but your safety and wellbeing should not be loosened. Be mindful of your neighborhood, your neighbors and your property. Always.

I want to end this subject with this:

If you do not practice scenarios, do you believe you would have the mental and physical ability to come up with options that can save your life? Even if the threats ambush you and are now trying to gain entry at each one of the doors? How capable are your children to remain calm and LISTEN to you if they suddenly get surprised (and scared) that some scary people are banging on the window and trying to get to them? Do you think, if you don't practice, that your children, when faced with such scenarios of fear, will hear you at all?

With practice comes reward. It doesn't take much effort or time to complete short practice sessions. You have to leave the vehicle to get into your home anyway, right? Main point being: if you don't practice, you run a higher risk of becoming the victim and creating victims out of your children. At least with practice, you increase your odds of success-fully saving your children and yourself. I'd much rather have safe, yet scared children inside the home and the police coming, than to have to plead with criminals to spare the lives of my children.

PS: If, right now, you are saying "That's why I carry a gun" but you've not practiced consistently each week (dry fire/range time), and never have had actual defensive training with a firearm, then you will probably die horribly if/when faced with a weapon-carrying threat. Defensive tactics is a subject for another book, but my point being: you don't know how you'll react to a stressful situation when your life is threatened (or your children's lives), if you've never trained in such conditions. This is where ego hinders common sense.

Practice often, practice different scenarios and practice with your children if you want to increase your chances of survival. If you don't practice because you're lazy or feel like it's not worth your time to practice, there's no 'do over' or 'respawn' in a real-life deadly situation. You cannot call a time out. You cannot press pause. You cannot say anything to the criminal that values your objects and money over your life. Think about that and then ask yourself if you could spare a little time each week.

FOOT/VEHICLE TRAFFIC

Paying attention to your home as you approach is vital, yes, but paying attention to the activity outside of your home is just as important. Threats understand that most people today are burying their heads into their phones. This makes it easier for criminals to scope out your home while you're inside. We are all creatures of habit and it is because of that fact, that criminals only need to spend a minimal amount of time watching your home, to gain your everyday patterns. This opens up opportunity for criminals.

Be aware of the vehicles that your neighbors have in their driveway. I am not directing you to spy on your neighbors, nor am I suggesting you sit by your window each day, with binoculars, to watch your neighborhood. I am also NOT suggesting anyone nail up a 'Neighborhood Watch' sign around the neighborhood. If you don't have a neighborhood watch group organized, perhaps speak with your neighbors and ask them if they are for or against the idea.

Once you know the vehicles around your community, it will stand out more if there are any staged vehicles around the area. Technology today allows criminals to park a car and walk away, while the camera(s) inside the vehicle streams around-the-clock information about your patterns. Criminals could swap vehicles out, change locations, and capture a week's worth of data about your home (and your neighbor's homes) with relative ease. If you don't think this is a possibility, you are refusing to open your eyes.

During warmer weather, some communities have frequent walkers around the neighborhood. There may also be some walkers during the winter, but depending where you live, it could be entirely too cold for people to go out for a stroll. This is important to mention, because if it is extremely cold outside and you see someone walking slowly by your home, that could prompt you to pay closer attention to that person. Did they glance at your home? Did they slow down as they arrived at a certain spot in front of your home? Did they stop? Are they speaking on their phone and looking at your home? Did they get into a vehicle close by? Was that vehicle running? Was there another person? Did that same person walk by your home in the other direction? Do you recognize that person?

Again, this doesn't mean sitting at your window all day, watching everything and anyone that goes by. You do that and the community around you WILL label you as the crazy/nosey neighbor! You don't want that, however, you do want to be aware of your environment and what is considered 'normal' traffic. For some who live out in the wilderness and/or outside a city, traffic would/could be minimal, versus those who live closer to a city. If you see movement, pay attention and take a mental snapshot of what you see. If it's suspicious, write it down.

If you have dogs in the home, they are great first-alert systems. Anyone that walks by, if they proceed to bark to warn you of a stranger, do not reprimand them for barking because it's their mission to protect the household and alert of danger. Rather, get your dog to respond to your commands by praising them for the alert. With adequate training, once you give your command for the dog to stop, the dog will watch the stranger outside quietly (until that stranger approaches the home). Having a dog could give you the needed time to gain access to your defensive tool, if a threat were to invade your home.

Seasonal clothing can be expected for the area, such as: winter jackets in the winter, shorts and t-shirts in the summer, etc. Seeing someone walk by in shorts and flip-flops when it is negative twenty degrees Fahrenheit outside should set off warning alarms in your head. Someone wearing a long, wool trench-coat in the middle of summer should set off your alarms also. Paying attention to these things are important and are a big part of remaining aware. Most people are complacent at home because they live with the mindset: it's my home and no one WILL break into it! Sadly, that has been the final mindset for many people who didn't live through a home invasion/violent encounter.

Action will ALWAYS beat reaction. Never forget that.

Here is a quick example on why it is important to remain aware while you're at home: After moving to another state, I was standing on my front stoop looking around the immediate area of my neighborhood. I've done my due diligence before moving here, I researched the area, the crimes, etc. and this neighborhood was small, quiet and in a nice location, bordering on the nearest city (which is barely a city it is so small).

I caught movement to my left, down the street, and noticed a white pickup truck driving slow and close to the curb, and stopping at each mailbox. This truck stopped at a mailbox. The person in the passenger seat reached into the mailbox, grabbed the mail and brought their arm back inside the vehicle. Nothing out of the ordinary, right? It could have been their house. They could have forgotten to get their mail before leaving their house and decided to grab it as they were passing by. That was not the case.

At this point, I noticed the truck but wasn't focused on it, per se, until the truck repeated that action at the next mailbox. In this neighborhood, the mailboxes are for the house across the street and your house. Each house has two mailboxes at the end of their property. Again, even if it was the neighbor pulling out of their driveway, pulling close to the curb where their mailbox resides to get their mail, they would not have done the same action at the next set of mailboxes.

As the truck stops at the next mailbox, which was my neighbor's mailbox, I stepped off of the stoop and slowly descended my driveway with my phone in hand. The truck driver nor passenger could see me because of the trees and shrubbery on the property, so I was shielded from view. The truck pulls away from their mailbox, accelerates slightly and begins to decelerate as they approach my set of mailboxes. As the truck moves closer to my mailboxes, that was when they spotted me.

The driver, trying to act normal, gunned his accelerator and pulled away from the curb. Too late. I immediately held my phone up as the truck passed me by, and I continued to step down my driveway and into the road. I kept my phone up and pointed in the direction of the quickly-accelerating truck. The truck drove to the end of the street and quickly made their escape. I returned to my stoop, sat down and waited to see if the truck returned to see if I was still here. They didn't return.

Why did I put my phone up and towards their direction? I wanted them to believe I was recording their actions. I know (and I am sure they knew) that taking someone else's mail is a federal offense. I know my phone was NOT recording (wish I had been quicker to activate my camera and actually video them, but was not) but they didn't. Remember, criminals/threats have a big motivation: don't get caught! I sat on my stoop for approximately forty minutes, hoping they would do another pass.

After that time, I went inside and harnessed my dogs and took them for a walk around the neighborhood. I went looking for that vehicle. I remembered the color, make/model and the identifying marks on the truck. I did not get a good look at the driver and the passenger turned their face away as they drove by, quickly indicating the driver spotted me and warned his passenger. I went looking for the truck, but I didn't find it. It didn't reside in my neighborhood.

When my neighbors got home, I made it a point to go out and speak with them. I asked them if they knew anyone in the area, or anyone in general that drove the vehicle I described. I then proceeded to tell them exactly what this driver and passenger were doing. They were amazed that someone had the audacity to perform such actions during the day. Each neighbor then thanked me for being observant enough to catch them in the act and deterring them using my phone to look like I was videotaping them.

People today are not like people back when I was growing up. Neighbors commonly communicated to each other. If a neighbor caught me doing something wrong, I could put money that I was going to be in trouble when I got home, because they were going to call my parents immediately! In those days, neighbors would catch up with each other each week, sometimes daily and if something was off, someone in the area would be checking on them. That doesn't seem to be the way it is now, not where I currently live, anyway.

Regardless of where you live, if you do not tour your neighborhood, you would have a difficult time making the distinction between a visitor and a resident. Whether it is a visitor or a resident, neither should be removing mail from anyone else's mailbox. Not all neighbors are good people, and not all shady-looking neighbors are bad. Looks can be deceiving, which is why it is important to know who your neighbors are. Bring some muffins to your neighbors and let them know who you are, it could be the start of a great friendship.

If/when you take the time to get to know your neighbors, your neighbors will start to grow their awareness also. This is a good thing, because then the neighbor is more motivated to step outside their home to approach a work vehicle parked in your driveway, to ask them if they are there to do any work and if the homeowner knows they are there. I've done that for my neighbors at every location I've lived.

If you spot a vehicle that does not belong and you have not seen anyone in or around it, speak with your neighbors to identify if it belongs to one of them. Sometimes their child returns from college, or a family member is visiting. There are valid reasons for a vehicle to be parked on a street. If it seems out of the ordinary, write down the specifics of the vehicle: license plate, make, model, color and identifying marks (dents, scrapes, missing lights, etc.). If it is nothing of concern, you can cross out that information or note it as a vehicle belonging to a neighbor's family or child.

Having a doorbell camera can be helpful to record visitors, but it is advisable to not have the settings at a distance that captures vehicle traffic. This will wear down your battery quickly and fill up the history folder. The main mission to this topic is to grow your awareness so if/when anyone walks by slowly, scoping out your home, or drives by slowly with a camera pointed at your home, that you would/could quickly obtain that specific information and write it down. Some share that information on community social media applications.

As I've stated elsewhere in this book: prepared and paranoia are two different things and being situationally aware is not being paranoid. You may get scoffed at when you pay attention. I have been scoffed at, until something happens and I'm prepared, but others were not. Then they realize how preparedness equated to having working plans for most situations, and also retaining specific information that they never absorbed. They were frozen mentally because they were not aware enough (or at all) to identify a bad situation unfolding, which meant they had no plan A, B nor C.

This does not mean you have rush to the window for every person that walks by, it means the more awareness you practice, the safer you will be. It doesn't take much effort. It takes more effort to read this book, than it does to become proactive about your safety and security.

DENTAL FLOSS

Dental floss is an inexpensive way to be alerted to an intruder waiting for you, hiding in the shadows, inside your home. Being aware, as I know you are by now, you feel confident that your home is just as safe as you left it. You haven't seen any signs that an intruder has entered your home (none of your curtains have been disrupted) and you feel safe. Super! But what if there IS someone inside your home?

A couple pieces of scotch tape and a short piece of dental floss is an easy way to gain valuable information. This is a low-cost solution and is easy to achieve. One thing to remember about what I am about to provide you, is to never become complacent. It's when you get complacent that you become comfortable that your security is top notch and impenetrable. That's about the time the threat lands on your doorstep (or inside your home) and you cease to exist.

There are a couple of ways to set a trip alarm and it is up to you to change things up, to avoid it becoming a pattern out of comfort or convenience. Below explains the process:

Take two pieces of scotch tape and a piece of floss. The length of the floss should be approximately 2-3 inches longer than the width of the inside of your doorway/door frame (if your frame width was 24 inches, then your floss is cut at 27-28 inches).

-Take one end of the floss and tape it to one side (inside) of the door frame. The floss should be a couple inches from the floor and held taut by the tape.

-Extend the floss to the other side of the door frame and tape it.

Here is where variation comes in: on one side of the doorframe, have the floss end pointing upward, so the remainder of the floss is below the tape. Then, on the other side of the frame, the floss would be taped with the end pointing downward.

Why?

As I have mentioned numerous times: we are creatures of habit. A criminal/threat who enters your home, is going to make entry where they feel they have the easiest access. If this is your front doorway, the dental floss can/will be pulled away from the frame as the threat's foot enters the doorway. IF the threat feels the snag, or hears the tape come off of the doorframe and attempts to replace it, they will replace it however they feel it was placed originally. That means there is a great chance the criminal will place the piece of floss with both ends facing downward (how they would do it).

Vary the patterns. Now, at this point you are probably saying: "Duh! There's only two ways to put the floss up and the criminal could get lucky and accidentally replace the floss in the same way I set it up" and you could be right...but, there is more than one way to approach this. One way is to have two pieces of tape on each side of the doorframe and have the ends do an 'over/under' pattern. Another way is to set a 'dummy' line eye level, which can give the criminal the idea that more trip lines are ahead, which could deter further progression into your home (and could maintain their focus at eye-level and miss the floss at the bottom of the frame).

The 'over/under' pattern is as follows and you may need to read this a couple of times to get the idea. This isn't to say you're not smart enough to understand, it is merely saying the description sounds a lot harder than it is physically to achieve, so it could sound confusing until you perform it.

Over/Under Technique (you'll need a longer piece of floss for this technique):

-On the left side of the frame, place the floss against the frame and lay a piece of tape across the floss. Leave a couple of inches of floss below that piece of tape. The 2-3 inches of floss that has been taped, is secure and pointed downwards.

-Take that excess 2-3 inches of floss that is currently taped to the frame and pull it upwards over the piece of tape. Now an excess of about 1-1.25 inches of floss is pointing upwards and in front of the first piece of tape.

-Take a second piece of tape and tape the upward-facing end above the first piece of tape.

At this point, you have completed the 'over-under' technique on the left side of the frame. You could do the same thing to the right side of the frame, or you could reverse your pattern on the right-side frame.

Using the over/under technique allows you to vary the directions of the floss, which only you would know that pattern. This provides options, options a threat would not get right, especially if they are in a rush. If the threat were to pull the floss away from the frame, there is little chance the threat would accidentally figure out your 'over/under' technique.

Are you getting the idea now? Using floss is an inexpensive solution that can give you a peace of mind, but also alert you to a possible danger awaiting you inside your home. Using dental floss is not the only item that works. Fine fishing line works really well. Thread used to sew, also works extremely well. Point being, it doesn't have to cost a great deal to increase your awareness in and around your home.

But...doesn't that border on being paranoid?

Being prepared is different from being paranoid. Being paranoid means you are obsessed with something that hasn't yet happened, but your fear is so great that you obsess over it and that runs your life. Paranoia is created when you are vulnerable because of lack of knowledge on how to counter the fear(s). Utilizing tools to help ease your concern is important for your peace of mind and wellbeing. It is, however, up to you to be proactive and pursue these solutions. You cannot afford to wait until something does happen before you become active in your own safety and security.

Using the dental floss, thread or fishing line would/could work on windows also. Scotch tape is not expensive, nor is thread or floss. If you keep it simplistic, it makes it easier for you to set it up. Again, and I cannot stress this enough: do not get lazy or complacent and begin to feel like it is a waste of your time to set up trip-alerts. When you drop your guard, that is when you are at your most vulnerable. Unfortunately, we live in a society today where people do not believe they need to think about safety and security.

If you live in an apartment complex, using the dental floss/thread technique can alert you to someone being inside your apartment when you aren't home. In the USA, the apartment complex/administration office notifies the lessee/renter whenever maintenance needs to gain access for repairs. This is not always the case. This technique is how I caught maintenance personnel breaking protocol. The office of the complex tried to insist no one had entered the apartment while I was gone, however, after explaining things in detail, they withdrew their comments.

The apartment complex I lived in was not in a bad neighborhood, but some of the occupants were shady at best. It was because of this, and another occupant who commented to other neighbors that maintenance likes to come and go as they see fit, that I set up trip alerts inside my apartment. I knew where the circuit-breaker panel was located, and the filters for the heating system, so there should be no reason to go into the bedroom or the closet, right? Right. I set up trip alerts using floss in my closet and bedroom. That's how I knew they were inside my apartment and in a location they shouldn't have been.

The trip system doesn't have to be at the bottom of the frame, either. The floss or thread could be placed at the top of the frame, so if the door were to be opened, the floss would be pulled through the small piece of tape, thus indicating someone entered the bedroom. Use your imagination and take the time to set yourself up for success (and safety)! Avoid becoming complacent and remain vigilant.

NEIGHBORS

I mention neighbors in another section, but that's for the sake of watching your home while you're away, and you watching their home. This section is important (as is all of the other information provided) for many reasons. You would need to get to know your neighbor(s) in order to trust them, and them you. Some neighbors want to be left alone, while other neighbors can be friendly. Some neighbors are chatty, while others are odd. We're humans and some of us are just plain weird. That being said, trust is a very important aspect to safety and awareness.

If you become friends or friendly with your neighbors, build that trust if it's possible. If you don't trust them after giving them a chance, so be it, leave them alone and identify how to deal with them. Neighbors you can trust can provide a safe haven to you and your children if you were in danger. If you trust your neighbor enough to consider them a possible safe haven away from danger, then you should work hard in building their trust in you. This gives them a safe haven from danger as well, which is only fair and neighborly.

Some neighbors are not good neighbors and over the years, I have seen numerous examples of neighbors who were not good/nice people:

-A neighbor was watching his neighbor's home while they were on vacation, but when those homeowners returned, their house was sold and emptied of all contents. Their neighbor emptied their house and sold all of their valuables, their furniture and their heirlooms, as soon as they left for their vacation.

-Two neighbors were friendly with each other, but not close. One neighbor always worked in his garage, had a wall full of tools, nice tool cabinets and worktable, and the neighbor would come over and talk over a beer or two. The one neighbor started to notice that he was missing some tools. He thought he just misplaced them, as happens to most of us, so he would buy replacement tools. Then the habitual vanishing of tools prompted him to become suspicious and he set up security cameras inside his garage. He was expecting to catch a neighborhood teen breaking in through the dog door, but instead caught his neighbor sneaking in almost nightly, to take a couple of tools.

-A homeowner lived down the street from a known 'biker house', where one of the local biker groups would frequent often for loud parties and fighting. The bikers always had people stationed on the front porch as the parties were going on and the neighbors, despite not liking the loud noise and fighting that occurred frequently, tried to ignore their behavior in fear of retaliation. The homeowner packed up the family in their RV and proceeded onward to their vacation destination: two weeks camping in the woods. Upon returning, the house was emptied of all contents and was put on the market by some of the occupants at the biker house. The bikers admitted to casing out the house and watching the RV leave on vacation, they denied emptying the house, but were later arrested for the robbery when security camera footage from the neighbor's house was anonymously provided to the police (they're neighbor gave it to them).

Having their house put on the market by someone who didn't own the house was incredibly daring. I don't know if they truly thought they would get away with selling someone else's property, especially without providing paperwork or evidence that it was their property, but when questioned, the gang stated it was a practical joke. Great neighbors, right?

Trust, as mentioned, is very vital when speaking about safety, security and awareness, because if you have children who know to rush over to the neighbor's house if they are in danger, you wouldn't want your children to be in danger because of that neighbor. This is why I state you should build a relationship to gain the trust (works both ways) and once established, you either trust them or you don't, but at least you know.

Just like you would have code words with friends and family, you would have code words with your neighbors. This way, if they were in danger/trouble, they could indicate that over the phone with you, hoping you would contact the police. What if your neighbors were elderly? What if they didn't have a cell phone? How would your neighbor signal you, to alert you to their situation? These are the question you should ask yourself, to find the solutions. They are not tough questions, but are very important.

Codewords used can be private to your specific neighbor and your family. This way you could appoint a different codeword to a different neighbor. In tighter communities, having a backyard get-together with the neighbors could be an opportune time to discuss a code word change. If you have fewer neighbors, or some you don't trust, then maintain the code word protocol you have in place and hope you never need to use it.

Trusting or utilizing your neighbor's home as a safe haven is not just in the event you are in danger from an intruder. If your home was on fire, during the winter, you would want a location to get to for warmth and safety. If you do not have neighbors, or the ones you do have you don't trust, then a solution should be identified now, rather than trying to figure it out as your house is burning to the ground during negative temperatures. Plan now and hope you won't ever need to implement that plan, rather than trying to think straight while your world is in chaos.

Now, back to the subject of elderly neighbors without cellphones: how do you communicate with your elderly neighbors? What options exist? Something I used when I lived in a different state involved using lights. I lived in a neighborhood primary filled with elder, retired folks. Many of these people were extremely nice, appreciative that a neighbor cared about them and welcomed the suggestions on how to signal if in danger. Some neighbors were not as personable, some didn't speak fluent English and a couple neighbors wanted to be left alone. As mentioned previously, you will run into all sorts of personalities.

For the elderly neighbors, especially those without cellphones, I would inquire if they had any Christmas candle-lights in their home. This was a single candlestick light that some people had in their windows and would plug in each night. The bulbs were different colors and the lights were available in different sizes. For the neighbors that couldn't afford those lights, I provided each one a light. It was important for me that they had a solution if they were in trouble. These lights plugged into the power outlet, which was close to the floor.

These lights were barely identified in the windows during the day and during the night, the light was bright. If it was not Christmas time, they would leave the light off, but the candlestick would remain plugged in and in the window. If there was a situation at their home, all they had to do was turn their light on. During Christmas time, the specific light had a different colored bulb than the rest, if they had any lights up. For those who only had this one candlestick in their window, it didn't matter what color it was.

Whenever I would walk by the window, I would always check their windows to look for that light. No light meant no danger or problems inside. This was an appropriate option, only because the light was located in one location and if they had fallen in another location, I wouldn't know because the light would remain off. Using a remote adapter for that outlet is beneficial because the occupant could click the remote to turn the light on from a different location within the house.

It doesn't have to be the candlestick light, a homeowner could use a dual light option for the front of their house. This way they can control which light they turn on with a switch inside the home. If the occupants become victims of a home invasion, they could flip the switch that activates their red lightbulb, thus alerting the neighbors that there's a problem inside. Many solutions are available and they can be low cost, you just need to think things through.

Main point: Know your neighbors well enough to determine if you trust them, and if you do, communicate with that neighbor to see if their home can be identified as a safe haven for your family. This goes both ways: let the neighbors know that your home is a safe haven for them also. Have code words with your neighbors, which can indicate you are in danger and trying to warn them, or you are in danger and fleeing from it.

Have other options thought out, such as using lights to signal danger or needing help. Think things through to find the solution that works the best. Another low-cost option is to use glow sticks to alert the neighbors, but that would require the stick to be retrieved, snapped, shaken and then tossed in a location that alerts the neighbors. It is a solution, but one that requires more action to activate.

-

3

INTERIOR OF THE HOME

The interior of the home may feel secure, safe and your safe haven, but that feeling of safe is only because you know you and your family are the only ones who should be inside. You, as well as most everyone else, know that your home is just that: your home. No one else has the right to just walk into your home, uninvited. This grows a false sense of security and could be detrimental to the wellbeing of your family.

It's true that no one outside of your home has any right to enter your home without permission, but that thought is why if/when a threat was to invade your home, you and your family are most at risk to become victims. If training, education and practice is not pursued and implemented, your response is nonexistent. With education comes knowledge, with knowledge comes practice, and practice creates response. Even the worst response is better than no response at all.

Home invasions are very real, and threats know that most people are not worried about their home (because 'nothing ever happens to them' in their home). Some people believe their home is secure because the occupants carry firearms, are hunters, were in the military at one time, etc. These are all poor reasons to justify not needing education and training on this subject. Even the 'toughest' person who believes they are prepared if someone were to attack them, are humbled and hurt when a threat actually attacks. All because the ego said "you're ready for anything" but the mind said "I don't have any experience or education to draw a solution". No solution equals instant victim.

Your home is your safe haven and should be a location your family and yourself feel the most secure. It takes knowledge of what 'could' happen, to properly create solutions that can increase the safety of your family and yourself. With minimal effort and maximum imagination and commitment, you and your family can be safe and secure...even if your home were to get invaded or burglarized. Don't wait until a threat has your family on their knees with guns trained at their heads before you realize you should have had a plan and trained the family.

It is my hope that you read this book and start on the road towards preparedness. It's better to have the knowledge and never need it, than to need it and never have it. Watching videos from the 'professionals' without knowing if their information is valid or pertinent to you, will only give you that false sense of preparedness and safety. There is an over-abundance of really bad information on the internet, and it smothers the honest, valid content from people who are passionate about putting out the right information.

Hard to tell what is good and what is bad? I agree, it is. So many people will give their allegiance to those with flashy videos, to those who compete professionally, to those who teach law enforcement, to those who boast they are the best in the industry, etc., but should you give your trust to these people? Some are valid and very good at delivering the information. Some get some information incorrect. It's hard to tell what is what and who is who. Here are some indicators that should throw up warning signs:

-No actual background in the subject they are teaching

-You hear them say "Just post yard signs for security companies and threats will stay away"

-They say: "NEVER use a [insert model/caliber/shape/whatever firearm here] because you need [some other firearm here] to stop the intruder with one shot!"

-They commit to a specific tactic without applying caveats to other possible people the information would/could/will reach (such as stating: "this is the best stance when confronting a threat" and "you should use this technique when a threat breaks into your home" or "this is the best weapon to use against a home invader" without adding information that fits others, such as: elderly, handicapped, house design, etc.)

I've seen many videos that are designed to get you to buy into their channel and pay for a subscription. I get it, it's business. My motivation for providing information is to actually give the information to the person, so they can apply it at home, not wait a week to get another clue to make it work. There's a lot of 'professionals' out there, I've had a few social media battles with some of those 'professionals' and their feelings got hurt because their egos overran their abilities/knowledge.

Main point to this is as follows: gather information from as many sources as possible, to learn and/or get ideas from them, and then work through those ideas to make it work for you and your home. Same goes for defensive tactics inside the home. No one can say "You need to do this in your home, if you want to survive" without actually talking with you and your family, AND seeing your home. Gather the information, see what works and what doesn't, then implement what works into your training at home.

With little effort, you and your family can have solutions embedded into your being. This is what could save you when an immediate, and unplanned, home invasion/burglary were to be initiated. Without a plan, your family may freeze in place, and this would make it much harder for everyone to survive the encounter (if it were to turn deadly). Gain the knowledge, train and practice...in the hopes that you never need to use what you learned.

DOORS

In other sections I speak about how to open the door, how to approach the door and how to identify those on the other side of the door, but this section is to go further in depth with specific information with door security.

FRONT DOOR

For increased safety and security, there are multiple options for front door access. In my previous home, we had a steel-reinforced door. It was very sturdy and durable. If anyone wanted access, they would have had to drive through it with their vehicle! Otherwise, to gain entry, it would have taken a very long time with tools. The only thing I didn't like about it was the glass in the center panels. I'm sure the glass was made of a material that didn't break easily, but it was still a weak point in my mind. What did I do? I installed a bulletproof storm door.

The storm door I installed had shatterproof glass, two panels, which would impede anyone's progress if they managed to get through the outer-most panel. It also had a three-position handle, which would activate either one lock, three locks or two locks, depending on how you lifted the handle. That was a great door, unfortunately I installed it before we moved. I wanted to leave the new homeowners with a dual security system they could trust.

Once we moved, our new house needed some upgrades to its security, and the front and back door needed replacing. I replaced the front door with a steel, reinforced door and frame, with shatterproof windows on the side and a security storm door (durable). I have may have mentioned this previously, but will mention this again: there are manufacturers out there that make/sell a film that is placed onto the glass and designed to stop someone from breaking through the window. Another low-cost option to think about.

If the front door is not used, there are security devices that exist that help maintain the security of that door and deter entrance by anyone attempting to break in. An extendable security bar is an inexpensive option and stops the door from opening. Decent locks can accomplish the same thing. We use our front door, so that is not a viable option for our home.

REAR SLIDING DOOR

In my previous home, the sliding glass door was of poor quality and antiquated (but a definite learning experience for me). It had one door that you would slide open to exit the home and the other side was a solid-glass panel. It was my assumption that the glass panel was immovable. I was incorrect in my assumption. When I was inspecting my glass doors, I noticed the grooves were extended for both doors, which I found curious. I stepped outside, placed my palms against the glass and 'shimmied' the panel, and watched as it moved along the grooved runners.

I was horrified that someone could have accessed my home with ease, just by gently shifting their palm-pressure on the panel. Since the main access door (the sliding door) was the one with the lock, I knew I could cut a piece of dowel-rod long enough to stick behind that door to stop it from opening, but it didn't provide a solution to stop the panel from being moved (and placing a dowel on the outside would do no good, since a criminal could easily pick it up and gain a weapon). My solution was two-fold:

First, I purchased a battery-powered sensor alarm for that door. I mounted the sensor on the glass panel and the base onto the frame. If that panel moved far enough for the sensors to separate, the alarm would sound. This was a low-cost solution that only required me to change out the batteries every couple of months.

Second, I was not going to glue the panel to the frame, I felt that to be a bit drastic and could think of an easier plan. I determined that I could use small hinges to secure the panel. I knew it was a temporary solution until I replaced the whole door and frame, and it would be cheap. I purchased three, small hinges, which I screwed into the frame and to the panel. This made it secure and immovable (temporarily).

The solution worked well, long enough for me to change out the entire door and frame. In my new location, I changed out the sliding back door with a new one, and this glass panel is part of the frame.

Not only is the panel secure, but the sliding door has a 3-position foot switch that you can step on, to lock the door in a specific position (closed fully, or opened in phases). Just by pressing the front with your foot, it will deactivate the lock and the door can be opened. The door has the regular lock by the handle that can be used, as well. Overall, it's a great and secure door.

There are a variation of designs, which is why you should do your research and find the one that fits your budget and fits your security/safety needs. They vary in size, lock options, UV protection-rating, colors and materials. As time progresses, the technology will advance. I've seen some designs that have a 'drop-bar' installed on the frame, which allows the user to drop the bar and stop the sliding door from opening, or raise the bar and the door can move. My only issue with that option is: if, for some reason, that bar was to drop while I was outside and the door was already closed, I would not have the option to open that door. That's what the bar is for: to stop the door from opening.

One other thing to think about: outside views. I would always recommend some level of shading (curtains or blinds) for the sliding doors. Some door-designs have built-in blinds, which some may like, but I usually have curtains or shades. To each their own. My concern and questions I ask: Can anyone see in? If someone were a great distance away and using a scope or binoculars, could they see into my home. I had to think about what options existed for me to reduce the chance of someone spying into my home.

There are options for those types of problems. Tinted/mirrored window tints exist, just like they have for vehicles, and can be installed easily by the homeowner. Mirrored window tint would deflect the sunlight and stop anyone from seeing inside my home from the outside (during the day). I had the concern of weather, or a person physically removing the window tint. I identified a tint that could be installed on the interior side of the glass, instead of the outside, and that removed my concerns.

It's important to be realistic with solutions, because for some solutions you may need to invest more money to gain the best solution, for other options you can achieve the solution at no cost or low cost. Having curtains over your doors can stop someone from seeing inside your home when it is dark outside and the lights are on, inside your home. If someone were to stand outside your glass door during the evening and the lights were on inside your home, you wouldn't see that person if you're on the inside looking out.

I am quite sure I shouldn't have to say this, but: locks don't work if you don't use them. Investing in good locks and longer screws is an investment into your protection and peace of mind. If you install good locks, but don't actually use them, what good are they? It's just like someone who has a security system, pays the money for monitoring each month, but doesn't ever set it. They feel secure 'just having it if they ever need it', but if they need it, it'll be too late. If you are going to put your hard-earned-money into an alarm/security system...please use it.

ALARM SYSTEMS

Alarm systems come in all shapes, sizes and prices. The more you add onto a system, the more expensive it will be. One of the great things that has evolved in the world of alarm systems, is the elimination of the hard-lined communication cable. Most (if not all) systems today are cellular, and each system has a backup battery in the event the power goes out. This is beneficial to the homeowners for a couple of reasons: alarm can still be triggered and monitored if the power goes out, and emergency services could still be initiated with a touch of a button.

In the past, alarm systems were hard-lined in, both power and communication. Criminals could cut the wire and the home would be defenseless, because signals couldn't go anywhere. Now that it's all cellular, the signal can go out. Pricing of alarm systems vary and there are numerous options for the homeowner. It's wise to do some research online and read some reviews for the companies in your area before you commit to a contract with a specific provider. It's also recommended to check what your city has regarding their policy, if police have to respond to an alarm at your home.

CITY REQUIREMENTS

In the city I used to live in, if the alarm went off, the police would come and check around the house. No charge. If the alarm went off three times, a letter would be sent from the city explaining the cost of ten dollars for every response after that, will be charged to the home. Ten dollars each time if the police had to respond to an alarm at my house? Yes please! I had zero issues with that because it was worth the money. Why? Because the police responded and took the time to check the exterior of my house (yes, they actually showed up and did a perimeter check). The ten-dollar fee was applied only until the new year, then it resets the counter (three visits and the $10 charge begins again).

In the city I currently live in, the city sends you a notice after the first visit. They explain the first visit is free, but if the police have to return, it's a charge of seventy-five dollars (if I recall correctly). After that, it jumps into the hundreds of dollars and climbs exponentially each time after. It also resets after the first of the year. This is an example of greed within the city leadership. It also increases the odds that someone's security will be breached.

How it plays out: think about it like this...if you know that the city will charge you upwards of over seven hundred dollars each time your alarm goes off, what is your motivation to activate your alarm system? More and more people will refuse to arm their systems in fear of the alarm going off and the city billing them. What excuse would city leadership have to justify such fees? The letter sent by the city explained the cost is due to taking the officer off of their patrol.

What?

My first response to that excuse was not a calm one because in my mind the officer is doing his/her job by being on patrol. Part of that officer's job is to maintain peace in the community. Part of the job description is to investigate crimes, maintain peace and safety within the community, which means to get out of their vehicle to check around a house that has an alarm going off. I was especially peeved when the pricing was listed out, and since I have a doorbell camera and it never recorded any officer walking around my property, that made me more aggravated at the greed.

Moral: Research the city requirements and billing specifics, specifically: responding to alarms.

MOTION SENSORS

Motion sensors are great with alarm systems because if someone were to break into your home, their movement could trigger your alarm. Most alarms have a 'home' setting and an 'away' setting. The home setting is for when you are home and don't plan on going outside again. Oddly enough, many people would ask: "Why would I set it if I'm at home?" and my response is simply: "Do you not think a home invasion is real?". The home setting is also for when you are sleeping. If someone were to break into your home, the sensors are probably going to set off the alarm well before you wake up. That should convince you of its worth.

Motion sensors, as stated, are a great thing, but you need to take into consideration where to place them, especially if you have pets. There are settings for these sensors so the sensitivity can be reduced if you have pets of average height. Unfortunately, if you have larger breeds, such as a Great Dane, it may be difficult to have effective sensors if the Dane roams freely about. If you have a large breed, it's quite easy to crate-train your pet, or isolate them into another room when it's bedtime, and this action can ensure your sensors do its job.

BROKEN GLASS SENSORS

Broken glass sensors work great, but as with anything, there are pros and cons. To be effective, the sensors need to be in a location that can detect the decibel level of breaking glass. If the sensor is too far away, it won't trigger. Another downfall is: if you drop a glass and it breaks, it will set the sensor off (same goes for ceramic plates). If anything makes a sound the sensor is designed to be triggered, it will. Think about placement locations before committing to the broken glass sensor, and realize it is an addition fee for most programs/systems.

WIINDOW SENSORS

Some systems have window sensors that tie into the program. These sensors are attached to the window and the frame. Once the sensor moves away from the base (on the frame), it triggers the alarm. I know some movies show a gum wrapper placed between the sensor and the base to disarm the sensor looks legitimate, but a more realistic concern for you should be about a criminal breaking the glass and not trying to open the window at all. With a window sensor, the sensor and base need to separate, which means the window has to be opened for the alarm to trigger, but it can be easily seen and is a good deterrent.

DIY SYSTEMS

There are multiple Do-It-Yourself (DIY) systems in existence and many allow you set up your home however you wish. This can be beneficial to many, depending on the size of the home, because you can assign sensors wherever you feel you need them. Just realize that even with DIY systems, you would still have to pay a service to monitor your alarm. This is the only way to alert the police that an alarm has been triggered at your home. There are pros and cons to most systems.

Do your research and review quality systems. When it comes to security, it's highly advisable to avoid going the cheapest route when selecting your security system. This doesn't mean to pursue the most-expensive system on the market, because just because it's expensive doesn't mean it's a good system and it definitely doesn't mean it's the perfect system for you. Read reviews, look through technology and security sites that outline their top ten systems and then read the comments. Online reviews are present for everything nowadays and it takes little time to read them. It is well worth your time to do so.

COMBINATIONS

Many systems today can be linked with other systems that exist, such as doorbell cameras and exterior systems. Having a system that can grow to your needs is invaluable and a good investment. Again, it doesn't have to break the bank to serve its purpose for your needs. Personally, I love my doorbell camera. I avoid stating specific opinions on brands because what works well for me and my home, may not work well for the reader(s). My goal is to put out information that I have discovered over the years, to all that desire to remain safe and secure within their home.

DOORBELL CAMERA

Personally, I use the RING doorbell camera/system. I want to explain why I love my doorbell camera system. The system is easy to maintain and has an accompanying application that can be downloaded onto your phone (as most apps are nowadays). The application informs me of many things: battery level, alerts, missed doorbell, and much more. It also has an IR camera and audio recording. It is also easy to recharge when the battery life gets low and I receive an email telling me it's time to recharge the doorbell.

ALERTS

One of the many great things my doorbell camera does is: it is motion activated and it alerts me whenever the boundary (which I set) is breached. My phone alerts me of motion, then I can initiate the application and go to a live feed to see, in real time, who or what is outside my door. If need be, I can also press the call button and speak to whomever is there. This can quickly scare an intruder who wandered onto the wrong property in the early morning hours, or can speak to a delivery driver who is innocently trying to drop off a package, but may have a question.

If criminal activity occurs within a five-mile radius from my house (and reported), I get an alert on my phone. Since it identifies by area, if anyone who has the same doorbell brand has issues (a car break-in, loiterers, thieves, etc.) and recorded something, they can upload that video and share it with the community. This helps to identify criminals in the area and hopefully get that person arrested for their crimes. I can control which videos I keep; I can track the logbook of the motion activated alerts, and do so much more with this one device. The battery lasts quite a long time and the camera/video is high quality. I do not regret investing in this doorbell camera.

TECHNOLOGY

As the world continues to advance technologically, there are some of us who are leery of the progress of some items. I am not a conspiracy theorist, I am not worrier and I am not against all technology, but I am quite leery about technology that can listen to me. I do not trust these objects to shut off (or not listen) when I am not speaking directly to it. If it can hear me on command, it can hear me whenever it desires.

What does that mean?

Good question. What it means for me is: I am cautious what technology I use within my house. I realize my phone has a camera and a microphone, but I also know that phones can be hacked (if someone were so inclined) and conversations and environments can be spied upon...even when the phone is off. What? That's right, if you doubt me, please research the televised investigation into technology where a disabled phone gets hacked from miles away. It was eye opening. Speaking of my phone, there are items that can be purchased that can shield one's phone when needed.

What sort of magic is this?

There are bags that exist, most use them for family time or dinner time, when the parents want a quiet dinner with family, with no one staring into their phones. The bag shuts down all communication, in and out, on the phone(s) and makes it impossible to send/receive calls or texts (it's not identifiable by cellular towers). These bags are marketed for family game nights and dinners and are inexpensive. This is not a recommendation to invest into one of these bags, I am merely mentioning they exist and are useful for many situations. Use your own discernment.

The moral: Having an alarm system increases your safety and security, but only if you actually use that alarm system. If you are willing to pay for a service, you should use that service as designed. Do your due diligence and research the different brand names, the ratings and reviews before you invest your money in any alarm system. Remember you will have to still pay for a service to monitor your alarm system, even if you use a DIY set-up.

Safety and security begins with you, and having the luxury of walking up to a control panel, pressing one button and having a firetruck or ambulance respond is invaluable. It works that way with calling/notifying the police also. The sensor location(s) should be considered, especially if you have larger pets, and even if you have smaller pets, you should make sure the person installing the system programs the sensitivity of those sensors, to avoid it being set off by their movement.

Walk around your home and determine where your weak points are and where, if you were a criminal, would you try to enter your home and what sort of alarm devices you could/should install there. Once you have your system, when you place your window stickers and yard signs up, you can do so with confidence that you are doing it because you actually have a system in place and not because you're trying to 'fake out' a criminal.

KNOW THE SOUNDS IN YOUR HOME

Every home has its own unique sounds it makes. Sounds vary depending on weather and seasons and knowing these sounds help to identify sounds that are out of the ordinary. The house settles over time and makes unique noises, but internally, knowing the sounds of someone walking in certain areas of the home is beneficial to the homeowner for safety/security reasons. It doesn't take much effort to know the sounds in and around your home, just time. Apartments are trickier because there are sounds created, sometimes on all sides.

SHADOWS

It's recommended to know the natural shadows that exist through-out your home, from the sunlight outside. In other words, if you have trees or tall shrubbery, know what shadows they cast within the home, to know what you could consider 'normal'. This can allow you to spot anything out of the ordinary, which could be someone hiding within those bushes. Those shadows will change over the seasons, but also when the light changes. Know those changes.

Nighttime is another time to identify the shadows. Moonlight can be quite bright and can cast shadows into the home. If you add wind to the equation, you can get some spooky situations where it looks like a witch waving at you from outside the home. I've experienced some odd shadows and MOST of those shadows were from outside objects and the moonlight. Most of those shadows.

Should you get up every hour, each night the moonlight is different? Not necessarily, but you could get a great idea by paying attention when you go to bed and have all of the lights off in the house. This can give you an indicator as to what things look like projecting into your home. The thing about moonlight brightness is that many criminals don't think about the shadows they may cast inside the home, while they are still outside. This is why the advantage goes to the homeowner and their knowledge of their home.

Does it make it any less dangerous to spot a criminal outside your home, just because you know the shadows? Not at all, but what it does do, is allow you to be prepared to defend your home until the police arrive. You see a shadow of someone lurking by your windows, you can immediately call the police and have them on their way as you prepare to secure yourself in your safe room (or prepare to defend). It is always recommended to go to your safe room and lock the doors, to protect yourself from danger. You can replace objects in your home, but you cannot respawn your life if you die.

If you can recognize the shadows and the sounds of your home, these two bits of information combined can help you identify where someone is located, in relation to your position inside the home. Knowing the sounds of the home also means knowing the sounds the windows make when they are opened, as this will indicate a breached location by an intruder and allow you to change your egress plan. This is why sounds are important.

Think about where you spend most of your time while in your home. The dining room? Kitchen? Living room? Bedroom? Bathroom? Most of us spend the majority of our time in two locations (unless you have an office in the home): the bedroom and the living room. The dining room and kitchen are used, but are used for minimal amounts of time throughout the day. The living room and the bedroom are where people spend the most hours at a time. Think about that for a moment...when you come home from a long day, what is your routine?

The reason this is important, is because occupants need to identify the sounds throughout the house from the locations where they spend most of their time. This means to know where the sounds are coming from as you are sitting inside the bedroom and/or in the living room. Your carry-on plan depends on knowing what you're hearing. You would not want to rush out of the bedroom after hearing a sound and stop abruptly because you are now face-to-face with a couple of intruders, would you? Probably not.

Think about your home. Do you have stairs? Do you have hallways? What type of flooring do you have? Wood? Tile? Linoleum? The difference each makes is noteworthy. It is also wise to recognize your patterns. What patterns, you may ask? Think about it: if you were to walk down a hallway, how would you do it? Don't cock your head at these words and think "What? Are you an idiot?" because this may seem like common sense, but in reality, nothing is common sense until someone educates you on the subject. After today, this will be common sense for you.

When you walk down hallways, I'm pretty confident that you walk down the middle of the hall. I am also confident that you are not thinking about where you are placing your feet, nor are you thinking about the impact your foot has on the floor, or the sound it makes. The more people walk in/on the same path, the looser things get, the squeakier the floor gets and that noise is quite distinct. This is especially true on wooden floors and staircases. Do you walk up the middle of your stairs at home? Probably, right? Why would you ever place your foot anywhere else but the middle, unless someone else is walking down the stairs at the same time you're trying to walk up?

These sounds are very distinct in your home. Your basement floor won't make any sounds when walking upon it, because it is concrete. Your feet may make sounds, but an intruder can walk softly on cement and not make much, if any, sounds as they move. On concrete, weight is not an issue of concern for an intruder. Wooden floors, laminate floors, linoleum floors and some tile floors would be a concern. Time loosens things up, even with some tile floors, and that looseness can create sounds. These are the sounds you should be familiar with, throughout your home.

If someone is inside your home and you cannot get to your saferoom and have to change your egress plan, knowing the sounds of your home (and where those sounds are the loudest) can help you navigate through your home without making much, if any, noise at all. How? Think about what I had just mentioned about where people usually walk: down the center of the hallway, up the center of the stairs? Remember? I hope so, because that location in the hallway and on the stairs is important to remember when crisis hits.

Stairs are usually made out of wood, sure there are some steel stairs, but steel makes a much different sound consistently, whereas wood will change noise the more worn it becomes. Impact on the treads and on the floorboards in the hallways remains in the middle, and over time it weakens the board(s). This is what makes the boards creak as someone steps on them. Weight differentials creates different sounds on the same treads and floorboards, but they still make sounds.

What do you do in the event someone is inside your home and you have to move?

If you have to move throughout your home, to evade a threat or escape to your saferoom quietly, this may sound odd, but I recommend you try what I am about to tell you. Once you try it, I am sure you will trust what I tell you a little bit more. Knowing the boards will make a sound by stepping in the middle, it makes sense to steps closer to the ends of the boards, to use the stronger areas of the wood. This does require your feet to be spread apart as you move, but that shouldn't be too much of a concern.

If you are able to spread your footing and can set your feet as close to the ends of the boards as possible, you will notice the sounds your feet make diminish, if not disappear entirely. This may not be enough to just spread your footing to the outer-most part of the boards, and you may be concerned at the loud sounds your feet make when they impact the floor. This is a real concern, but not something that cannot be solved. When moving, when you step, if you allow your heel to impact first and the remaining portion of your foot 'rolls' downward and forward, your foot will make less of an impact sound.

Using the outer areas of the treads and the flooring helps to reduce the noise, which masks your travel and your location. Rolling your foot-steps help in that endeavor. If a threat were to identify your location, they could attempt to rush to where you are. At that point, the threat is not concerned with you knowing they are there, they are more concerned that you could stop them, or they could get caught. Either way, criminals do not want to get caught. Ever! Rolling your feet can allow swift movement, up or down stairs and hallways, to get you to a safer location and away from the threat(s) unnoticed.

Knowing what the home sounds like from the different locations within your home allows for accurate planning for egress and safety. Most parents will tell you they know what trouble the children upstairs are in by the sounds they hear on the floor above them. I do agree with that, but I have used the knowledge that the child's silence is a sign they are getting into trouble, because that was the case with mine. I could, however, identify where my child was from where I was located, just by listening to the sounds being made.

Knowing the shadows outside your home (and inside) can help you identify where the threat may be, but I need to add some information to that thought as well, because I've met too many people who were told what I am about to tell you, and could end up getting themselves killed because of that thought process. Let me expound on that comment:

Many people believe that having a shotgun inside the home for protection is recommended by everyone. Many believe that to be so because of what was told to them by someone they believe to be knowledgeable in self-defense or home protection practices. Some believe it because of someone who worked behind the counter at a gun or sporting good store. Those who know little to nothing about home protection or defensive tactics will absorb the information coming from someone at a gun store, a gun range, a sporting good store, former/current law enforcement and/or former military person.

Let me put that thought process into perspective for a moment: you're told your appendix has burst and you need emergency surgery or you're going to die, but the only doctor available at that moment is a veterinarian. Still a doctor? Still a doctor that has done surgeries, but on animals. Still a viable option for your survival? I hope your answer is a loud NO!

If you go to a gun range and ask the person behind the counter what they recommend for home protection, they may try to feel you out to identify if you have any knowledge at all. Once they identify you don't have any defensive knowledge, they may either try to sell you on an expensive firearm, be it a shotgun, pistol or rifle, or they may try to sell you on what they, themselves, have in their home. Does that benefit you in your home? Does it make you any safer? Again, the answer is no.

As I am trying to keep this book entirely on the subject of situational awareness, I am going to put what I am saying into perspective after hammering on the following points: just because something works for one person, doesn't mean it'll work well for you. Just because someone says they were a (fill in the blank: military, law enforcement, security guard, etc.), doesn't mean they know how to defend themselves adequately (remember, many in those fields learn how to use their firearms fresh and absorb everything told to them, which becomes their "this is the best way to do this" and "this is the best weapon for defensive purposes") nor does it mean they methodically ask you important questions to determine your knowledge level and abilities (to include your restrictions and limitations).

Perspective I wanted to leave you with:

Many, and I have heard this with my own ears, have heard the person 'behind the counter' say (with a pump action shotgun in their hands): "Any burglar in your home hears this (person cycles the slide on the shotgun) they will run away quickly!". Please re-read that about fifty times and ask yourself:

-Does this make sense?

-Have I heard this before?

-Why would the threat run away from that sound?

-Would the threat know that sound?

-Would the threat be scared?

-Would it need to be loaded to sound more convincing?

-Do I believe that statement to be true?

-Who have I heard this from?

Now, onto the perspective part of things...let's put it into a real-world scenario. Real world-scenario means what could actually occur and not what Hollywood has embedded into our brains. I break into your home. I don't know your home, I only know how many occupy that home, where the weak points are (because I did my surveillance) and I know your patterns. I am inside your home...and I hear the floor creaking close by. What do I do? Nothing, that's what I do.

You, on the other hand, heard the window break and know someone has broken in...but you don't know where I am. You have your shotgun in hand (because you trusted the store/gun shop/range personnel) and you stop to listen. I stay in the darkness to listen for location and if you're still coming closer. You don't hear anything so you 'rack the slide' (cycle the slide), to announce you have a weapon. Now I am definitely not moving. Why? Am I scared? Am I concerned your weapon is better than mine? Not at all.

Think about everything that has just been mentioned. With this information, I know the following things for certain:

-You have a shotgun

-You are close by

-You suspect someone is inside your home

Here's the most important thing:

-You do NOT know where I am (but I KNOW WHERE YOU ARE)!

Am I going to throw my hands into the air and give up? Am I going to call out to you and say "please don't shoot, I won't steal anything, I won't hurt you"? No to all. What I will do, being a criminal who has broken into your home and not wanting to get caught or killed by you is: I will wait in the shadows. You see, I know WHERE you are and WHAT you have to defend yourself with, but you don't know where I am. You only suspect that someone has broke in to your home, but you're not positive. Once thing for certain is: you won't just go back to bed and worry about it in the morning. You will throw some lights on and investigate your home to find the broken window.

At this point, my eyes are adjusted to the darkness because I've been awake the entire time, whereas you just woke up. This means your sight is not as keen as mine currently is. You may have a shotgun in hand, but my gun is poised and aimed in the direction your footsteps told me you were coming from. Who has the advantage? Who has the upper hand? You may think you have the high ground, but in all reality, I am the one holding the winning (and deadly for you) hand!

How's that shotgun sound going to help you now?

I hope this makes sense to every reader that has this book in their hands. Will it hurt some egos? Yes indeed. Will it cause some readers to use the following statements?

-Anyone breaks into my house, I'll shoot them dead

-I'll kill anything that enters my house uninvited

-Break into my house and it'll be the last house you do

-I don't have to be accurate with a shotgun, just close

-I only have to shoot the intruder once with a shotgun

YES, IT WILL!

Is the shotgun a recommended tool for defending your home? Depends on you, your training, your abilities, your limitations and how your house is designed. Training is paramount, practice is vital and recognizing/embracing your limitations is key to properly train for dangerous situations, but training and practice are an ongoing necessity. I've tried to arm students with the knowledge of: if someone tells you a shotgun is the only weapon for home defense, or use the racking of the slide as a convincing action to cause criminals to run from your house, then you should step away from these people and not listen to them.

Knowing the shadows can give you a heads up that someone is sneaking around the outside of your home and it would be safe to assume that person will eventually attempt to break in. This gives you time to call the police and get you and your family to your saferoom(s). Knowing the sounds of your home can alert you to the location of possible intruders and how to navigate your home as quietly as possible, to get away from said-intruders. This is something that costs nothing but time and effort and I'm quite sure you can make time for that.

If you live in an apartment, you would need to be concerned about using a weapon for home defense, especially if you are not trained appropriately. You should be skilled with any defense tool (because you constantly practice to maintain that skill). Your concern should be your neighbors and what happens to them if you were to miss an intruder. Some apartment complexes have thin walls and weak construction. If you were to fire at an intruder, miss your target and the bullet were to travel through the wall and into the child sleeping in their bed next door, you will go to jail.

YOU OWN EVERY BULLET THAT COMES OUT OF YOUR FIREARM!!!

SAFEROOM

A saferoom is a location that occupants can run to, to be safe and aware from harm. It is usually the master bedroom in a house, or the bedroom in an apartment, either way, it's a room that allows occupants to be safe from home invaders and/or dangerous events. It is wise to evaluate your home and its design, to identify what you should consider the saferoom. It's not only the room that provides the most safety from a threat, but should also be a location that allows for egress from the home, if needed. Is this still going to be the master bedroom? Maybe not.

If there are children in the home, sometimes two saferooms are needed, just in case the children are not able to get to the master bedroom. This could also be in case the parent(s) cannot get to the master bedroom and rushes into the child's bedroom to keep them safe. Having a primary and secondary saferoom also provides options if you cannot get to one of those rooms because of the threat's location. Identifying these rooms costs no money, just time and imagination. Making these rooms truly safe and prepared may cost some money, but it doesn't have to break the bank.

PRIMARY SAFEROOM

As stated, the master bedroom is usually identified as the primary saferoom due to its size. Regardless which is identified as the primary saferoom, an egress option out of that location is also important. Criminals/threats may have more than burglarizing your home on their minds, and you want to maintain the option to escape the house entirely, if need be. When you identify your saferoom, keep in mind the difference between cover and concealment. This is important knowledge.

An easy way to remember the difference between cover and concealment is: concealment 'hides' you from view, whereas cover can provide a layer of protection between you and an attacker (and their weapon). Example: If you go into the closet and hide behind a dress that's hanging up, you are hidden from view, but not protected against anything if an intruder were to fire their gun into the dress. For cover, if you were behind a dresser and a threat were to fire their gun, the dresser could provide protection and hopefully impede the speed and trajectory of that bullet. That is the difference between cover and concealment, which will help you as you evaluate your saferooms.

Most bedrooms have a bed inside, which can provide cover and concealment. Also, inside a bedroom would be a dresser of sorts, which can also provide cover and concealment. Some master bathrooms are windowless, which makes it a dead-end and you don't want to end up in a dead-end. A bathroom should be considered a last resort location. Using the bed and/or dresser for cover and concealment can allow you a location where you could defend from, if you had to. If a bullet were fired at those cover locations, hopefully the bullet would divert from its intended path (because of the barriers inside the bed and inside the dresser).

DOORS

Many doors inside the home are hollow. They are lightweight and low cost for the builder, but they don't provide much protection from a home invader. A hollow door does not provide any protection from a threat with a weapon. A solid wooden door can be installed with relative ease, but you must ensure that solid door comes with a reinforced frame. You want to make certain that door cannot be kicked in, and a solid frame can help with that. Good locks are worth the investment, so are longer screws for the locks, hinges and bases for the hardware. Longer screws equal greater hold/strength.

SAFEROOM ITEMS

In your primary saferoom, it's wise to have items are the 'ready' just in case an emergency were to arise. These items can be used easily and would not take up much space. It is always better to have these items ready and never need them, than it is to need them and not have them. Some items recommended include:

-Flashlight: I recommend you carry a flashlight on your person at all times. A flashlight can be used to illuminate the area in the dark, but can also be used to stun an attacker and/or used as a defensive tool. In this case, a spare flashlight would be recommended to store in the saferooms (primary and secondary).

-Cell Phone: Many people keep their cell phones next to their bed anyways, but if you have an old cell phone that you don't use any longer, if you keep it charged, it will still work to call 911. Most phones nowadays have that option. Then, you could store your active cell phone next to your bed, so you can grab it and go, if you needed to. Cell phones can be used to call 911, can be used as a defensive tool, can be used to signal someone outside, and many more uses.

-Spare House Keys with a glowstick: Having a spare set of housekeys attached to a glowstick allows the homeowner to crack the glowstick, shake it to get it glowing and then drop it out of the window so the police can find it when they arrive at your home. Dropping keys into the snow, or on a snowy evening, could be close to impossible to find (especially if it's deep snow), but with a glowstick attached, it makes it easier to locate. The spare key can help the police gain entrance into your home without you having to leave your safe room, which could put you at risk for an ambush.

-Self Defense Tools: There are many things that can be used as a self-defense tool and it would be up to each household to identify which tool(s) would be best to use, taking into account if there are small children in the home. Some people choose oak dowels, some shotguns, some pistols, some bear spray, and some get creative in their choices.

Identify what you're comfortable with AND could use if in a defensive situation, and go from there.

SECONDARY SAFEROOM

Usually, a spare bedroom or a children's bedroom would be identified as the secondary saferoom. This would be a room that the occupants could use to keep threats away from them, in an emergency situation. As with the primary saferoom, the door is the first hurdle to overcome. The door should be solid, with a reinforced frame and longer screws in the hardware. It should also have a good lock installed. If this is the children's room, the parents may want to use a key lock, just in case the children think it's funny to lock you out when they're in trouble.

I cannot assume anyone would want to house any weaponry in a secondary saferoom if it houses the children. It is a saferoom, so any item inside the saferoom could be used by the children if they needed to defend themselves. You can teach your children how to use their lamp as a projectile, their pillow as a deterrent, their shoes, their toys, but most importantly: use whatever they need to, in any manner they can, to keep a threat away from them. It's a scary thought, but if you don't teach them that it's okay to use what is around them to keep themselves safe, chances are they won't think of something when/if that moment occurs.

Anything could be used as a defense tool in any saferoom, as long as you identify it as a possible tool. To be honest, if the only thing I had on my dresser was a can of wasp spray, I would use that. I'm not advocating the use of wasp spray, especially since the print on the can does state 'it is illegal to use for anything other than what it was designed for', however, if it's the only thing at my disposal, I don't think I would hesitate one bit to use it to protect my family. Again, I AM NOT saying to use any insect spray against an attacker.

EMERGENCY LADDERS

If the saferooms and/or the bedrooms are on the second floor, it's advisable to have egress ladders. KIDDE makes inexpensive ladder systems that can be installed underneath the window and/or hidden inside the wall. When it is needed, you open the panel, pull the ladder out of the bag and toss the ladder out of the window. The ladder is designed to unroll with gravity. Keep in mind, just having the ladder will do you no good. The ladder must be adequate for the distance and the occupants inside the home. This is quite important and should be discussed now, instead of finding out when it's needed.

If you invest in a KIDDE egress ladder, ensure the ladder is rated for the weight of the occupants. The entire household would not be egressing at the exact same time, so it is not a cumulative weight that is needed, but the estimated weight of the heaviest person who may have to egress, plus a bit more. Why add more weight? There is a good reason to add more weight when estimating the rating of the ladder and it may surprise you, especially if you have children in the home.

In emergency situations, children tend to freeze. In some house fires, the children perished because they ran and hid inside their closet so they didn't have to see the fire or smoke. Eventually, the fire and smoke found them and they died because they were so frozen with fear, they went to what they considered to be the safest place for them. For those in the household who do not practice for emergency situations, there is a greater chance they too will freeze when faced with a traumatic situation. This is why practice and training are so vital.

Knowing now that children have a tendency to freeze up when faced with emergency situations, if the children were to run into the saferoom where the parents are sleeping and alert them of the emergency, the parents would need to guide the children through what is needed for egress. Some may think the parent would go down the ladder and wait at the bottom for the children to descend, but if the children freeze, they could remain in the saferoom and perish. Not a good solution.

How to solve the problem:

If you have children in the home and their bedrooms are on the second floor, the following will work to get them over their fears: take the time, when nothing is going on, to show them how to toss the ladder out of the window. Then the parent should climb out of the window and onto the ladder. Once outside, on the ladder and looking into the open window at the children, the parent then should coach one of the children to join them on the ladder. The parent remains in place as the child climbs out.

At this point, the parent would have the child on the inside of their location and holding onto the ladder with them. Then, together, the parent would calmly speak to their child and coach them downward, to the bottom of the ladder. Once at the bottom, the child steps off, the parent climbs back up and repeats that process with the other children, one at a time. By doing this when an emergency is not present, the children solve a problem they haven't encountered yet. By being successful, that action and experience is now embedded into their brains, where it will be saved forever.

This works well because if the children are stuck in the secondary saferoom and the parents are stuck in the primary saferoom, the children could still escape their room, the house and to a safer location without needing the parent to be there. The emergency egress ladders have directions on installing the base onto the studs in the walls (for some models). The occupants only need to toss the ladder out of the window and it will unravel for them and remain securely anchored. Other models have the base extending outwards, wider than the width of the window, so the framing around the window keeps the ladder secured.

Having an option to escape is realistic, especially if the only other way out is through the smoke and fire-filled house. It is an inexpensive option that you only need to purchase once for your home. It can give you the peace of mind that your children are safe and if you needed to egress quickly, you are safe also. These are the small things that people think about as they are standing in front of smoldering ashes of where their house used to be. Sadly, that is a true statement. Use this information to be safer and better prepared for emergencies that are realistic, before you need to deal with them.

DEFENSE

I do not want to go into great detail for self-defense tools, such as: shotguns, rifles, pistols, knives, bats, etc. for a couple reasons:

-This book is about awareness and protection

-This is not a self-defense book

-Laws change everywhere and what may be recommended now, could be illegal next week.

I will say the following: if you do not practice with whatever tool(s) you have for home defense and safety, you will not be proficient with said-tool when the time comes. If you do not continue to practice with that tool, your skill(s) will diminish over time. Just because you had a positive training session once with your defensive tool, does not mean you maintain that skill forever without practice. Practice different scenarios, practice different locations and different tools, for 'just in case' situations.

With the above said, I will be working on a defensive book later on down the road, in the hopes that many will invest in it and practice what I suggest. However, I am realistic in my thoughts and know that oh-so-many people will NOT purchase a book about home defense. Why? It is because their ego will not let them, because in their mind(s) they believe they are well-equipped to handle any situation that appears in the home. They also believe that, because they've used that tool for many years (by used I mean: perhaps once a year, and/or they carry it daily...key word: CARRY) and are taught to believe whatever training they've received in the past is good enough to protect them in the future.

I have dealt with these people and even when they, being as hard-headed as they were, were shown how poorly their safety and security would be in a violent/traumatic situation, they still walked away saying "I'll be okay". At that point I watch them walk away. Why? It is because

I have adopted the philosophy a long time ago: I cannot/will not reach everyone. I want to, I try to, I even approach the realism with kid gloves in anticipation of their reaction, but cannot reach everyone. I can sleep at night knowing I at least tried to reach them.

If you live in an apartment and live on the second floor, the emergency egress ladder option is a viable option for your as well. If you go to the KIDDE website and look at their egress ladders, they have them for all lengths and situations. If you live in an apartment, you cannot cut out a section in the wall to install an emergency egress ladder (however, you should ask your landlord/leasing office if they would pay to have one installed if you were to purchase it, or maybe they may purchase it. You don't know until you ask) usually, so that option may be off the table. You also wouldn't want to have a bag sitting on the floor, under the window and in the way. KIDDE does make ladders that would still work for that situation.

If the leasing office/landlord refuses to purchase an egress ladder and/or they refuse to pay to have an emergency egress ladder installed, then purchase the ladder that is stand-alone. This means, you unzip the bag, pull out the ladder, extend the ends (this part would stay on the inside of the apartment and anchor to the framing of the window) and you would toss the remaining ladder out of the window. It will unravel to the ground and allow for easy egress out of and away from the situation. I would hope an apartment complex would invest in such devices to bring insurance costs down, but perhaps they haven't thought about that yet, but you have!

Overall, if you were in a traumatic event this evening, would your children make it out safe? Would your spouse? Would you? If you hesitate for a moment, use that alert to signal your answer. A little time to organize items, a little time to run through a possible scenario with your children, could be the deciding factor between living through the ordeal, or found in the ashes the next day. I prefer you take my warning and train your family, instead of the alternative.

Ultimately, the choice is yours. Choose wisely...your life and the life of your family depends on it.

TYPICAL HOUSE SETUP

Most homes have the same items inside: couch, chairs, tables, eating utensils, plates, glasses, beds, sheets, pillows, television, computer, papers/magazines, lights and phones. Does that sound about right? Some homes have more items inside and some homes have less. The main thing is: there are items in the home for comfort that could be used against a threat. Those that avoid identifying possible defensive tools from their everyday objects will be in a tough situation if the time comes when they need it.

Let me expound on that a little. Criminals follow patterns and those patterns occur in cycles. When was the last time you heard about a home invasion? What about a car-jacking? I could put a bet down that you've heard of a bank robbery occurring more than a home invasion. Why do you think that is? I have many reasons in mind, the main point is that these crimes do still exist. Are they popular? Maybe not, which is probably why you'll see more reports about what is popular for criminals at THIS MOMENT IN TIME.

Case in point: It seems that criminals have taken to stealing catalytic converters off of vehicles and selling them. Who knew there was such a market? Sure enough, I've seen a lot of RING videos and discussions online regarding the stolen converters. I've seen the videos that people post, trying to identify the criminals and they've truly gotten this thievery down to an art form. One pair of criminals had one person jacking the car up, as the other person swiftly cut the converter off. From start to finish, these two were in and out of there within a couple of minutes.

Do you see my point?

The point of me starting this part out like this is to awaken your awareness in your home, where most people are happily unaware. They are unaware because of a false sense of being protected because they are inside their own home. Again, the head in the sand syndrome, but this situation is more of a blind ignorance that there's no possibility that someone could break into their home because it is NOT their (the criminal's) home! I've seen and heard it from students, who have all changed their thought processes after they sat through this situational awareness seminar.

This moves the conversation towards how is your house set up? When you step into the front door, are you in the living room? Are you entering a hallway? Are there stairs? These are important questions. Why? If a threat were to kick in your door, that threat could continue quickly towards the occupants, regardless where they are. If the front door enters into the living room and you and your family are sitting there watching television, what are you going to do? The criminal knows what they are going to do, and what they are willing to do so they don't get caught (and to eliminate witnesses).

You have options in your living room. If you have a couch, you probably have pillows. If you have a television, you probably have a remote control. If you have a phone, it is probably close to you. This will differ per household, but the basics are there. You have options. If a threat were to kick in your door, they are doing so because they know their action can, and will, beat your reaction. If you have never trained for that situation and it were to happen, you would be frozen in fear. Data overload (your brain trying to decipher the action and make sense of it).

The criminal is relying on the fact that most people are so consumed with things (television, computer, social media, phone, etc.) that most will not take the time to practice different scenarios to find the failure points, to work through what could/would be successful. I said most people, but I didn't say all. There are some, and I can praise most of my students for taking this for action, who receive the information and realize how unaware they have been living. They then make the change(s) in their life to be more aware and protected in their most vulnerable location: their home.

You have two choices at this point: freeze and become the victim and hope you survive, or choose to be better prepared and use the tools around you to create the action the criminal needs to react to. The choice is yours. I hope you choose wisely.

When sitting on your couch, it's as simple as looking at where the door is and looking around for objects you see daily, which could be used as a tool. A magazine sitting on the coffee table? That's a great tool. A pillow on the couch? Another great tool. Your cell phone? Laptop? Remote control? All great tools. If a threat were to rush into your home, uninvited, you could toss an object directly at their face and that would immediately cause that criminal to protect their face. You can use that distraction to get away to your saferoom. If you cannot get away, it allows you some time to close the gap to gain the upper hand.

Some people have closets close to their living room. A closet can house numerous tools: an umbrella, hockey stick, bat, etc. Anything that could be used as a defensive tool against an intruder who's trying to do you harm, is an effective tool. Anyone that has anything thrown towards their face will instinctively cover their face to protect their head. Their brain knows how important it is and wants to protect it all costs. This means to turn the head away, throw one's hands up and cover their face and head, and sometimes duck out of the way. This could give the occupants time to escape. I've proven this in class using a tissue.

Tissue example: I would walk up to a student, show them that it was just a tissue in my hand and then I would underhand toss the tissue at them. They would instinctively reach up to catch the tissue before it arrived at their face. Instincts can be used to your advantage.

Each of your rooms has options, even if you live in an apartment. If you have a kitchen, you have: plates, glasses, mugs, cups, sponges, knives, forks, spoons, pots, pans, lids, mail, candles, napkins, and so forth. Each can be used as a tool. Bedrooms have: pillows, sheets, blankets, pants, shirts, shoes, socks, underwear, candles, clocks, and so on. Bathrooms have: soap, toilet paper rolls, trash cans, toothbrushes, toothpaste, cups, face cloths, towels and so forth. Even cleaning items can be used to defend against a violent intruder. Point being, if you identify what can be used, you're not going to have to think about it if/when the situation comes up.

Walk through your home and ask yourself: What could I use if the intruder came through my kitchen window? Through the front door? Through the garage? Through the basement? Through the bedroom window? Also ask: where would I go if an intruder came in through those locations. This allows you to identify alternate solutions, which is important because you should never assume it to be just one person, nor should you think you would always be in one location when an event occurs. That's what many people do, and are unhappily surprised to find out it was the wrong way to think.

RULE OF 3's

I live and teach the rule of three. This means: If there is one threat, there has to be three. I do not let my guard down until I identify all three threats are gone or neutralized. There may only be two threats, which means I stay alert and continue with my plan until all three are neutralized or gone. See how that works? This allows me to not let my guard down prematurely. I don't want to be surprised with an ambush by the threat's entourage. Preparedness!

Caveat: Unfortunately, with all of the movies in existence, we have absorbed the 'Hollywood' scenario. This means, there is a good chance that someone who is not educated/trained in situational awareness and/or defensive techniques would neutralize one threat and then let their guard down. This is a very real scenario and occurs frequently. The report(s) have included the victim statements of: "I didn't know there were more than one…" and "I thought I was good after taken the threat down, so I put my weapon away…". There are more stories (unfortunately) that gain new additions each day because people 'celebrate' after the immediate threat is neutralized. They never see it coming.

Once you identify the defensive tools in each room, you can now start planning different scenarios to think through. Then, all you would need to do is walk through your scenarios. Walk them out as if it were happening, and talk yourself through it:

"I'm sitting on the couch, a threat kicks in my door, I immediately throw the pillow at their face as I stand. Threat ducks as I race up the stairs, down the hallway and into my saferoom, where I shut and lock the door and call 911. I then move behind my bed for cover and set my phone in front of me as I reach for my defensive tool and plan my next move".

Walking through the scenarios allows you to identify weak points in your egress and/or defense plan. This gives you a chance to find a solution to those problems. By merely walking through your scenarios, you are better prepared for something to happen (and hopefully nothing ever happens), more-so than the average person, who will freeze in fear because their brains have zero successful scenario walk-throughs completed. This works well for those who take the time and work through the 'what if's'.

ANSWERING THE DOOR

I know it may sound simple, it may be a subject you have no interest in reading, but if you continue reading I'm sure you'll gain some information that you can apply in sketchy situations. Is it about answering the door? It is, but it includes a bit more. Please continue reading.

There are many techniques/tactics used against innocent homeowners by criminals that understand natural reactions. This means: if someone knocks on the door, many people would open that door to see who is on the other side (seems like a normal reaction, correct?). Once that door is open, the threat has full control because they have the element of surprise against the homeowner. Can this be avoided? Of course it can! There are many options for the homeowner and it's wise to note them.

If someone is knocking on your door with some sort of emergency, do not open the door, and pay close attention to the sounds around you (reread this sentence until fully absorbed!). A popular tactic by criminals has been to keep the homeowner occupied at the front of the home, while an accomplice breaks in through the back door (or window). Be loud, be assertive and ask them what they want. They may have a rushed tone, an emergent need for you to open the door and possibly use words that make no sense (which could cause you to open the door to hear better). Do not open the door! Instead, in a loud voice, inform the person that you've called the police to get them help.

If someone were to knock on your door and you don't have a peep-hole, or windows to look out to see who it is, again, ask who it is and be assertive. If you have a bad sense that something is off, act like there is someone else in the house. For example: Someone knocks on the door.

You: Who is it?

Person: Please let me in, my car broke down!

You: Do you need me to call (turn your head and speak loudly and sound irritated) WHAT? It's someone at the door...No I don't know who it is, I was asking them now (turn back to the door and sound exhausted at the situation) I'm sorry, what's the problem? Do you need me to call the police or a tow truck?

The threat could think there was someone else in the home, when they assumed it was only you. Making them think/believe that someone else is inside the house could cause them to rush away, to avoid getting seen or caught. This works well.

If you do feel you need to open the door, place your non-dominant foot about 4 inches from the door, lean back and crack the door open slightly. If the threat is going to try and surprise you with an ambush, them rushing the door will cause the door to impact your foot hard, but stops the door. At this point, the threat is not stopping because their force is moving forward and they will run into the door, thus sending them backwards. At that point, you can shut and lock the door! You can then call 911 while you rush to your saferoom to grab your defensive tool, and lock yourself inside.

It is important to lean back so you do not get hit by the door as the threat rushes forward. You don't want to knock yourself out when the door flies open, just the threat. There are many tactics that criminals may try to use to get you to open the door. For example:

-Threats have used a recording of a crying baby outside the home. The homeowner opens the door, steps outside and gets ambushed by awaiting criminals/threats.

-Threats have sent a 'bloody/battered' female to the door crying, saying she was beat up by her boyfriend/husband and needed shelter from him, to get the homeowner (usually a woman) to open the door to let her inside. Women are more likely to open the door to protect the young girl, but that girl is a tool used by the threats/criminals.

-Threats have used a car seat set on the grass, with the back to the house and a recording of a baby crying set inside. The homeowners see the car seat, rush out of the house and get ambushed by the threats/criminals.

If your home has a peep-hole, use it. If you don't have a peep-hole, there are doorbells that allow video and audio communication with whomever is on the outside of the door. If you want a decent peep-hole because you don't have a video doorbell yet, there are video peep-holes where the screen is mounted on the wall and the camera is in the center of the door. This way, the homeowner doesn't have to be behind the peep-hole directly. If the threat were to kick in the door, the homeowner would not be in the direct trajectory of that door.

The main take-away from this section is: Do not immediately open the door when someone knocks. Check the windows, check your video doorbell, check the peep-hole, and/or ask who it is before you think about opening that door. Once the threat hears the lock unlatch and the door release, they may force all their weight against the door quickly (their ambush). If your foot is not there, the door could impact you and cause you to reel backwards. Then, the threat/criminal has the element of surprise and full control of the situation.

If you have a bolt-lock on the door and a lock on the doorknob, you could loudly unlock the doorknob and pull on the door so it makes a sound. If the intention of the threat is to bust in once the door releases, you'll know it because they would try to bust in at that moment. The bolt-lock will hold the door closed, and now you know exactly what their intent is. This is why you should put effort in your protection and safety by investing in a good bolt-lock for your door. You should also use longer screws for the section that bolts into the door frame (longer screws equal stronger grip).

I would advise against a bolt-lock that is key-only on both sides. The reasoning behind this is because of how difficult it is to manipulate during an emergency situation. When adrenaline and fear are front and center during an dangerous situation, it would be very difficult to insert a key into the lock to unlock your only safe exit. A key access on the outside with a knob on the inside is typical. That configuration works adequately and maintains the safety and security of the home. Be aware of any windows by that lock. If there are windows framing your door, a threat could break the window, reach in to physically unlock the bolt-lock and just open the door. So, what happens in that situation?

If you cannot avoid that situation, a good bolt-lock is still advisable, but there are other ways to secure the door. If need be, the homeowner could install a small door lock at the bottom of the door, where it cannot be reached from the outside (if the threat were to reach inside a window). Now, no one wants to have multiple locks on their door, but if it is the only choice to provide proper security (shy of replacing the entire door and frame with one without windows), you do what you have to.

Lastly, there are sheets of protective film that can be purchased and placed onto glass that will withstand impact. Some locations use that technology because the location is prone to hurricanes and tornadoes, some locations use it due to it being in a high crime area. If someone were going to attempt a break-in through a window, to reach inside to unlock the door manually, they would have to spend some time hammering at the glass before anything would give in (which could/would create noise, which the threat does not want). By that time, they would probably run away. This is a low-cost option, rather than having to replace the entire door assembly.

Just remember: you do NOT have to open that door. If someone knocks and you ask who it is and the reply is: "Police, please open the door", ask the person to show you their badge, as you dial 911. As the 911 operator answers, explain who you are, your address and details about the 'officer' trying to get you to open the door. Gain confirmation that their officer is actually at your door. Ask the operator for the name and badge number of the officer, then ask the officer what their name and badge number are. If the name/badge number doesn't match, 911 is already on the phone and help should be forthcoming.

Threats want to target those they feel are easy marks and they do not want to get caught. By applying these techniques of: keeping your ears open (listening for a threat trying to enter your home from another location as the main threat tries to keep your attention at the front door) and having your phone in hand, your safety can be reinforced. Know the sounds of your home and remember: you DON'T have to open the door!

HIDING SPOTS

Throughout the home, there should be multiple locations that seem like an adequate choice for hiding. Now it's time to expand your thought process using 'what if' thinking. Case in point: a closet. A closet could be an adequate hiding place, if you are playing hide-and-seek with your child, but is it a viable location if criminals invaded your home? Could it work? Possibly, but if criminals are breaking into your home, chances are they are there to burglarize your house, to sell the stolen items later. This could mean the closet is going to be ransacked. Now is it a good place to hide?

If the closet is a last resort location, which could happen, what are your options if/when the threat(s) enter? You cannot just hide inside and hope for the best, you must believe they will find you there, and this is why you need a plan. What can be used in your closet as a defensive tool? Some people might say: "that's where I keep my home defense weapon", which may be okay in this specific scenario, but probably not for others (will discuss that in a different book).

Let's assume there are no firearms in the closet for you to use against the criminals inside your home. What next? Are you able to egress from the closet and out of the home? If so, that's the plan, execute the plan. Don't think about it. Don't over think it. Make sure the area is clear and go for it! What if you cannot escape and you're stuck inside that closet? Again, what tools do you have at your disposal? What about the coat/clothes hangers in your closet?

Coat hangers, be it plastic, wooden or metal, hurt a lot when someone smacks you in the face with them. Grab a clothes hanger and be prepared to swing like your life depends on it...because it probably does. You may also have shoes inside that closet. Shoes work also, and remember, anything thrown at the face, will cause that someone to duck, cover their face, and/or move their head to avoid an impact. That could be the break you need to escape the area. A closet may not be the ideal place, but could be an option (depending on your home).

Under the bed? Would that be a good place? Not so much. Criminals breaking into a home to burglarize it are going to look in the dresser drawers, closets and, yes, you guessed it, under the bed. Hiding underneath your bed could trap you in that location. Even if you wanted to, you wouldn't have the ability to scramble away from that location with any relative ease (or speed). Another note on using underneath the bed: If you know criminals will look underneath your bed for items they can steal, think about what you place under there and avoid storing valuable objects in that location. Why make it easy for the criminal(s)?

What about the bathroom as a viable hiding place? It depends on the situation and the layout/design of the bathroom. If a burglar were to break into your home, they may pop their head inside the bathroom to look quickly around the sink for any jewelry that may be set there, but they won't stay long in that location. It is unusual that anyone stores valuables (except for what was just mentioned) in the bathroom, so it could be a viable hiding place.

If your bathroom has a stand-up shower with sliding doors, it should have a handle on the door closest to the shower entry. Some people use that handle to hang their towel. If a large towel is hung on that handle and the door is open, an average-sized person could hide behind the towel, crouched down inside the shower.

In my last house, I slid the shower door to the side to open it and had my wife crouch down inside. My wife was able to hide inside the shower, behind the towel that was hanging on the outside shower door-handle. Upon entering the bathroom, I could not see my wife and would have never assumed there was anyone hiding inside.

Why?

With the doors open, it provides the appearance that it is an empty shower. If there was a cloudy curtain around a bathtub/shower, the criminal could/would probably swipe the curtain wide, to ensure no one was hiding inside the bathtub. Why? Because the criminal(s) could not see inside the tub/shower. With the stand-up shower, I set the scene where the glass above the towel was unobstructed. The criminal could see inside the shower and the shower door was fully open, which pro-vokes an immediate assumption that the shower was completely empty (despite there being a person crouched behind the towel).

If there is a window inside the bathroom, there is a possibility that the occupant could use an emergency ladder to escape a second-floor bathroom window. In that scenario, it is important to recognize the sounds that would be created when someone attempts an escape out of an open window. The bathroom door would need to be locked, to impede any entry into the bathroom. This limits the escape opportu-nity for the occupant if the threat(s) hear noises coming from another location. They could/would rush to see what that noise was (again, they don't want to get caught).

In my previous dwellings (apartment and house), I had a dedicated linen closet. My child was small enough to fit inside this closet. We practiced the egress many times, and I set up that closet to look like an ordinary closet. My child could sneak into that closet, hide behind the large package of toilet paper and not worry about being spotted. If a threat were to open the closet, they would see the linen and the toilet paper and move onto more lucrative locations. If it appears to not be lucrative for the criminal(s), they would move on, thus leaving my child safe inside.

You know your house and apartment, which means you know where ideal locations may be for your child(ren) to hide. If you practice scenarios, you imbed viable actions into their brain, thus allowing them to retain a possible location to hide if a threat were to invade the home. The practice is important. You cannot just tell a child that a hiding-location will work in an emergency, you have to have them proceed to that location and hide themselves. Otherwise, the action of a threat busting in the door could cause them to freeze, instead of acting. Kids are smart, but if they haven't practiced anything, their brains must (just like an adults' brain) process the data coming at them before they come up with a viable solution.

Hiding places can exist wherever the homeowner needs them, with prior planning. By simply stacking cabinets a certain distance from a wall, it could provide an escape location for the occupants without being seen or heard. This allows the occupants of the home to have another option if they are unable to get to their primary/secondary saferoom location. You can create your own safe-havens throughout your house without having to invest a lot of money. Think out of the box and identify those locations.

Could you invest in having a saferoom constructed in your home? You sure could, for many thousands of dollars, but know this: many constructed saferooms have one entry/exit and that is it. Many safe-rooms that are constructed inside the home will have one door and no escape. Sure, the saferoom may have its own ventilation, but what happens if your home is on fire? Are they fireproof? Most are...but what if something happens with the ventilation? What if the smoke were to encroach the air ducts? Depending on where the saferoom is constructed, it could be worse for the occupants to remain in the saferoom.

Ultimately, the choice is yours. If you are proactive enough, walk around your entire home (including the garage) and identify locations where you could hide from intruders. Even behind the couch in the living room is a viable option. Threats are not very likely to look behind the couch for valuables, but they may crouch down to check underneath. If you crouch and look underneath the couch, can you see the baseboard or the wall behind the couch? If so, attach fabric so it impedes that view. A low-cost idea and minimal effort could easily provide the solution.

Some children are small enough to fit underneath counters and/ or inside cabinets. That's a thought, but keep in mind, although the criminals may NOT look in the kitchen cabinets, there is a chance they might check them. More importantly, you would need to have a space already set up for the child AND ensure there was something that could be placed in front of them (in case the threat was to open the doors to that cabinet). See the problem? Most people would eventually use that cabinet space.

The main purpose of identifying hiding locations and creating your own hiding locations throughout the home, is to be better prepared if a home invasion occurred. Knowing the safe spots throughout the home also allows the occupants to act, rather than freeze (if they come home and suddenly encounter a burglar inside their home). These scenarios occur each day and do not always end the way good people wish they would end. This can be prevented by taking a moment and identifying the possible locations, then practicing the egress action(s) with the occupants.

Wishing an evil person would leave you alone, leave your house alone and leave your children alone, will not deter an evil person from doing so. Practice will not guarantee your safety (nor freedom), but it will greatly increase your chances of survival. Your chance of survival without practice and without thinking about possible solutions, are much less than if you had. You can hope nothing bad happens to you and think that is enough, but if it does happen to you and you never took the time to think about the scenarios and identify solutions, you will forever regret it. Again, the choice is yours. Choose wisely.

Each possible hiding location should be assessed fully before committing to it. As a last resort, you may not have a choice and may need to hide in a location that does not provide an exit, but it would be beneficial to the occupant(s) to identify all locations and then write down the pros and cons. This process allows the occupants to talk through possible alternatives and exit strategies. If there are 'last resort' locations, ensure there are tools in that area for whomever hides in that location and defensive actions are needed.

Dead-ends should not be the first choice for any occupant. Identify each location and assign a priority number. Practice scenarios with the occupants of the home and critique each scenario by allowing each occupant to assess their locations. By conducting the scenarios, using 'what if' situations and critiquing the actions, each occupant can identify possible alternatives. They could then verbally identify the tools they could use for defense and how they would use it against a threat.

Remember: concealment hides, cover provides a level of protection. Take the time to fully assess your location for possible hiding spots and practice using those locations. Involve all occupants and critique the scenarios. If any deficiencies are identified, fix the problems or remove that location as a possible hiding spot. Being proactive by initiating scenarios and fixing problems identified, if/when a real emergency is present, the occupants have solutions at their disposal that they know work.

DISTANCES INSIDE THE HOME

Some people may think it silly to know the distances throughout their home, but there are reasons why it should be known. If you are thinking I am going to speak about home defensive distances while using a firearm, this is not the book. It IS a very important subject to cover, but this book is about situational awareness in the home, but that book will be forthcoming. No, distances inside the home are important (or should be) to the whole family, if they want to survive.

Sounds dramatic, right? It should. Now, I first want to state that there have been reports of schools that have provided the students a blank floorplan-template, for them to go home and draw their home floorplan and bring back to school the next day. This was an assignment. Sorry, there's no possible way I would provide my floorplan to any-one outside of my family. The prints exist already if you order/request them, but why would you? If the floorplan for your home exists in an unsecure location and happens to get stolen, the household is at risk.

Is that what the assignment was designed to do?

I would hope a school would not deliberately set out to place the household of the student at risk. I would hope. In our current society and with what is exposed daily, I would not remove that possibility from the list of possible scenarios. The floorplan assignment was for the students to draw their egress plans at home, in the event of an emergency. To be honest, the parent of each child should educate their children on egress options in the home, not the teacher and not the principal. Yet, here we are.

In this scenario of the student bringing home a blank template to draw a floorplan of their home, I would direct my child to draw a floorplan that exists on their favorite television show, or make up their own floorplan. The parent could then look at it to ensure it resembles a realistic floorplan of a home (that was not their own) for the project submission. At no time would it be okay to allow a floorplan drawing to be done outside of the home, which is something each parent should also advise their child(ren).

Why does knowing the distances matter?

If there were a fire in your home during the overnight hours, how would your family handle that? Would the kids rush into their closet and hide? Would you rush around throughout the house, eventually succumbing to smoke inhalation and dying? Would your spouse rush around through the fire to look for you, find you and succumb of smoke inhalation also? Does any of that sound like a solution that would work for the entire household? For me, the answer is a resounding NO!

Knowing the distances in your home allows you to navigate your home throughout any condition, just by counting your steps. You should know your average stride distance (for most it is between 2.5 to 3 feet) and if you don't, I suggest you measure it out and remember it. If the house was filled with smoke (it is wise to remember that smoke rises), it is important to get/stay low and egress from the home.

As much as I love my pets, survivability is important and that may mean you must leave your pets behind. My pets are like family, which means I would try to get them out, but only while I am trying to get my family out. If I am successful, I will be much happier, but if the goal is to survive, I may have to leave them behind. Children are more likely to grab a pet and keep them hidden inside a closet, to protect their pet from harm. Then your child and the pet will perish. This is not a win-win scenario.

By knowing the distances in the home, I can estimate how far I need to crawl before I must turn. I know how far I have to run, to get to the emergency ladder in the spare bedroom. I know how far I need to crawl to get to my children. It also allows for accurate counting of the stairs you must descend to escape the danger. Knowing distances is extremely helpful to get the family to safety during an emergency.

What else?

Knowing the distances throughout the home can also provide you with vital timing-knowledge, and not just for escape-purposes. If you know the distance from the living room to the upstairs saferoom, you can estimate how much time the threat needs to rush to your location. This allows for reverse planning. Knowing the distances allows the occupants to plan a defense and escape strategy. There are endless amounts of 'what-if' scenarios and we cannot plan for them all, but we can plan for what we consider the worse scenarios.

You can time yourself getting from location to location. This becomes an estimation for anyone else that may try to navigate your home in the dark. To the occupants, this is beneficial to understand because someone less-knowledgeable of your home and floorplan would take longer because they do not know your home. You safety move around the objects you navigate daily, but a threat who doesn't know your home will not be as graceful, and this would make their timing longer overall. This knowledge also benefits the occupants.

Know the distances in your home, to aid in egress and for timing a threat that is already inside your home. Knowing the distance your stride takes can help know the step-count needed to get out of your home safely. Know the children's strides and educate them on knowing their step-counts also. An educated and trained family has a much better chance of survival.

WINDOWS

Newer windows today have evolved greatly from the windows of old. I can remember my windows at the house I grew up in, where you could use a library card (for the kids today...a library card is what you needed to check books out of the library...*sigh*...a library is a location which stores books for people to check out and read...I feel old) and unlock the window. The securing device was a lever that was easily moved (if not new) by a thin card (or other object thin enough to move through the space between the inner window and the outer-upper window).

The older windows allowed criminals to gain access into a home with relative ease. This is not a good thing. In order to be secure in your home, back in those days, other security protocols needed to be implemented to avoid a break-in or home invasion. Why does that matter today? Some houses still have older windows installed, so this is quite relevant. New windows and installation can be quite pricy and some people cannot afford to replace all of their windows, especially those people on a fixed income.

Window construction has changed over the years and the science behind windows today is quite impressive. As technology evolves, newer, more energy-efficient windows will be available and designs can be tailored to the customer's preferences. With this evolution of windows and materials used to construct them, safety features will vary also. Some safety/security features allow for the window(s) to remain open, allowing the homeowner to enjoy a nice breeze.

The variation of security features would be moot in this book, only because the designs, locations, and specifics involved will change over time. The windows I had in the house I lived in previously had security tabs in the top window (framing). The tabs were easily pressed in to open the window fully, or could be released to allow the window to remain open a couple of inches. These tabs were small and looked thin enough to break if great force was applied. Those tabs were quite strong and durable and if anyone were to pry the window open enough to break the tabs, the noise made would/could be enough to wake the household (and hopefully scare the intruder away).

The tabs on these windows were located a couple of inches above the moveable window (inside the home) and inside the upper window (some of those windows are immovable while others can be manipulated to open). The window design I had didn't allow the upper window to move. Some designs allow the upper window to release and pull inward, for ease of cleaning. The tabs were strategically located at a distance that would allow the inner window to open slightly, but not enough for an intruder to gain any upward momentum to break the tabs, and/or open the window fully.

There are much smarter people than I working on these designs. I give them accolades for designing security tabs at a distance that an intruder cannot gain easy entry into the home. Some windows have tabs on top, ends of the window, while other windows have security tabs in other locations. The main importance is the window should have security devices in place to impede/stop an intruder from easily making entry when the windows are open.

What if you have older windows and cannot afford new ones?

OLD WINDOWS

While teaching the Situational Awareness seminar, I had this tiny, quiet elderly woman who sat in the front row and was laser-focused on everything I said. As I began to speak about the window safety and security, she got a sad look on her face, so I stopped and asked her why. Her reply was: she was too poor to afford new windows and was on a fixed budget, but she really enjoyed opening her windows in the spring through summertime. I stopped for a moment and noticed others were paying closer attention at what I might respond with.

I smiled at her and told her that there are solutions which can achieve the result she was looking for, while saving her from having to install brand-new windows. She perked up, as did the others. I then asked her if she had anyone at home that could do repairs or small home construction jobs, and she admitted her grandson likes to do things for her. I then proceeded to slowly explain an option, while she wrote it down step by step. The instructions are as follows:

-Go to a hardware store and purchase a length of a wooden dowel rod. Dowels are commonly used in closets to hang clothes on.

-Next, if the hardware store does not carry Velcro, go to an arts and crafts store, or a department store near you, and purchase a roll of Velcro. Again, not pricy at all.

-Go to your window and open it approximately two inches or so (however high you want the window opened, but remember: the higher the window, the larger the access) and measure from the top of the inner window to the inside-top of the frame. Let's say it's twenty-four inches for the ease of this example.

-Take the dowel rod and mark off twenty-four inches and cut that length.

-Cut two-small lengths of Velcro. The Velcro has both the male and female parts, so make sure they remain together when you cut them (to make sure they are the same length).

This next part can vary depending on the design of the windows and frames:

-Look at the frame to identify two spots, one higher up and one lower, where the dowel can fit into the frame. If the dowel doesn't fit into the frame due to the depth of the frame, consider using the window frame that faces you, on the upper window.

-Take the Velcro and attach it to the dowel, pull the back off of the other section of Velcro (that protects the glue) and place the dowel into position, and press the Velcro into the rear frame.

Repeat with the upper Velcro.

Side note: If you want to protect the finish/material of the window framing, there are felt covers that can be found in hardware stores and some department stores. These felt pads have peel-off bottoms so the pad can be stuck onto an object. These are used for the bottom of chair-legs, to stop the chair from scratching the floor. These same felt-pads can be used on the ends of the dowels to achieve the same intended result. Keep in mind, your dimensions change because of these felt pads, so please keep that in mind when you do your measurements and cuts.

The above solution, which worked great for that elderly woman, is quick and easy. It also allows the window to be raised without the fear of an intruder lifting the window any further. If an intruder tried to lower the window and raise it quickly, thinking they could knock the dowel off or jar it loose, the Velcro would hold the dowel in place. If the homeowner wants to open the window fully, they just have to pull the dowel away from its location and set it aside. A quick, low-cost solution that can be easily achieved.

Newer windows can be a great benefit because the gases used between the window panes can deflect heat from the sun, conserve energy and last for many years. In another house I had, in the first winter we endured, we had ice on the inside of the house. The windows were not new and their effectiveness had failed. We were losing heat, which meant our furnace was running more often, which equaled higher utility bills.

It was more cost-effective to replace my windows, than it was to pay elevated bills each winter.

Moral of this: if you cannot afford new windows, look at your windows and get creative in your solutions. It doesn't have to break the bank, it just needs to keep intruders out and allow you the breeze you desire.

TIMERS

Using plug-in timers for lights and other items are a great way to deter criminals from targeting your home when you are away. This is an effective option for those who go on vacation and/or those who have to work during the evening. Timers, however, do have their downside and that is the timers are set for specific times. If you use a timer on a specific light source and that light pops on and off at specific times, if anyone is watching that house, it could/would be detected as a timer-initiated light.

With technology growing as it does, there are many more options today for such needed solutions. Having a timer that initiates power at different times throughout the night, allows the home to look as if someone was turning on lights as they travel through the home. Doing this shows the appearance of different light sequences and provides the illusion that the home is occupied. This could deter a criminal.

Another option, when speaking of deterring criminals, is a fake television. It's a low-cost light machine that, when turned on, changes light patterns to appear as if someone were watching television. It lights up the room and changes colors sporadically, and to anyone outside the home, it would appear that someone was watching television. If you are curious about what 'changes the light sequence' means, here is a task for you:

-Tonight, turn on your television and tune in a typical evening show. Pick a sitcom or series.

-Go outside and look at the windows of the room that has your television. Notice the changing colors. That fake television projects changing colors and mimics the same lights you witnessed.

The fake television works well because it eliminates the need to have your television on a timer. It also makes it easier to convince a criminal that someone was still inside the home and is currently awake watching television. That projection makes your home a harder target to hit. Criminals like easy targets (with no one home preferably) where they can quietly get in and get out with whatever they can carry.

Using timers can be beneficial to the homeowners and can provide a peace of mind when away from the home. Timers are also helpful for those who come home after work after the sun goes down. During the winter, it gets darker much earlier than in the summer. Using timers can allow the homeowner the luxury of illuminating his/her home prior to arriving from work. This way, if the homeowner were to arrive home and notice most of the lights are off, they are alerted to the possibility that someone is (could be) inside their home. That allows for a quick call to the police, so they can clear the home and ensure no one is hiding inside.

Again, technology being what it is, there will be greater advances as time progresses. So many applications are now activated and manipulated by the phone. I'm sure at this point in our age of technological advancements, there are now timers and lights that can be manipulated through our phones. Personally, I choose to avoid some of that technology because of the downsides, but I am sure I will warm up to some of them in the future. Having a light that is controlled by your phone could be useful, and could allow you to turn lights on and off sporadically, to avoid the programmed timing of an actual plug-in timer.

Do your research and shop around for the best rated deals. As with many things: just because it's expensive, doesn't mean it's the best, and just because it's cheap, doesn't mean you should buy it. Do your due diligence and research. Read. Ask questions. Then invest.

ARRIVING HOME FROM [...]

It doesn't have to be a date, it could be arriving home from visiting a friend, or whatever reason you are returning home. Today, it is important to have safeguards in place to ensure the safety of you, your friends and your family. Having a simple 'check in' to a friend or family member could be the one thing that saves you.

Why/How?

Let's say you arrive home and there's a threat inside your home. Convincing the threat you have to call your friend/family because they will call the police if you don't, could be the one thing that saves you. Having a check-in saves you whether you make that call-in or not. If you do not call in and your friend is expecting that call, your friend knows to call the police. If the threat tells you to call your friend, but 'don't be stupid', which means: "don't tell anyone that I'm here", now you can implement the call and coded message. Win-win situation.

Setting it up:

When setting up a call-in/check-in protocol with your friends and family, it's wise to make the codes simple and easy to remember, yet innocuous. You can't say there's a threat next to you, because that threat could then cause harm to you. You cannot sound like you're sending a code to your friend/family, because, once again, the threat could/would recognize the coded message attempt and cause you physical harm. Your codes should be simple and easy to remember, yet be something the family reacts to immediately and doesn't get confused.

Examples:

Let's say you have a daughter, we'll call her Angel, and she's at a college located in a state too far away to respond to. You know she is going out on a blind date and is planning to be home by 10 p.m. her time (so let's say 9 p.m. your time). A simple scenario without concern or worry would look like:

[Phone rings]

Mom: Hello dear, how was your date?

Angel: It was okay, we ran out of things to talk about.

Mom: Sorry to hear that, maybe next time.

Angel: Maybe

Mom: You going to bed now, dear?

Angel: I'm going to stay up a bit and watch some TV and then hit the bed.

Mom: All right, dear. We love you.

Angel: Love you guys. Goodnight.

Mom: Goodnight.

[Phones are hung up]

In that scenario, it was a blind date that turned boring. Angel got home safe and was going to watch some TV and then go to bed. What sort of codes could be used if the blind date followed Angel home (or dropped her off and forced his way inside the home)?

[Phone rings]

Mom: Hello Angel, how was the date?

Angel: It was okay. The restaurant was new so...

Mom: New? What'd you order?

Angel: I wanted mussels, like what we had at that place on the Cape?

Mom: Mussels? They didn't have any on the menu?

Angel: Since it was new, I figured I'd order the chicken salad, just to be safe.

Mom: I understand, dear. Glad you are home safe. Are you going to bed now?

Angel: No, I think I'm going to stay up for a little bit, have a glass of wine and maybe start the book series I've been putting off.

Mom: Okay, dear, we love you. Goodnight.

Angel: Love you, mom, goodnight.

[Phones are hung up]

Breaking down the conversation, Angel begins by telling her mom that the restaurant is new. Her mom would begin to catch on that something was 'off', because Angel avoids new restaurants because she likes to wait until they are established before trying them. Let's say mom missed that hint. Angel mentioned she wanted to order mussels, like they had on the Cape. Her mother would know that Angel despises mussels, or perhaps is allergic, which should prompt mom to begin jotting down some notes.

If the blind date was standing there, listening, he was obviously present during the date, so the following would/should sound normal, because he observed it in real time. Angel tells her mom that instead of ordering the mussels, she ordered the chicken salad (or whatever was ordered). This is done to add authenticity to the conversation between Angel and her mother, and since she DID order the chicken salad, no suspicions are provoked. Hopefully. Angel's mom asks if Angel is going to bed and Angel replies that she is going to pour herself a glass of wine and start reading a book that is a part of a series.

Angel's mom would know that Angel dislikes wine, thus prompting another red flag for the mom to catch onto. Her mom would also know that Angel doesn't like books that are parts of a series of connected stories. Perhaps Angel's mom knows that Angel doesn't read in the evening because it makes her vision fuzzy. These are the specifics that can be used to provide information that would 'calmly' alarm her parents. During the conversation, once the mother understands the message, she can jot down "Angel is in trouble. Call 911 to her home" and rush it over to a family member or spouse, to have them call the police in Angel's location.

While the mom and Angel are talking, someone else in the house could be calling 911 in the state Angel lives, and report that she is under duress. If the threat were listening to the conversation and doesn't identify any red flags, then he may get bored and relax on his attentiveness. He could get aggravated and wave at her to get off the phone, but then Angel can roll her eyes while pointing at the phone and make the 'blah blah blah' hand signals to the blind date, acting as if she was trying to get off the phone, but her mom's a 'talker'. Again, normal actions that would not raise alarms.

If the check-in is with a friend, the same concept could work, but let's use a texting situation/confirmation with the friend. Same blind date scenario and the date, let's call him Bob, forces Angel inside her apartment. Angel's friend, Ann, knows Angel's blind date ends at 10 p.m. Angel and Ann have a code system they use to indicate they are home, alone and safe.

[Through text message at 10 p.m.]

Ann: You back yet?

Angel: Just got home.

Ann: How'd it go? Was he nice?

Angel: Super nice! Almost too nice (winky face emoji)!

Ann: Are you going to see him again?

Angel: I hope so, but next time we'll do dinner and dancing!

Ann: Sounds fun!

Angel: Should be, I just have to convince him to come see me again.

Ann: That shouldn't be too hard, you're a great catch.

Angel: Aww, thanks. Love you too.

Ann: Okay, I'm going to bed now. Talk with you tomorrow?

Angel: Sure thing, love ya! Goodnight.

Ann: Love you too! Goodnight.

[Texts stop]

Between Angel and Ann, they have codes within their conversation, to indicate if the date went well, if she was alone, or if she were in danger. Ann asks if Angel is home and if he, Bob, was nice. Angel replies with "super nice" and follows that up with "almost too nice" and adds an emoji at the end. Keeping the codes simple and both parties assuming there is someone watching the phone over their shoulders, the codes should be natural to the conversation. It was a blind date and friends ask each other about the person that showed up and if they were nice, etc. By Angel saying the word "super" and followed the line up with an emoji, Ann now knows that the date isn't over and Bob is inside her home. The indicator that she was under duress was when she mentions "dinner and dancing", because only her friend knows that Angel hates to dance, and especially hates dance clubs.

The codes should be something that both parties would catch onto. Not calling at all is a prompt to call the police, but in the event the person is inside the home with an intruder or threat, the best bet is to convince that threat that if she doesn't text her friend/call her family to tell them about the date and that she's home, they would call the police immediately. That concept is not foreign to the world. Many friends/families will request a notification that their friend/family member is okay, especially after a blind date, because that date was with a stranger.

We live in a dangerous world where bad people do bad things and want nothing more than to get away with it so they can continue doing bad things. Being prepared and aware of these things means to think of all angles. What if you just arrived home from work? It's dark when you leave work, you get home and your house is dark, quiet and 'empty'...or so you think. You enter the home and what is the first thing you do? Drop your keys onto the counter, take off your coat and turn on a light? What if, when you flip that light switch, there's a strange man standing there with a knife/gun in his hand?

At that very moment, you would/should be frozen in fear. Why? Because you were not expecting anyone to be there. What do you do? This is why thinking about these things now can benefit you if this situation were to occur. I can honestly tell you, the reader, that I hope with all of my heart that nothing remotely like this ever happens to you. I truly mean that. Being realistic in our thinking means we must think about it, so we can create a solution. That solution may need a lot of 'what ifs' just to see options, but it doesn't take any money, takes little time and provides a mountain of benefit IF the situation were to present itself.

If you have read this book, you realize that part of the awareness lessons includes identifying defensive tools everywhere throughout your home, just in case it is needed in that area. Wherever you are, there should be something that could be used to defend against an intruder, anything. Having your cell phone on your person is important because it can be used as a defensive tool also, and used to send a code to your neighbor/friend/family, to signal that you are in danger and need help now.

In trying to keep communication natural, just in case the threat is watching your texts, your codes should be something you're not quick to forget when in crisis-mode. Since I was prior military, there's lots of acronyms that could be used to signal an SOS. Military lingo to a civilian may not be well received, so should be avoided (in this sense, a civilian is referring to someone who has never been in the military). If you don't think you'll be able to convince the threat that you need to make a call, have a text code backup.

Examples:

Peanut Butter: Texting Peanut Butter to your friend can signal you are in duress. If you received a text from your friend, but were unable to talk or spend time texting, but you were not in trouble, your reply would be: "CUP", as in Peanut Butter Cup. It completes the text and tells your friend that you cannot talk, but are not in any trouble. It could have been a great date and the conversation was still ongoing. One can talk on speakerphone and text at the same time.

Mickey: One would presume MOUSE would be the return code, but it doesn't have to be and who else would know? Between two people, how they put their call and reply codes in effect is on them. If your friend were to text you MICKEY and you were home with a threat present and that threat sees that text, the threat could/would ask what it was about. You could then tell the threat that you have communication with your friends each time you go out, and if you don't reply, they will call the police. The threat would then tell you to reply.

Now, between you and your friend, if the code used is MICKEY, you could make it so you would reply with MOUSE, because that would be normal to those who don't know. This could alert your friend that you are in danger. If you are not in danger, but on the phone, your reply to signal you cannot talk at the moment, but are at home and safe, could be MINNIE.

Variations of codes are limitless and only hampered by your imagination. The codes should be changed every so often, just so it doesn't become something you forget about, and think about providing a small itinerary to your friend/family when going out. This information does not need to be intricate, just informative. By providing an itinerary, you are letting your friends/family know where you are going to be and about what time, so if anything were to happen, they have locations to search and gain information from.

Itinerary information could be as brief as: 8 pm dinner at The Steak House on Burger Street. Movies at 915pm and home by 1130pm. If you were to go on vacation and wanted friends and family to know where you were going and so forth, it would be advisable to include a planned code word-text each night to signal you are back at the hotel, safe and sound. An itinerary could/would look like:

Monday: 1pm hiking at Big Mountain. 5pm dinner at Taco Hut. 8pm back to hotel for drinks. 10pm confirmation text.

Tuesday: 11am jet skiing on Wet Lake. 2pm hiking Big Mountain. 5pm dinner at hotel restaurant, followed by drinks. 10pm confirmation text.

Wednesday: 9am leave hotel to go to the airport. Flight 111 at 12pm. Arrive at home airport 4pm. Home by 530pm latest. Confirmation text by 9pm in case of delays.

In the above examples, the confirmation texts were at 10pm while on vacation, which allows you to send a text code if you are in trouble, just by sending the text earlier than planned. This is a way to alert your friends and family that you are in danger. They can look at your itinerary and see that you should be hiking Big Mountain at the time you sent your 'last text of the evening' text. This gives family and friends a location to provide to local law enforcement.

The main point I am stressing here is to be prepared for events you cannot plan for, and communicate information without the 'bad guy' knowing you are alerting your friends and family of the situation. If you popped on a light and an intruder was standing there with a knife or a gun, you probably are not going to get away with saying "I'm going to order us a pizza". That would be an unnatural act in that situation/ scenario. There is a chance you could play it off by saying you were very nervous and lightheaded from not eating, and then ask if you could order a pizza (through 911). That may work, but the main point is to know what your options are, create code words between you and your friends/family that would prompt them to know you are in danger, and have the state of mind to activate those codes when needed.

IF FIREARMS ARE USED

As I mention in other locations, this book is not about firearm defense or defensive tactics inside the home. That being said, I feel it is important to state some things in this section, in the hopes of breaking through some egos, some diehard believers of whoever taught them, dedicated pupils of who they consider 'gun Gods', those who have 'been shooting their entire lives' and those who are hunters, law enforcement, and/or military or veterans. I suppose I should also add that I hope to break through to the ignorant, also (and I don't mean that to come off disrespectful or insulting, by ignorant I am referring to the untrained/ unknowing).

I am definitely motivated to write a home defense book, truly, but I have encountered too many people who live in a bubble and believe they are much better prepared to defend themselves than they really are. This means they could die a horrible death because they believe they are adequately prepared. I had some success in the past, but the majority of those I've tried to reach who fit into those categories I've mentioned, walked away still believing they were still 'good to go' in the defense realm...despite their targets telling them different.

TEST

If you REALLY believe you are adequately trained and efficient with your firearm to defend your home from intruders, then try this little test and prove to yourself that you are correct in that thought process. Those of you who read this section and say "This is crap, I know my skills" have egos that will cause you to lose your defensive action(s) against intruders. Those that say "I don't need to train, I'm a [fill in occupation: cop, security guard, military, veteran, instructor, etc.]" are fooled into thinking what you currently know is good enough to protect yourself from harm. Does that sound like a positive thing?

If you store your firearm inside a lockbox, to be used as a home defense tool when a home invader enters your home, is it close by or in another location?

If you store your firearm inside a lockbox and that box needs a key to open it, are you proficient in retrieving the box, unlocking it and retrieving the firearm quickly?

If you store your firearm inside a lockbox that has biometrics (using a thumbprint to open), have you tried to open that box with a bloody thumb? Do you know if it is possible?

If you store your firearm inside a lockbox, but store your ammunition in another location, have you timed yourself getting out of bed, retrieving the box, unlocking the box, rushing to the ammunition, loading your firearm and preparing to defend your position? Do you think a threat or group of threats could reach you before you achieved all of those actions?

Have you ever tried retrieving your firearm while under duress?

Have you thought about everything that you need, to defend effectively?

Have you thought about: how long does it take me to be fully wake, after being woken up by a strange sound (or a reason not known because I was sleeping)?

Have you thought about the effects of adrenaline?

Have you thought about a smoke-filled house with threats inside?

These are all important questions to ask yourself now, rather than when faced with those situations and have to figure it out as the footsteps of many criminals get louder to your location. Still, some will ignore those questions and live with the false sense of being adequate with their firearm for defensive purposes. You are the ones I worry about when I am out and about, not because of your lack of training or abilities, but because you are probably going to shoot a lot of innocent people in your response to a bad situation you are not truly proficient in defending against. Sad but true.

THE TEST

What is this test I want you to do? It's a test to hopefully show you where your failure points are, where you need to make corrections, but most importantly to hopefully wake you up to the realization of your skill level. That's my hope for you. Here is the test I want you to try:

-Place an object in the location you usually store your firearm (i.e. a dollar bill, a hair brush, etc.).

-Place your firearm in another location, away from the location you usually store it. If storage is inside a lockbox, remove the pistol, make it safe, place the object you are substituting for your firearm inside the box and lock it.

-Again: objects you can use to replace your firearm: a spoon, a wallet, a pair of socks, a dollar bill, really anything that fits into your hand.

-Once the replacement object is inside the lockbox, or at the location your defensive firearm is usually stored, lie down in bed.

-Set your alarm for a minute, or a minute five seconds, or whatever, but minimum a minute for this test.

-Once the alarm is set, set your phone down and think about something else: sports, yardwork, locations you've traveled, anything but the alarm.

-When the alarm sounds, spring up, get your object and point it at the door.

Questions:

-Were you able to get that object pointed at the door before the alarm rang three times?

-Were you extremely shaky trying to get to your object?

-Were you fumbling around with the object before you gained control of it?

-Did you accomplish your goal before a threat could get to you?

PERSPECTIVE

Now put things into perspective. You were not asleep when you attempted this test. You were already awake and aware of what you needed to do, which means you should be super-proficient in retrieving the object and pointing it at the door with speed and efficient movements. No fumbling. No 'sausage-fingers'. No hesitation.

Was that the case?

SOLUTIONS

Training and practicing accuracy, control and ALL of the fundamentals as often as possible is a step in the right direction. Is it costly? In can be, so what's another solution to reduce the costs? Simple, dry fire practice at home. Practicing the actions of retrieval and aiming at home. Practicing at home, without ammunition loaded into the firearm, can increase your proficiency before you need to apply it in a real-world scenario.

The benefit of trying this test is you get to identify where your weak points are or your failure points, and allows you to change where/how you store your firearm. It also allows you to identify movements and possible solutions to impede the progress of an intruder, while you retrieve your firearm. I hope I've made my point, and definitely hope you purchase my home defense book when it is written, because it will help you for sure, but you have to want to accept that help. That can be hard for many to accept.

I want to add, again, the importance of flashlights and especially mounted flashlights. Some people have mounted flashlights on their home defense firearm. If you use a flashlight, practice holding the flashlight while shooting. If you use a mounted flashlight in a house and you fire the pistol, the smoke will fill the area and the flashlight will blind the user by bouncing back (reflection) from the smoke. This is why a mounted flashlight is not recommended (by me) for home use. Outside, a mounted flashlight would/should work fine, but I continue to prefer to hold the flashlight in my supportive hand, so I can control the beam and apply the tactics I've practiced for years (it also allows for me to have a striking-object in one hand, while pistol in the other).

Note: It is a personal preference and application. I've had my flashlight beam reflect back from gun-smoke and that brightness caused my pupils to constrict. Constricted pupils made me 'snow-blind' and my ability to identify the target became greatly limited. If you believe your flashlight skills are good enough, or your comfortable with the 'what-ifs' during a smoke-filled encounter, then do what you have the most faith in.

I will end this section with this: for the many thousands of students that I have had the privilege of training in my classrooms, I would tell them all the same thing. That was: It's not common sense until someone tells you about it. Once told, though, it THEN becomes common sense. This has a powerful impact on those who were distraught that they were taught poorly, had bad information or was convinced of the wrong thing.

I would hear: "I feel stupid for not knowing that" or "This is a dumb question, but..." and "I should have known that". I would quickly correct them by informing them that if it is a question that pops into their heads, it's not a dumb question. If convinced to not ask questions because it would be looked at as stupid, then whoever pushed that upon you is not a good person. They exist, more prominent than I'd like to acknowledge. Moral of the story: I've given you the information, which means you cannot say that you were not told about it. After this book, it will become common sense.

PRACTICE AND DRILLS

I cannot stress this enough through this book: practice, practice and practice more. This practice is for inside the home, and with the children (if applicable). Practice embeds solutions, even if those solutions seem 'clunky', they are still solutions. Each practice brings about clarity of what works and what doesn't. This is where change can occur: to make better decisions that produce better outcomes. Practice does not have to occur nightly, but should occur. I say that because most would shy away from the thought of having to invest time into practicing for something that 'probably won't ever happen to me'!

CHILDREN

If you have children in the home, it is important that those children react to the commands of their parents. If you give a command, they need to respond and not stand there asking "how come" or "why do I have to do that" and so forth. Now, I know what you're thinking: "If I could get my kids to respond to my commands at all, that would be a huge accomplishment", but this is where parenting is needed. You should explain to your children the importance of responding to your voice when a command is given, versus questioning everything. Once you explain that their safety would be in jeopardy if a threat were to invade their home, they become a little more invested.

No one is saying it will be easy.

This is where the practice comes in and hopefully pays off. Children/teens need a reward for their efforts, otherwise they may not be invested. This does not mean to buy them something when they do something correct, it means to be smart about what that reward is. If you involve your children in the plans, they become invested because now they had the ability to choose something or be a part of something. It was theirs and theirs alone that prompted the scenario. This is where praise comes in (which young children respond well to) and sometimes a different reward (such as: an dish of ice cream, their favorite cookie, they get to stay up an extra 30 minutes after their bedtime, a toy, etc.).

When practicing for scenarios, a family meeting can take place, let's say in the living room, and you discuss what the scenario will be. At this point, you could turn to one of the children and tell them that they get to choose the scenario next week, but it must meet the criteria AND they must accept criticism so solutions can evolve. Criticism for a child/teen is tough, because they could take it personally because they created the scenario. Let me give you an example of how a simple scenario can unfold:

I collect the family in the living room and explain the scenario. In this scenario, a home invader kicks in the front door, but doesn't gain entry on the first try. When I yell "RUN", everyone scrambles to their saferoom location and proceed with their protocols. Our protocols are: the kids rush into the main saferoom with my spouse. My spouse dials 911 as the children get behind cover, close to my spouse. My spouse simulates speaking to the 911 operator while listening for my follow-on voice commands.

"RUN"

Everyone proceeds as planned. The reason I am not in the saferoom with everyone else is: I am ensuring they get to the saferoom and prepared to lock the door, as I leave a small gap so I can defend my family if the threat gains full entry. If I have to command the threat, my spouse can relay what I am saying to the operator on the phone. I rush into the saferoom and lock the door.

Once the door is locked, I unlock it and we all meet back in the living room. This is where the questions come in: what did we do well? What did we do that needs work? What could we have done if we couldn't get to the saferoom? Any question that can be asked about that scenario, should be welcomed by any/everyone in the family. Criticism (respectful) is important and should not be stifled. Criticism allows for change, which is needed to fine-tune actions. The criticisms should be acknowledged and explained further, if a child's criticism is not realistic. Be honest but do not make the child feel like their answers or criticism was unimportant or 'stupid'.

By involving the children in the scenario-creation and criticism, you are welcoming their investment, showing them that their opinion and views are valid and important. Especially if the children are small (young in age), it will be very important that they remain interested and invested. They also need to understand why they should respond, instead of remaining in place trying to process the drama themselves. Ice cream is a great reward, by the way, when they finally get the process and do well in their immediate response. Just saying...ice cream is a great reward for everyone!

As practice continues and becomes a common occurrence in the home, advancing the scenarios to involve contingencies is very important. Nothing (usually) ever goes 'perfect' the first time (or when you really want it to), so adding contingencies is needed to encourage the growth of the family. It is advisable to contain the scenarios and debrief into a dedicated period of time and try not to exceed that time. If practice gets too long, too involved or seemingly impossible, the occupants (especially children) will lose interest and end up 'going through the motions' just to get through the practice. Keep it interesting.

CODE WORDS

Code words are used to relay information to others in the home, without giving away the information. What this means is: it gives you a chance to alert those in the house that you are under duress as you enter, thus allowing them to quickly egress to their saferoom locations. Keep the codes simple and proprietary to the household. It is important to not divulge the code words and challenge and reply information, which means it is very important to explain to the children why it is vital to keep it private.

Only allow the immediate circle of family in on the specific home-codes and have simple code words for the outer-circle of friends/family. You wouldn't want someone to drive up to your small child and have them say "Your mom is sick, in the hospital and she needs you! Get in!" because the first response of the child, naturally, would be to rush to their mom's side. You should want your child to respond with:

"Blueberry" to see if that person knows the correct response. It is very important that the words or phrases do not make sense, such as: Peanut butter and jelly, or apple and pie. Make it unusual and hard to guess.

Code words and challenge and replies can give a lot of information without sounding out of the ordinary. For example, a husband arrives home, steps into the house and calls out to his wife: "Hey honey". The wife responds: "Did you remember the ham?", quickly alerting the husband that there is someone inside the home and has the wife stuck where she's at. If she responded with: "Did you remember the biscuits?", the husband would know there are multiple threats inside the home. How? A ham is singular, biscuits plural, and by speaking in a normal manner with an ordinary subject, the threat(s) would not catch onto their codes. His response would be: "Darn it! Sorry, I'll go grab it now".

In that scenario, the husband can then open the door and slam it loudly. He then stands still and listens. The threats will be listening to the door slam, alerting them that the husband had left. Not hearing a vehicle pull away, they will question whether or not they heard the car leave and head to a window and/or check the garage. The husband knows to wait out the threats to gain the advantage. He would have the element of surprise, thus creating the action to cause the threat to react. This could give the husband time to grab a defensive tool in preparation of the incoming threat.

Another scenario using a codeword/challenge & reply for children, is as follows: Father returns home and gets ambushed as he enters his home. He quickly calls out to his daughter: "Sammy, I'm home, you better not have that cat in your room!" and continues slowly into the home. A criminal could know he has a daughter named Sammy, but it's unlikely the threat would know about a pet, nor would the threat realize there is no pet in the home at all. Using that phrase alerts Sammy that there's a threat inside the house and she is to rush into her saferoom and lock the door. If the threat forces the father to the daughter's door, the father can still provide coded information while sounding like a typical father:

-"Sammy, you ruined my favorite blanket with that cat, if you ruin another..." and if the threat coerces the father to get his daughter to open the door:

-"Sammy, open the door right now or you get no ice cream after dinner!" knowing Sammy doesn't like ice cream, but the threat does not.

This would alert Sammy that the threat is still there and has her father in a position by the door, where he is still in danger. Sammy now knows to not open the door. She can then pick up her phone, call 911 and speak in a low tone while hunkered down next to the bed. This keeps her away from the door and allows her to describe the events that are occurring, while giving important information to the 911 operator (i.e. her address. Status of her father, entry points at the house, etc.)

If the father is taken away, but returns and he taps on the door and says:

"Sammy, you get chocolate chip cookies tonight!" Sammy now knows the threat is gone, because her father knows those are her favorite cookies and they use that as the 'all clear' signal for her to open the door for him.

Change the code words for the family every couple of months to avoid anyone from gaining that information on accident. Do the same for the secondary code words with the children. This way, if a stranger, or a neighbor that you don't know, pulls up and tries to convince your child to get into their vehicle, the child will have the most current code word or phrase to throw at them. It could go like this:

Stranger: Bobby, quick, your dad needs you. Get in the car.

Bobby: Mister Greg, Mickey

Stranger: Mickey?

Bobby: Codeword for Mickey?

Stranger: Mouse, now get into the car Bobby!

Bobby knows to now run away and get an adult to help protect against the neighbor. Mouse is an obvious reply to Mickey, but this is why we make sure it doesn't match or come close. Involve the children in creating the codes, it makes them feel like they are participating, but also empowers them that they were the ones that chose the words (they get to act like a spy). This simple solution can save lives and with the amount of kidnapping and child trafficking occurring throughout our world, it is more important than ever to put safeguards in place to protect the children.

One more example: Mother comes home, gets ambushed and forced inside and she announces her arrival to her son.

Mom: Randy, I'm home. You better not be playing that PlayStation.

Perhaps Randy doesn't have a game system or he has an Xbox. Main point is, mom just alerted Randy to lock his door.

Mom walks to his room with the threat directly behind her. Mom knocks hard on the door.

Mom: Randy! Open this door right now! Open it! If you don't open it, you are not going to the movies with Brian!

Randy now knows the threat is at the door with his mom and he knows not to open the door. This alerts him to enact their protocol of phoning the police and giving the information to the 911 dispatcher.

It is important to make it interesting when you practice. It is also important to reward successful practice, especially with children, but avoid making it playful to the point where it loses its seriousness. Keep it difficult and challenging for the movement, add an obstruction in their path to the saferoom, split the kids up from the parents during a practice and so forth. Change it up, reward success, be gentle with the criticism/but honest and continue to change the code words with the family. Doing this increases success against a fast-paced, dangerous real-world home invasion. You want action/response, not frozen and instant victims.

If you have smaller children, you want to avoid scaring them into learning. What I mean is: instead of saying a man kicks in the door with a chainsaw to kill us all, you could just say the family is going to practice fire drills. Or if that child watches a show that has a character they don't like, have that character come through the door to steal the child's candy. Be creative, but avoid giving the child nightmares that they will be murdered in the night. I'm pretty sure, as a parent, you would not want years of a repeating nightmare that keeps you up. Pretty sure.

Start your practice slow to ensure no one gets injured. Make your scenarios realistic and challenging. Identify the items you would use to throw into the face of an intruder and practice on each other with a pillow, but not too hard. Main point is to get the action practiced, without destroying your stuff. If an intruder kicks in your door, you should grab the first thing close to you and chuck it at their face. You may practice with a pillow to not break or injure anything/anyone, but should grab the first thing available without a concern that the object will break, or hurt the intruder. This is why practice is important.

It is advisable to advance your scenarios as the occupants of the home grow in experience. This means to wait until the occupants are comfortable (and competent) with the current scenarios before you eliminate lights. Avoid practicing scenarios in full darkness until the occupants become proficient in their movements. Once the proficiency increases, it would be wise to begin scenarios with less light and incorporating a flashlight into the scenario(s). A flashlight, again, is a highly useful and recommended tool, which every person should have on their person at all times (in my opinion).

WHY FLASHLIGHT?

I know that some may be questioning why I push having a flashlight onto everyone, but let me expound on the subject in a manner that you can connect with:

If you and I were standing in front of each other and I reached down, withdrew my flashlight and held it up, where would you look? You would look directly at the flashlight for a moment before shifting your gaze back to me. Why? You would look directly at what was in my hand because it's a NATURAL human response. If I pulled out a dollar, a coin, a pen, whatever, and did the same action, you would look up at whatever was in my hand. It's a natural response!

Now that you know that, let's say you're a threat. You enter my home and are facing me. I pull out the flashlight and hold it up while depressing the switch to 'flash' the light. You look up at my hand (natural response) and directly into the bright burst of light that my flashlight gives off (because that is the job of the flashlight after all). At this point in time, your pupils will constrict because of the bright light. This creates a 'snow-blind' situation where you are not able to see well until your pupils normalize to the lighting in the room.

As soon as I initiate the light, I know I have about 3-7 seconds (depending on the level of darkness in the surroundings) to rush from the scene because you cannot see well for that time. By the time you're able to see well, I'm already away from the area, and safely inside my saferoom. The darker the environment, the longer the 'snow-blindness' will be present.

If you (again-as the threat) enter my dark living room and I perform the same action(s) (while your pupils are dilated more than they would be with light present), I can gain even more seconds of advantage. It will take your eyes much longer to focus back to 'normal' in that scenario, which gives me more time to escape the situation.

A flashlight is important!

USING THE PHONE

Just reading the title, I'm sure some reactions may be: "Duh, I know how to use the phone", but do you really? What about in a situation where criminals are running around? Does it matter? Of course it does...if you don't want to be identified by a threat, that is. Knowing how to use the phone could save you in some really dangerous/bad situations. I would suggest reading on.

If you are in your saferoom, or hiding elsewhere in your home and there are threats inside the home, you would want to contact the police.

When calling the police, you should make sure your ringer is off and phone is not set on vibrate. A vibrating phone can be heard through the silence. You would dial 911 and want to start regurgitating what you know about the situation. This part is hard for those under duress and caught by surprise.

When speaking with the 911 dispatch, you want to avoid whispering. A whisper has an 's' sound that's made when whispers occur (go ahead and whisper and listen to the sound...try to whisper: "There's a man in my house with a gun and he's trying to harm us"). Talk low, as calmly as possible, but speak in a low tone (now try to repeat the same sentence by speaking low and not in a whisper). The dispatch officer will still hear you, but the threat(s) shouldn't. Talking low allows you to speak even if the threat is close. A whisper is a quick way to get caught/located by the threat(s).

While speaking to the 911 officer, you would give them the information you know: your name, your address, the situation (threats inside the home), how many threats inside the home, if there are any armed threats, where you are within the home, if there are children inside the home, and if you are going to drop keys down to the officers when they arrive. Some people say to tell the dispatch officer if you are armed. I agree that should be mentioned, but only after the vital information is given.

Once the important information is given, then provide the dispatch with the information that you are armed (if applicable). This allows the dispatch to give the arriving officers that information, along with where you are located. Once the threats have been cleared from the home (either from escaping or being arrested) and there's a knock on your saferoom door, now is the time to gain confirmation of who is at your door.

Having someone knock on your saferoom door, when threats were just inside your house and you've been at a high level of fear and stress, can cause the occupant to hear that knock and have a sigh of relief that they are now safe. What if the knock on the door is a threat acting like the police? Many people would be so thankful the bad event is over, they would rush to the door and open it. Then, in walks the threat(s), and that would be bad for everyone inside.

If there's a knock on the door, ask who it is, then confirm it with the operator. The conversation should go like this:

Homeowner: Who is it?

Person: Officer Johnson

Homeowner: (to 911 dispatch) What is the name and badge number of the officer at my saferoom door?

911 Dispatch: Badge 1234 Officer Mike Johnson

Homeowner: Officer Johnson, what is your badge number please?

Person: Badge number 1234

Homeowner: Okay Officer Johnson, thank you. I am going to set my pistol/rifle/shotgun away from me, on the floor.

By confirming with the operator that Officer Johnson is who he says he is, the homeowner can ensure their safety and the steps to take next. If the reply from Officer Johnson was "Badge number 9999" then the homeowner could ask the dispatch to confirm Officer Johnson's badge number again, just to make sure they did not make a mistake. If they did not make a mistake, then the homeowner would inform the dispatch operator that someone was at the door saying they were Officer Johnson but with the wrong badge number.

Why is this necessary?

Think about it this way: if, somehow, one of the threats ambushed Officer Johnson as he was approaching the front door. Now Officer Johnson is compromised and would probably be held in another location, handcuffed outside, or something along those lines. Officer Johnson's nametag would be easy to find, but the threat(s) may not be quick to think about the badge number. This is why you confirm the badge number, along with the first/last name of the officer. The name tag only has the last name of the officer, so a threat would have to know the officer personally, to know their first name.

If you are at home and are ambushed inside your home unexpect-edly, one thing to think about is: you are not beat yet. This means, you still have options. One of those options in this traumatic scenario, is to convince the threat(s) that you would need to order some food before the kids get home, or it would look suspicious. Then, call 911 and order some pizza. This tactic was developed years ago and was a brilliant idea.

Many years ago, calling 911 and ordering a pizza was specifically designed for women who were threatened by their husbands or violent boyfriends. It was created to appear like they were ordering food, but in reality they were informing the police that they were under duress and fearful for their life. The dispatch officer would understand imme-diately and begin confirming the address and ask if the woman could talk. If the woman begins ordering specifics (large pepperoni pizza, large cheese pizza) the dispatch officer would try to get a confirmation from the woman, but would scramble officers to the address on their computer screen.

This worked/works well. In the event the threat snatches the phone from the woman's hand and starts asking who is on the other end of the phone, the dispatch officer would play it off as if they were from a legitimate pizza shop/restaurant. This tactic was helpful in saving many women from dangerous/deadly situations. Even today, calling 911 and ordering a pizza would prompt the dispatch officer to probe for more information. The key to using code is to not sound like you are actually using code, and to get the point across.

If I were trying to give clues to my current environment, while threats were present and threatening me, my conversation would be as follows:

Me: Yes, hi, I'd like to order three large pizzas.

Dispatch: You called 911.

Me: Yes, that's correct, three large pizzas.

Dispatch: Are you in trouble.

Me: I am, I am paying with my card.

Dispatch: How many threats are there?

Me: Three large pizzas.

Dispatch: Can you confirm your address?

Me: Yes, delivered to 1234 Smith Street

Dispatch: Do they have weapons?

Me: Lots of pepperoni on the first one, please.

Dispatch: Officers are on their way.

Me: The other two pizzas are just cheese.

Dispatch: Are they listening?

Me: Of course (fake laugh) lots of napkins, please?

As you can see, the dispatch officer would ask many questions, but depending on the situation and where the threats are, minimal clues can be divulged without tipping the threats off. The goal is to alert the dispatch officer of the threats, try to give them a total number of threats present (3 large pizzas) and answer with typical responses to their questions (Dispatch: Are they listening? Me: Of course (fake laugh) lots of napkins, please?). This helps to disguise the answers. If the dispatch officer is aware to the clues, they will have all of the important information to relay to the arriving police.

There are options, even when scary things are happening fast, there are options if you embrace them. This means thinking about the scenarios I've provided in this book. Think about the training and practice. Think about fortifying the saferoom, after you have identified it appropriately. Think about setting you and your family up for success by being proactive and aware of your surroundings. Your health, safety and security are important, but you have to make the effort.

I want to close this section out with an important note: if the police have to come to your home because you are under duress, the police do not know you. This means: when the police arrive, do not get offended, or be surprised that the police put you onto the ground. Their guns will be out and they will be suspecting everyone inside the home as the threat(s). This means you are considered a threat also. They will scream at you to lie down with outstretched arms. This is for their safety and protection.

There have been many people who scream and yell that the police treated them like a criminal. Obviously, once the adrenaline settles and the heartrate lowers, those with sense will see that the police reacted appropriately. If I was a police officer showing up to a scene where there are home invaders, armed intruders or violent threats inside the home, I would put everyone on the ground first. This includes those inside saferooms, because how would I know what you consider your saferoom? You could be a threat pretending to be an occupant of the home.

Note: I am not saying that ALL of the people who claim to be abused by the police were/are lying, nor justified in their claims. There are good and bad people in every job in existence and in some cases there have been bad people doing criminal (or beyond protocol) actions against someone else.

The moral of the story is: Do not relinquish your defensive tool until you've verified the officer on the other side of your door through the 911 dispatch on the phone. Once verified, place tool away from yourself and be prepared to be put on the floor and searched for a weapon. Do not make sudden movements, do not threaten or fight with the police. This is why practice is important, and knowing what to do when law enforcement arrives is very important.

VACATION PLANNING

When you go on vacation, you do so to get away from your life, away from your everyday stresses and most of all, you go to relax and not think about home for a few days. This is where you can utilize your neighbors for damage control and awareness. I realize in our world today, knowing your neighbor is definitely not like knowing your neighbor in the years I was growing up. In those days, if you were doing something wrong, your neighbor would straighten you out and then your parents would straighten you out when they got home. Today, not as many are friendly with their neighbors, and that is sad.

Take some time and get to know your immediate neighbors, not just for you to have someone who can watch your home when you're away, but also to form a friendship because you live close to each other. Bake some cookies and bring them over, invite them over for a barbeque dinner, or hang out with them around a fire pit in your backyard. If you can form a friendship with your neighbors, you gain so much more and so do they. Just know this: there are some people, who may be your neighbors, that you won't like, know or trust. That is also okay, but you won't want to ask them to watch your home when you're away (or your children).

WHY ASK YOUR NEIGHBORS?

If you are going away for a span of time, if you don't want to ask your neighbors to watch your home and are concerned with your mail piling up, you could put a 'stop delivery' on your mail at your local post office. Main point here is to either ask your neighbor to collect your mail daily, or stop it from being delivered while you're away. An overflowing mailbox and/or boxes piled at the front door is an indication that the homeowners are not home. That is what criminals look for. If your neighbor could collect your mail while you're gone, it reduces the chance of a criminal knowing you are away.

If I was asked by a neighbor to watch their house while they were on vacation and collect their mail, here is what I do:

-I will collect their mail daily as I collect my mail, so it won't be noticed.

-I will walk around their home once every couple of days and look for things out of the ordinary (footprints in the grass/snow, windows opened, windows broken, etc.).

-I will pay attention to any vehicles that seem to be loitering around their home.

If you are friendly with your neighbors, you will become familiar with the vehicles that are usually visiting or parked next/close to their houses. My neighbors will inform me when they are leaving town and when they are returning. They will also inform me if any family member/friend(s) will be staying at their house while they are gone, or if a family member will be checking on the house every once in a while, while they are gone. This is why I pay attention to the vehicles that are normally there. It allows me to identify anything out of the ordinary.

During the evenings, I would make it a point to periodically glace at their home, specifically for movement or unnatural lighting (flashlights). If they have lights on timers, I would see them come on at the same time. If someone were inside with flashlights, the flashlights would light the house differently and I'd be able to identify the movement of the lights. Once I identify abnormal lights, I can give the police a quick call and inform them of possible intruders in the home.

The main point here: get to know your neighbors (for many reasons, one reason being to be friendly, another is to get to know them and see if you can trust them) and gain a rapport with them. Watch their home when they ask you to, and you watch their home when they go on vacation. If you cannot trust or do not like your neighbor, move on to another neighbor (if you have one). Some people live where there are few homes around, others live where the homes are all very close to each other. It's nice to have someone you can rely on to watch your home when you are on vacation (or a business trip) and I'm sure they'd say the same thing.

It is not being too cautious to take the needed time to get to know your neighbors, especially today. If there are any warning signs, do not ignore them. Do not brush off any 'red flags' because you feel you are over-judging the person. Trust your gut and only give trust to someone when they have earned it, never before. It doesn't make you judgmental in a negative way, it makes you cautious. Trust yourself and embrace the warning signs as the universe sending you loud alarms.

MOTION SENSOR LIGHTS

Since there are many design differences between homes, it is important to mention another option: motion sensor/beam activated lights. For some, their bedrooms may be in the lowest level of the home, for others it may be at the highest. It truly doesn't matter where the bedroom(s) is/are located, what matters is what you install to increase your personal safety and security. This additional bit of information isn't just for bad situations, it is also for everyday use.

Motion activated lights can be a benefit for those who need to navigate through a dark home. If you got up in the middle of the night and decided to go to the kitchen, would there be enough light for you to safely navigate to that area? If you had a motion/beam activated light, your movement can initiate a small (or larger) light, which could illuminate the area you're in and make it safer for your travels. If you had friends or visiting family stay over, a motion/beam activated light could help light the area (they wouldn't know the layout of your home as well as you and your family) and decrease the chances of them running into a piece of furniture.

Stairs can be tricky to navigate in the dark, but can be deadly to navigate if you are half-awake and trying to ascend/descend the staircase. A motion/sensor activated light can help, even if the area was engulfed in smoke, by providing light in areas that alert the homeowner of existing stairs and/or towards an exit. These are the practical uses for motion/sensor activated lights. There is another reason for installing motion/sensor activated light(s) within the home: an unintended visitor (home invader/burglar/threat/criminal).

A motion/sensor activated light could provide surprise illumination to someone who is inside your home and not wanting to be caught or identified. If a threat, who shouldn't know your home well, were to break in and attempt to stalk through the home towards your location, the light would provide an immediate shock of fear to the criminal. As the criminal slowly creeps through the home, once the light initiates, that criminal no longer has the same night vision they previously had (nor the element of surprise). If you combine this motion/sensor activated light with a small motion/sensor activated alarm, you could gain a heads up that someone is inside your home, by the alarm that sounds near your head.

Once the threat passes through the invisible (IR) beam and initiates the light, they have a decision to make: progress towards their intended target or run away. If they progress towards your location, they still need their vision to readjust to the darkness. The smaller, remote alarm wakes you to an intruder, which wakens you and prepares you for a possible ambush. When you wake, your eyes may need to adjust to any remaining light within view, but your eyes are going to be adjusted to the darkness better than the criminal (because of the light they just experienced).

This doesn't mean you need to pursue the criminal, remember: the criminal may not know your home, but they know where they are and you may not. You know where you are. This means, if you are awakened by your sensor-alarm, you are able to prepare yourself by finding cover and/or egressing from the home. However you defend your home, you could be more prepared than the criminal believes you to be. This is why thinking about these things before they could happen is necessary. Your efforts towards planning and preparation now, could save your life later.

A motion/sensor activated light could also wake you, if you are someone who sleeps light enough to catch those differences. I'm a light sleeper, so any noise and/or any light differential that occurs will wake me. Having a motion/sensor activated light allows me to be alerted to the presence of an intruder. Since I do have dogs and cats, I have my sensors higher than the animals. This way they do not accidentally trip the beam. If you have pets, take their height(s) into consideration, to avoid them triggering the light.

With that information, if you want to step your 'game' up, might I suggest something: a motion/sensor activated light mounted on the side walls and a camera high up on the wall, close by. Now, that camera could be fake because no one would know for sure, but think about it: a criminal is tippy-toeing across the floor and down your hallway, trying hard not to make noise or get caught, and then they cross the beams. The light initiates, which causes fear/panic into the criminal as they shield their eyes against the light, and what do they see? They see a camera within view (but out of reach). Chances are, that criminal will want to escape your home quickly.

If you decide to use an internal camera system, you could incorporate a camera in conjunction with the motion activated or beam sensor lights. This way, the camera would record the intruder as they attempt to sneak down the hallway (or up the stairs or however you set up your system) and even if they trip the sensor (or activate the motion activated lights), the camera will continue to record. The criminal could destroy the camera, but they won't get the recording because the DVR would be located in a 'secret' location of your choosing.

As you can see, a motion activated (or sensor activated) light could be a first-alert warning device, but could also be a practical item for those who have to navigate through your home in the darkness. It is a win-win situation on this investment. The next decision you need to make is: to decide where you should mount the sensors or the motion activated light, and if you want to incorporate a sensor activated alarm alongside it. These are low-cost decisions, but do cost.

There are inexpensive, beam-initiated alarms that have a remote speaker and are easy to install. The beam-activated alarm is small and only alarms if someone breaks the beam. They make these alarms for exterior use, also. Some use these alarms at the end of their driveway, so if someone were to drive into their driveway, an alarm would sound at the speaker (wherever that is located). Break the beam, alarm sounds. Same idea for the beam-initiated lights. Motion activated lights and alarms work off distance and motion. Get within the distance while moving and it'll sound the alarm or initiate the light.

Do your homework and read reviews. Find the best one that works for you and your budget, and invest in your protection. Knowing that you initiated another safeguard within your home, to alert the household of an unsuspecting intruder, could help the household sleep better at night. There are many options out there and since I am not a salesman, I will not recommend anything specific to the reader, because I don't know the specifics of your needs nor the layout of your home. This is something to empower you with, it's your home and your decision. You got this!

4

ONLINE/PHONE SAFETY

ONLINE /PHONE SAFETY

This subject is much more important today than it was decades ago. Anyone that believes technology provides privacy obviously never watched a documentary about technology (there are many). The 'un-hackable' phones have been hacked, which means your phone can be hacked. There is a documentary where the camera crew were split in two locations and spaced 5 miles apart. The interviewer asked the hacker to show how he could hack the producer's phone, which was off. With relative ease, this hacker was able to initiate the producer's camera and microphone while the phone was off, and the camera recorded the whole ordeal (and audio to prove it was legitimate).

These video snippets and show segments are searchable online and on various video-based channels on the internet. Search: "Television interviews showing phone hacks" and "iPhone gets hacked" to see a list of recordings for proof.

I've mentioned this in a previous section but will mention this again here: there are bags advertised and found online on major retail sites, that can/will block calls/texts inbound and/or outbound. You cannot make a call while the phone is inside this bag, and calls cannot come in. It drops your phone off of the 'radar' until you withdraw your phone from the bag. Then, it can be identified again (the towers need to locate your phone again). They market these bags as 'family time' or 'game night' bags and with a short search, you can/will find them. They may be worth your investment if privacy is needed.

Note: To find these bags, search online: "Faraday bags for phones" and "EMF protection bags for electronics" and/or "Cell phone signal blocking bag" and you will see many listings for these bags.

Phishing scams and telemarketers still exist today, but most don't hear about it because of everything else in the news. If you don't want to watch documentaries about how marketing today is being conducted through technology, let me give you some insight, then perhaps you will begin to watch some of these documentaries on the subject. They are enlightening (and somewhat frightening).

SOCIAL MEDIA

Ever wonder why you see advertisements for things you were speaking about days before, or were searching for? Even if you were searching on a different computer? Were you ever curious? First off, avoid taking any polls online. By taking a poll, you are allowing someone else to create a profile on you. The way you answer the questions can/will provide the collection organization the information needed to accurately build your profile. This allows them to target you directly with ads you may like, services you may enjoy, how you feel politically, racially, publicly, etc. This allows you to be on a list.

People get too comfortable online, by posting their life stories, their movements, pictures and what they are eating. People post pictures at home and never choose the option to remove the geo-location on the image (also known as a geotag). This means anyone who wants to know where that picture was taken, could easily find it. That is what happened to Adam Savage, the man who was the co-host of the Myth-Busters show, because it happened at his house. It was because of this mistake that he went public with this problem...because a lot of fans suddenly showed up at his house.

Note: Online, search: "Web photo Geotags can reveal more than you wish" and/or "The dangers of Geotagging" and you will quickly find this article/story.

Despite the fact that it should be common sense to not divulge intimate information about your life or personal business, many people do not care enough to stop. If you think like a criminal, you may have a chance at avoiding having your house cleaned out while you're on vacation, but that's only if you take appropriate steps to avoid it. Here is an example of why you should not give out too much information online:

Note: online, you can search: "Women gets burglarized after posting on social media" for numerous examples of those who learned their lessons the hard way.

A woman was on a popular social media site, let's say her name is Beth, and Beth happened to post a status update such as: "Can't wait until Friday! Going to see [Band] at the [Location] at 9pm! Hubby and I are going to have dinner and drinks at [Restaurant] before the show and prime up before the concert! So excited". Can you pick out what is wrong with that posting? When Beth and her hubby got home from that concert, she came home to a ransacked house. Thankfully, she had an internal camera system, which recorded the entire event.

Beth and her hubby watched the video of her house being burglarized. Her cameras were placed in strategic locations and Beth was able to screen capture (creating an image from what was on the screen/monitor) the face of the burglar. She took that screen capture, saved it as a picture and then posted it onto her social media account. She then added "These guys robbed my house while we were at the concert! I can't believe it!". She quickly got a message from one of her friends, who replied with: "You should know that guy, he's on your friend's list".

You see, Beth had accepted a friend request from this guy a couple of months earlier. They went to kindergarten together, but beyond that, she didn't know him at all. By her posting that she was excited to go to that concert, she posted her comment with a picture of her at her home (geo-location). Beth also posted the time of the concert and that she was going to dinner before the concert. It was easy for this guy to gain a timeline.

Let's say it takes an hour for Beth to get to the concert location. Concert was at 9pm, they would need to leave at least by 7:45pm, right? How bad is the traffic on a Friday? Probably like it is everywhere else, horrific, but they were going to dinner and mentioned the restaurant. An easy online check could tell anyone how far that restaurant was from the concert venue. Walking distance? Perfect!

Concert is at 9pm, traffic is probably bad and they're going to dinner at a location within walking distance from the venue. Dinner would probably be set for 7:30pm, or close to it. That allows for an hour to eat and plenty of time to walk to the venue. A 7:30pm restaurant time would mean they needed to be on the road by 6:30pm at the latest. But, since Fridays usually prove to be heavy traffic on the highways, they would most likely leave around 5:15pm at the latest. Does that sound realistic? So, they leave the house at 5:15 p.m.

Concert begins at 9 p.m. and is at least an hour, but more likely 2 hours in duration. This means the concert will not end until 11 p.m. An hour drive back should put them at midnight; however, it takes a little more time because of the concert traffic, but let's say it only extends their drive by 30 minutes. They could be home by 12:30 a.m. They left at 5:15 p.m. and returned at 12:30 a.m. the following morning. How many hours was the house left unattended? 7 hours and some change? Do you think that guy on her friends list needed to do much more than what I just explained, to gain a grasp of what he needed to do and when, to rob her blind?

Taking pictures in your home could provide anyone who can access your profile and pictures, with valuable information about your life, lifestyle, and any expensive items within your home. The more data you provide online, the greater the chance of someone taking that data and using it against you. If your picture is out there, anyone who sees it now knows who you are, but you have no idea who the people are who have seen your pictures. Any of your friends could comment on your page, or share your picture, or tag you in a photo, which could allow anyone on their friends list to have access to that information also, and they don't know you and you don't know them.

PHISHING

Phishing occurs constantly online. Phishing is when someone contacts another and poses as a legitimate organization (or representative), to gain personal information from that person. For example: you receive a phone call from someone that says they are the fraud department at your bank and need you to give them the number on your credit card, the expiration date and the security pin. Perhaps they ask for your social security number, date of birth and address? They do this online, through emails, and other routes. Protect your information.

There are protections that exist, but you would need to pay for them. Identity theft is a very real threat today. Identity theft can occur if your computer is hacked, or if you fall prey to a phishing attempt. Personally, knowing I would still have a hassle to face if my identity is stolen, I made the decision to invest in identity theft protection. It's worth it to me to have something in place, in the event of identity theft. I also use a VPN service, so no one can see or track where I visit and what I do online. It's not that I am worried that someone could see where I visit, but if they can see the history, it means they could access my computer and the information on the hard drive.

Note: Think about what you do on your phone, laptop and desktop. Do you shop online? How many sites have you visited and made a purchase? If you made a purchase then you provided your name, address, telephone number, credit card number, expiration date and security number on the back of your card. That information could be used to create a large hassle in your life.

Note: You may notice I do not provide specific organization information of who I use for security alarms, monitoring, VPN services and so forth. Why? It is because you need (and should want) to research these different organizations to find the one that best fits your situation.

There are plenty of reviews for each organization (also chat rooms/comment sections) and should provide you with the needed data, for you to choose the best (and most affordable) product for you and your family.

Note: I do mention the RING doorbell that I have, but only as an example of what I look for and the benefits it provides to my household. I still will not promote any names.

Limit the information you provide on any/all social media site(s) and maintain a level of privacy to protect yourself. Phishing and coercion still works for the criminal-community and since I mentioned the hackers earlier (where they hacked a shut off phone 5 miles away), I want to add another television interview/documentary I had witnessed. There was another report on television that was recorded at a convention of sorts (a phishing/hacker convention perhaps). It may have been a security convention, but it was many years ago so I may be wrong on those details. It's the foundation of the story that is important. Here is what happened:

The interviewer (let's call him Bob) was speaking to a woman, let's call her Mia. Mia was explaining to Bob that it was quite easy to get the information off of his credit card without seeing the security numbers on the back and without using a skimmer. Bob was curious and said: "Okay, go ahead".

Mia: Okay, Bob, can I see your card?

Bob: Wait a minute, you said without seeing my card?

Mia: No, I said without seeing the security code on the back. If you pull your card out in a store, I would see and remember your name, card number, and date on the card. Is that fair?

Bob: That's fair.

Mia: Okay, let me see your card, please.

Bob: Okay (shows his card)

Mia: A [Credit Card: CC], Great!

Bob puts his credit card away. Mia calls the 800 number for the CC (it is not hard to get the number for Visa, Mastercard, etc.) and withdraws another phone and holds it in her other hand. An operator answers (let's call her Frida).

Frida: CC Check Card, can I get your name, please?

Mia: (sobbing) I'm sorry, my husband is going to be so mad at me, I think I lost the card but I need to get my shopping done!

Frida: Ma'am, I'm sorry to hear that. Do you know the card number?

Mia: (sobbing) I do...it's 1 2 3 4 5 6 7 8 8 ...and...(sobs)...expires on May of 1990 (sobs)

Frida: Excellent, thank you.

Mia: (sobbing) He's gonna be so mad at me...he gets so mad sometimes (sobs)

Frida: Is this your card, ma'am?

Mia: It's my husband's card...he's going to kill me (sobs)

Frida: I'm not supposed to approve it unless it's your card. Do you have a card?

Mia: I don't, I have to use...(sobs) he makes me use his card! His name is Bob (last name) (sobs uncontrollably).

Frida: I really cannot approve a transaction if you don't know the security...

At that moment, Mia initiates her other phone and the sound of a baby crying loudly bellows from the speaker.

Mia: (frantic) Oh sweetheart, mommy's sorry...almost done...(sobs)(to Frida) I'm sorry (sobs) my baby isn't feeling well and I have to get medicine for her...(sobs)(baby sobs)

Frida: I'm not supposed to do this, but I'll approve your purchase, go ahead and get what you need...but please make sure you call in and get yourself a card for this account, okay?

Mia: Thank you so much...(sobs)

Mia hangs up the phone, stopped the baby from crying on the other phone and smiled at Bob. Bob was beside himself that his card would have been used in a purchase without knowing the security number on the back.

Bob: That was incredible.

Mia: It's easy

Bob: But how did you know she would fall for it?

Mia: A woman answered.

Bob: Okay?

Mia: I preyed on her empathy that I was a woman in a desperate situation.

Bob: Why the baby?

Mia: She was hesitant to give me the approval, so initiating the recording allowed me to make it more stressful and emotional.

Bob: What if she wasn't a mother?

Mia: She may not have any kids, but since I was frantic and caught in a situation where I couldn't get something to help my sick child, her motherly instinct kicked in.

Bob: What if it was a man?

Mia: I have recordings for that also.

Bob: Incredible. It's that easy.

Mia: It's that easy.

This young lady was able to get an approval for a card she had seen, but did not have in her own name. She used techniques that would strike an empathic nerve in the woman on the phone and used the recording of a baby crying to seal the deal. The credit card company would not have called Bob, because she said she was Bob's wife. Bob would not have known about the purchase until the bill arrives, which could be weeks and by then it would be a big hassle to try and get that money back and/or dispute the charges.

TELEMARKETERS

Years ago, telemarketers had to physically call people to try and sell them things. As technology progressed, machines would generate the calls and if someone answered, the telemarketer's phone would initiate and they could begin their sales-speech. Nowadays, robocalls and machine-generated calls occur, but usually on landlines (hard-lined phones within a home) and not cell phones. Don't get me wrong, it still occurs on cell phones, but not at the frequency it used to. Years ago, there was a 'do not call' registry, where you could plug in your number and it would block telemarketing calls.

Note: With cell phones today, one could easily block numbers on their phone, but won't slow down the machine that generates the number shown on the phone screen. Can you block the numbers? Yes. I currently block these numbers that call, but I get numerous calls each week, so I am blocking numbers quite often.

As is with all things-technologically advancing, if there is a safeguard put in place, there is a workaround that criminals will find and use. If a telemarketer calls you and you decide to answer, ask them to remove you from their list. Your data has been sold to organizations that buy data to sell something. Social media sites have been getting in trouble for selling data to other companies, because that means your information is no longer private. Probing questions can gain more than just the immediate information, it can also profile you to better target the products offered (and worse).

ONLINE DATING

On the subject of online dating, I am not an expert or even generally educated on the subject, but this isn't about online dating, it's about awareness of what's out there and not becoming a victim. It is in that sense, that it's important to understand how fake many people are. There are some evil people online, who pose as a completely different person just to cause a crime (or injury) against someone else. Unfortunately, it is difficult to trust most everything you see, hear and read online, because it's hard to distinguish what is real and what is made up.

It is because of this deceit that I can provide some warnings. Communicating online with someone you don't know, trying to get to know them, but not knowing if they are telling you the truth (some of us are weird, so we may not want to lead with that if we're trying to get a date), is going to be a difficult process. Warning signs exist, but for those who are putting themselves out there in pursuit of a connection or love, or those who may be naïve to the evil, could easily fall prey to dangerous predators.

Warning signs:

-"How about I pick you up at your house? What's your address?"

-"How about we meet at this retail store parking lot?"

-"Let's meet at this parking lot at this park"

-"You can trust me, I'm a nice (girl/guy)"

-"How about I cook dinner for you at my place"

Those are some examples of warning signs. If you are going to do internet dating, pick a neutral location where there will be plenty of people around. A coffee shop is a decent place to meet up, to get to know each other. A dark restaurant you have never been to is probably not the best choice. Neutral means it's not in a location that is hidden and not private. I'd say a neutral location is one outside of both of your stomping grounds, but that option could be difficult in smaller cities and towns. The main point is: have witnesses/patrons around you, during the day and located in a very public place.

CODES

If/when you have your date, make sure you have a friend that you can contact when you get home. This is where the codewords and phrases pay off. You provide your friend with the vital information needed to identify the person, if it were needed. Give your friend:

-Name of the date

-Send a link to his/her profile to your friend

-Location of the date (plus the time of the meet up)

-Estimated time you intend to return home, or: a time for your friend to text or call you, if you do not text him/her at the designated time.

Again, make the codewords and phrases something someone would actually say in conversation when checking in with their friend. Then, if the date became a threat, they would/could pick up on that codeword/phrase.

The code words need to be simple to you and your friend, but not easy for someone else to guess. For example, if you text your friend: Blueberry, that may be odd because it doesn't make sense in any sort of conversation, especially if the date was violent. You couldn't just say "hey, hold up, I need to text my friend something...". That won't bode well for you. Use something that could make sense to the threat, without keying them in that you're signaling for help.

Another example is: if your friend texts you (because you were still on the date and missed your text-time): "How's the date? And don't say 1st OF MAY! Haha". It's not a good joke, but a threat would see that as only a joke, not a code. You and your friend could have it set up that they send you that text, and if you were to reply: "It's actually the 5th of July! Ha!", that would tell your friend that you need help. But if your reply was: "I'm allergic to DATES! Hahah" to symbolize your date is going well, it could still be looked at as a joke. The date would have no idea and it would only seem like a bad dad-joke.

There are many ways to create the codes, but until you know the other person long enough to actually know their quirks (their buttons and their anger), keep the codes and phrases going with your friend(s). You cannot be too safe, especially in our world today. Your safety and security are of primary importance and letting your guard down before you actually know the other person could put you at risk.

As in the older days, roofies exist even today. Many people have experienced being 'roofied' and wake up in a tub of ice, with a note next to them that tells them to call 911 to tell the 911 operator that your kidneys are gone. That's not a scenario I wish for anyone to experience, which is why I mention the importance of not leaving your food or drink unattended.

What if you need to use the bathroom?

If you have to leave the table to go to the bathroom, take your drink to the bar, ask the bartender to make you another drink and you'll pick it up on your way back. This keeps your drink safe. There is a nail polish that college students created, that when dipped into a drink will turn colors if there are drugs in that drink. I'm sure this technology will advance as well, but I think a fingernail polish is a great idea. All you would need to do is dip a nail into your drink and look at it. If it changes color, you know there's drugs in the drink.

What about the food?

As for the meal, what would I do if on a date with a stranger? I would push my food normally in a way which I could identify if it's been changed. I would set my fork and knife onto the plate and then depart for the bathroom. If my date were to try and hide drugs in my food, they would have to blend it in, which means disturb how I left my plate. This would give me the warning that something was done to my food.

Being aware of your surroundings may sound exhausting, but it is not. It provides you with the security of knowing your area is secure from threats at the moment. If anything dangerous were to set off your alarms, you have plans in place to act immediately. Your proactiveness now can save you today, tonight and/or tomorrow. You may never be placed into a dangerous or harmful situation, which I truly hope is the case, but if you do, are you aware enough to catch on that the danger has arrived? Did you plan for that attack?

It's better to have it and not need it, than to need it and not have it!

APPLICATIONS

There are numerous applications that can benefit you when speaking about safety, security and awareness. Each day, more and more applications are surfacing to mimic the existing applications and make them obsolete. That's business, of course. I will speak of a couple applications that I personally use and why. It's a personal preference and you should sit down and note what you are looking for in an application, search for the solutions that exist, and then pro/con each to gain a decision.

SPOTCRIME

By now there are probably a couple of applications that achieve the same result, but I have used SPOTCRIME for some time. This application allows you to search any area inside the United States, to see what the crimes are committed during a specified timeline. This application also allows you to create a profile and set the parameters from your home. This allows you to get an email alert when a crime is attempted within your parameters. I have my parameters set for a radius of 5 miles around my home. This application provides options to identify different crimes they would like to be notified about.

If I don't care about vandalism, I can uncheck that block and any vandalism within the 5-mile radius around my home would not be reported. The icons are symbols to allow the user to identify quickly, the crime(s) that was committed. For example: the icon of a fist is for assaults. A masked face is for burglary. A spray can is for vandalism, and so on. Using this application has multiple benefits for the user:

-One can type in an address they are going on vacation to, set the parameters for the past two months or so, and see where the most active crimes were and where they were conducted.

Note: this can help identify locations where crime is plentiful in the area. This is important when choosing a hotel/motel.

-One could use this to check out a possible neighborhood they would like to move to, to see where the most crimes are and what they were. This reduces the chance that you may visit the location on a 'good' day, buy the house and find out it's in a rotten location.

Again, useful in multiple ways.

NEXTDOOR

The Nextdoor application allows you to connect with your neighbors. Sometimes the local police will have an account in your neighborhood and report the crimes that occur. It also updates when someone reports a crime and alerts those that are signed up for those neighborhoods. It is less of a social media site and more for people trying to connect to their community. They share job requests, advice on contractors, report shady vehicles cruising around, crimes, happy thoughts and so on. As with anything related to the internet: unless you know the person, do not provide personal information on any application.

DOORBELL CAMERAS

The doorbell camera I use also has alerts if a crime has been committed within a couple of miles. With this application, those in the community who also have this technology, will post their videos of someone trying to break into their home, or screen captures of the person. They do this to share around to see if anyone knows who the person was. I've seen this get shared on the Nextdoor application, because videos can be uploaded as well. It has identified an elderly person who was roaming the neighborhood during a very cold evening, which saved that person's life.

5

DEFENSIVE OPTIONS

I've mentioned this in other chapters, but it is worth repeating: In no way, shape or form am I condoning or prompting violence against another individual. This book is specific to awareness, but it would be foolish to think self-defense topics are sunflowers and rainbows only. Defense can/could be nonviolent, but there are also situations where aggression and violence is necessary to defend against an attacker. Use your better judgement on these things and continue to cultivate your awareness abilities, so if you are faced with a situation, you can activate your plan A, B or C without needing a defensive option.

Sometimes violence/aggression is needed to break free from the grasp of an attacker, or attackers. How much is too much? A good rule to live with when asking yourself "how much aggression is adequate when dealing with a dangerous threat", is: use only the amount of aggression/defensive tactics necessary to break free from an attacker and flee the area. This means: if kicking someone in the shin causes a threat to release their grasp on you and you can egress away from the scene, then that is the amount of necessary defensive action/aggression.

Aggression is not the best word to use because it sparks a thought that one could lose control against an attacker and it would be justified. Those of us within the firearm realm understand the importance of only using appropriate-defensive actions to neutralize an attacker (and only when necessary). I've spoken to many conceal carry cardholders who believed they would/could fire everything in their pistol magazine (which could be 6-19 bullets) against an attacker. They were unhappy when I informed them that that would be considered excessive and they would be the ones going to jail (and probably brought up on murder charges).

Who's to say/define what is justified when it comes to determining what level of defensive action is appropriate for the situation? The courts? Well, it's not the courts that are currently surrounded by 3 drunk aggressors with knives and broken bottles in their hand, each slurring that they are going to cut your face off. In that scenario, being able to safely egress the area and avoid the situation may not be something you have the time to determine the appropriate level of defensive-muscle to apply to each threat. Confusing? Perhaps.

My main point to drive across here is this: each situation is/can be different, which prompts a mindset that each situation would require the same question but not the same answer. Since each situation is different, you must evaluate your options (quickly) and determine what is considered adequate. Will you always have that option? No, of course not. What do you do? You do whatever is necessary to break free from an attacker, to safely egress that situation, and get to a safe location to call the police. If someone points at you and says your level of aggression was too much, that's on them. We cannot always be 'nice' when faced with such aggressive situations where we feel our life is at risk.

Again, this doesn't mean you should automatically knee someone in the groin and rip their ear off, just because you felt there was a possibility they were going to be aggressive with you. That, in itself, would be too aggressive and unprovoked (and considered assault...which means you go to jail). An important aspect to being human is: we try to maintain personal space and hope others will also. This is not always the case, unfortunately, and there are some who do not recognize boundaries (or some who have had too much to drink and get too close to talk to others), which may require you to enforce your boundaries to them.

Remember: Assess the situation and use only the amount of defensive aggression needed to break free from an aggressor, and egress from the situation.

I have said this for a very long time and will continue to say this because it is factual and pertinent to this topic (and many firearm topics): Action beats reaction! Every time! So many conceal carry cardholders (whom I have dealt with) and officers (be it state, local and/or federal) were unhappy at that reality. Why? Some believed they knew enough to defend themselves adequately. Some believed their inner aggressive mindset and desire would match their skill level. So many found out the hard way, that their skill level definitely did not match what their inner self believed to be true. Some didn't survive their experience.

Action beats reaction, in the defensive option realm, means you must assess your situation in a dynamic manner. It might change second by second. It may remain static for a long time before it turns dynamic. The one thing you can be assured of is: what you plan for one second, may/will change very shortly. This ability to assess the situation and remain fluid in your options is what could give you the upper hand and attribute to your survival. If you don't assess the situation and a threat approaches you and punches you in the face, the threat has the control and you become the victim.

Again, this means you assess your situation and remain aware of your surroundings, so you do not miss vital information that could free you from the situation. If you are taken by surprise by someone grabbing your arm tightly, you may freeze immediately because you have not thought about it. Your ability to survive a situation is dependent on what you practice and think through. Sometimes, just thinking through different scenarios can offer viable solutions during high-stress situations.

What if that person who tightly grabbed your arm was trying to save you from an oncoming car they spotted, that you didn't?

What if that person grabbed you as you were getting into your car because they spotted a threat hiding in the back seat, but you were too busy talking/texting on your phone to see?

What if that person that grabbed you did so to pull you into their car?

As you can see, there are many 'what if' scenarios that can be played out in your mind. This is important to consider because these are very real possibilities. If a threat grabs you, they do so because they have targeted you as someone weaker than they are. They feel they have priority control over you, and that their actions will force you to comply with whatever it is they want from you. This is where your assessment skills come in, so you can determine what is needed to break free from this person and egress from the area/situation.

Anyone that gets grabbed suddenly would react close to the same way as everyone else: surprise glance at whoever grabbed them. Why? You'd be surprised because you were not expecting that action against you. You may have been walking to your car and thinking about where you needed to go next, or what you needed to do. What you were not thinking was: "I think someone is going to try and kidnap me as I get into my car today". No one would/should be thinking that (hopefully).

Helpful Note: Action beats reaction will be important to embrace and acknowledge mentally. This allows a person to realize the importance of their rapid assessment of the situation and initiation of an action to cause the reaction, rather than the other way around.

What possible tools do you have at your home if you were surprised by an attacker while you are inside? Think about your home and how you have it set up. Think about your closet. You have many things at your disposal, and these things could be used to level the playing field if a threat were to attack you inside your home. Let's break down some things that you have at your disposal, using what the average person may have inside their home:

Fingers/Fists/Hands:

-If a person is without tools within their reach to use against a sudden-surprise attack inside their home, the hands/fingers/fists are available. If the situation requires it, a person in this situation could close their fist to strike the nose, throat or eyes of an attacker. A strike to the nose can cause the eyes to water, which could cause the attacker to release their grip. An open hand could be used to 'chop' into the throat of an attacker. This strike could cause the attacker to lose the ability to breathe normally.

It should be mentioned that a strike to the throat could kill that attacker. Now, I'm sure someone out there reading this would say: "They attacked me, they deserve to die". This is a judgement call and yes, the attacker was inside the house and tried to ambush the occupant. If the only action available was a throat-chop to stop the attack, embrace that fact and ensure you have a lawyer by your side, because the system is not exactly built for the victim in all situations.

If you asked me: "Would you chop someone in the throat if they were attacking you", my answer would be this: "If I was attacked in my home by a someone that did not belong and my only available opportunity to survive was to punch/chop that threat in the throat, I would not hesitate to do so to survive the encounter and break free". That is me and only if the situation dictated that action. Use your better judgement for each scenario and stand by your actions.

Closing your fist and extending your thumb can provide you with a strike option that reaches deeper into the threat. A strike into the eye, behind the ear or in the temple in this manner can impact harder and could cause the threat to break contact with you, giving you the time and space needed to safely/quickly egress from the area. Remember, the purpose is to survive the encounter and escape, not go toe-to-toe with an aggressor.

Using your hands, if being attacked by a male, the groin is a great target area to squeeze, twist and crush. That action would undoubtedly cause the threat to release their grasp on you. They will probably drop to the ground in great pain at that point, giving you the opportunity to run away and call 911. You could knee a male in the groin to break contact also, but may be harder to accomplish depending on their proximity to you and/or angle. You could also slap/cup the ears, with great speed and determination, which can create immediate pain onto the threat and again, break their grasp on you. Multiple options exist, if you just think about them.

-Hockey stick(s): If you have a hockey stick in your closet, you have a far-reaching defensive tool that can keep a threat at bay while you attempt to egress from the home. If the threat were to advance towards you, a swift slapshot onto the shins of the threat could quickly drop that threat to the ground (in great pain). Once the threat is down, they are considered neutralized and any further strikes by you would be considered excessive (and cause you some problems legally).

It is advisable to not allow the threat to get a hold of that hockey stick in your hand because then they have control of your defensive tool and it no longer allows you the safety you once had. If a threat were to advance quickly, and you cannot think to do a slapshot onto the threat's shins, a chest-jab with the stick could knock the wind out of the threat. Taking away the ability to breathe normally causes people to rethink their life choices (and neutralizes them).

-Umbrella: Same as the hockey stick, the umbrella can be used to swing at an attacker to keep them at bay. Umbrella's usually have a pointy end, which can be used to poke at an attacker, if necessary, but could also penetrate the person. Remember: At some point you may have to defend your actions in court, be sure your actions are justified.

-Shoes: Shoes can be used in the hands, to swing at the threat, or thrown at the face. By throwing a shoe at the face of an attacker, their brain will cause them to protect their head. They will either close their eyes, duck, cover their face, dive out of the way, stop, or other actions that could give you a window of opportunity to escape the area.

-Jacket/Coats: A jacket can be used to defend yourself against an attacker with a weapon. Holding onto the sleeves in each hand allows you to use the coat as a buffer and deflect the weapon strikes. It is wise to hold up the jackets/coats in your closet to figure out the best way to hold it, to protect against a threat. Figure it out now, rather than trying to figure it out as a threat is advancing on you.

-Coat hangers: Be it wooded, plastic or metal, coat hangers hurt when they impact a person. They may not be long, but they sting and that sensation could cause the threat to stop their attack, thus giving you time to escape the area/situation. Metal coat hangers sting a lot and are very lightweight (which means easy to swing quickly). Wooden and plastic coat hangers can break upon impact, which is why its use should be considered a one hit option.

-Pillows (on couch): used to throw at the face of an attacker.

-Magazine: Same as pillow. To be thrown at the face of an attacker.

-Remote control: Can be used to throw in the face of an attacker and as a striking implement. If you must use a remote control, a firm grip is needed and quick, solid strikes to areas of the body that will create the needed results. If you must use a remote control, think of it as a harder version of your hand, which can strike at/in the same locations.

-Plates/Glasses/Bowls: Same as pillows and magazines: can be used to throw into the face of an attacker. This could give you the pause needed to break contact and escape the home/attacker.

-Towel: A towel can be used like a jacket/coat and a striking tool for defense. By twisting the towel, it can be snapped at a threat like a whip would, or can be used to deflect an attack.

-Cell phone: Can be used as a striking implement, same as your fist.

-Pepper spray/Bear Spray: Bear spray is usually larger and reaches further, so it is designed for outside of the home, however, it could be used inside. Be warned, though, that using pepper spray or bear spray inside the home where ventilation is weaker, could cause the occupant to be affected also. That being said, with pepper spray, one must get closer for it to be affective and that may not be the greatest option.

Pepper spray has an effective range. This means, depending on the platform, the threat must be a certain distance from you for the spray to take effect. There are platforms that mount on a key chain that can reach 5 feet. You should mark off 5 feet in your home and stand there to truly appreciate how close that is. Other sprays can reach 15 feet maximum, which is an okay distance, but again, realize that distance is not sustainable the entire time that can is being emptied. This means: your strongest stream of spray occurs in the beginning of the can initiation, but will weaken as it empties. If your attempts are not delivered accurately, the effectiveness lessens as it empties.

Pepper spray has an expiration date and I have met too many people who carried the same can for years. Once I informed them that their can has an expiration date, they checked their can and sure enough, it was expired. I had them go outside and initiate the can to see if it would do anything, and they all were confused as to why they couldn't get the can to initiate. Was the gas dead inside (the propellant)? For most the can was dead, but for others, they never learned how to disengage the safety lever on their spray. This allowed me to follow that epiphany up with: "What would have happened if you needed that can to save your life?". That wake-up call was one that prompted them to rethink how they approached personal safety and awareness. That was a win-win (they didn't need the can to defend themselves and discovered it during a class and not in a high risk, danger situation).

Lastly, on the subject of pepper spray, the spray affects people differently. In other words: it could take up to 45 seconds before it takes effect for some people. How much damage could someone do in 45 seconds?

Solution: If you decide you want to carry pepper spray, purchase the spray while also purchasing an inert can of the same design. Inert cans are filled with water. It can be used to practice withdrawing from wherever you carry it and initiated. This allows you to practice disengaging the safety and getting it into your hands properly. Remember: Pepper spray has an expiration date, even if you don't use it, you must replace it or it will be of no use to you when you need it the most (look up: What is Murphy's Law).

TEACHING CHILDREN:

I discuss the importance of teaching children in another chapter, but that is for approaching the scenario training inside the home, not defense. Children look to their parents for guidance and permission, and if a household were to avoid teaching their children certain topics, if the time came, there is a good chance those children will become instant victims. This is my attempt at trying to provide parents with information that increases the likelihood of success and less victims. That is my hope, but it begins with the parents (obviously).

How do you convince a society that wants to avoid thinking about the evil that exists all around us, that being proactive and taking awareness for action is important? Some will never believe they need this information. Some will remain with their 'buried in the sand' mentality, because nothing 'bad' has happened to them so "why should I worry about it now"? But let something bad happen to those households and watch how fast their screams of becoming the victim surface.

I will repeat this again: it is better to have it (the knowledge and awareness) and never need it, than to need it and not have it!

Teaching children must be approached logically, but in a way that will reach these children and allow them to understand the specifics. This is important because you do not want your child to go to school the next day and practice what you taught them on another student! That's a quick way to meet the Principal AND law enforcement (and angry parents of the child your child practiced on)! You nor I want that.

PERMISSION:

It's important to sit your child down and explain what permission means. Permission is the same for adults: permission to cause distress on another if that other person is trying to harm you (and ONLY when that occurs). By explaining to your child that what they learn inside the home, can and should be used only in emergency situations, it helps them understand. At this point, your child may not ask for you to expound on that sentence, so it is up to you to take it upon yourself and over-explain it. Emergency situations such as: a stranger tries to snatch them up, a stranger tries to hit them, etc.

Note: I am going to have another situational awareness book that covers teaching your children about active situations at school and their options, because this book is specifically awareness and safety at home. I don't want to go overboard with information that can be better received inside another book. Reason: The longer the book, the less likely more people are going to remain engaged with the information. Remember, no one likes homework, but my homework could save your life!

Depending on the age(s) of your child(ren), the information you provide them for options may differ. Smaller children do not have much strength compared to older children. This matters if a stranger were to attempt to snatch your child up and drive away. This is why teaching your child to be aware is very important. Teach them to keep their eyes up and their head on a swivel (which means, paying attention to where they are going, who's standing around in their path, identify anyone looking shady, any possible threats, exits, options, etc.) and not in their phones.

Smaller children may need extra assistance if an adult tries to grab their arm and kidnap them. Screaming is the first permission you should give your child. Some children will freeze up and remain silent from fear and no training. Data overload will/can cause children to shut down mentally. If this happens, there is a good chance the threat will take them away easily, and I won't give you the statistics of seeing your child again if that occurs. No one wants to see/hear that reality, but I'm sure you can guess it to be bad.

Teaching (and practicing with) your small child: immediately upon being confronted with a stranger that they feel is dangerous, they should scream "HELP" at the top of their lungs and keep screaming it. If the threat were to try and grab them up and quickly haul them away to their car, that is where/when the child should fight back. This means the child needs permission from you, to fight against an adult. When I was growing up, we were taught to respect our elders and such, but in the event a strange adult were to try and cause us harm, we were told to grab, squeeze, pull, punch and jab to break free, and then run away as fast as possible.

When you give your child permission to defend themselves against a stranger, especially an adult stranger, it empowers them with options that they know you will not be mad at them for. This is why discussion is so important. You want this conversation to occur face to face, close to your child, where you can say: "what do you think it means when I tell you it is okay to defend yourself against a stranger that is trying to hurt you". You want to know how your child's mind works and what they absorbed from the conversation you are having with them.

Children have lunchboxes and backpacks. Those haven't changed for many over the years. If there is a possibility that your child could face a situation, whether outside playing or at school, or at a friends house, or at the movie theater, then conversing about defensive options is a must. Carrying a backpack to or from school means they have objects they could carry in their hand to help them if they need it. Items, such as: pencils, pens, erasers (to throw), notebook (to throw), ruler, scissors (even the small, blunt scissors can be a jabbing tool), etc.

By identifying these objects, you can pull each object out and ask your child to show you how they might use it to defend themselves. If they have keys they carry to get into your home after school, you can teach them how to hold the keyring and where they should aim if they have to jab at an attacker. Each time an explanation is given, remind the child that these techniques are only if they have to defend against a stranger/strange adult that is trying to harm them. Reinforce what they learn at home is NOT to be used against classmates or friends, ever!

It is because smaller children do not have the strength to fight off an adult attacker, that defensive objects may be necessary. If they cannot withdraw an object to help them in that situation, show them spots to target with their hands or fist. Grabbing an ear and pulling downward, hard and fast, could be painful enough to cause the threat to let them go. Jabbing a thumb into the eye of an adult attacker could cause enough pain to stop the attacker. Kicking a threat in the groin is an option to break free from an adult attacker.

Reinforce the need to do whatever is necessary to break contact and flee from an attacker. I have a section coming up that explains an awareness game that you can teach your household, which can allow you to identify up to three people with great accuracy. I suggest you read that section and incorporate your children, to enhance their ability to identify a threat accurately (or/and their vehicle). The main mission is for the children to break contact by any means necessary, while screaming for help, so they can egress quickly and safely from the area, and pursue help from law enforcement or other adults.

Last case/worst case scenario: if they have to use their teeth or their head against an attacker that has them wrapped up in their arms, they won't know how hard to bite. This is important to understand, because your children are vulnerable to ceasing what they are doing if someone were to recoil and scream in pain from their actions. This is true even if they are under duress and bite the attacker. If the attacker screams in pain from their bite, there is a chance the child will stop because they know they caused that pain. This is why discussion is so important between parent and child.

Again, knowing your defensive options in the home allows you to teach your children what can be used. Practicing different scenarios with the family/occupants allows for a repetition of events (provides mental options in emergencies), but also allows for the household to critique the practice to find better solutions. Pulling out coats from the closet, umbrella and/or hockey stick (or bat, tennis racquet, etc.) and simulating what would occur, shows the limitations of the defensive tool. It is better to find those limitations now, before you really need to use the object, than it is to have to figure it out as a threat rushes towards you with their weapon poised.

Sit down and discuss options with your children, while giving them permission to defend themselves against an adult threat, but only if that adult is trying to harm them. Going over the objects they could use, areas of opportunity for them to target and their overall objective to break contact so they can flee the area to get help, can save their lives. Knowing the child is likely to stop biting a threat if the threat screams in pain, reinforce the need to continue defending by any means necessary if the threat continues to assault them. Their main goal should be to get away while screaming for help, and being prepared to defend if they cannot break contact with the threat.

I hope this point has been driven home for parents. I am a parent and my biggest fear was my child getting abducted while coming home from school. I taught my child about defense and the importance of not using it at school or against other children, even if they were trying to get him to fight. I empowered my son to defend by any means necessary if he was ever attacked by an adult threat. Today, in our society, those discussions are occurring less and less. Crime hasn't been reduced that much, and just because the media is not plastered with child abductions, human trafficking, murders, etc., doesn't mean the evil has stopped.

-

6

RESTAURANTS and OTHER LOCATIONS

This section is specifically for those who visit eating establishments (which would be everyone at some point in time) and how to be aware within said establishment. Some may scoff at this subject and turn their nose up at that thought of needing to be aware while enjoying a nice dinner with a significant other. It is at those times where those people believe nothing could possibly happen, and then it happens. You don't want to be caught off guard in any location, but to live in ignorance that a dangerous event will never happen at your location, will only set you up for failure.

When we go out to eat, we do so to enjoy the company, have a delightful meal and possibly tasty drinks, but what we are not expecting is something horrific to happen. Being proactive about your safety is not being paranoid. Paranoid means you feel that something WILL happen to you EVERYWHERE you go. Being prepared means you can still enjoy life while ensuring you are alert/aware of your surroundings. See the difference? I hope so.

If you are going on vacation and plan on going out to eat while you are there (which is pretty much everyone), do some research on the area and identify which areas are the best choices. One could easily look at the area on applications such as: SpotCrime.com, where you can look at a specific area during a specific timeframe and determine how bad that area is. From that little effort, you could quickly identify where to stay away from. If need be, I could check an area going two months back, to identify any criminal trends in the area(s) I plan to visit.

Another option is to go onto the internet and research the area. Look up those restaurants you are interested in on sites such as Yelp. This allows you to review the comments of others and get an idea of their experiences. Keep in mind, that there are many people on this Earth who make it their mission in life to cause hate and discontent wherever they go. This means: take the critiques with a grain of salt and remember that there are some people who deliberately try to screw over restaurants because they couldn't get something they wanted.

Sadly, that last fact exists in our reality. This doesn't mean visitors didn't have a negative experience, but it does mean that some people always try to get something for nothing and their purpose in trashing a restaurant online is mainly because that restaurant didn't cater to their complaints, called them out on their scam-attempt and/or refused to take their abuse. In the past, I had worked in the food industry and experienced those people myself, but they were not the majority.

In simpler terms: read the comments/critiques of those who ate at the locations you are interested in and look for a trend. If there are a plethora of positive critiques, gushing about the food, the service and the prices, but there are a couple of one-star reviews that go on and on about being overpriced (or whatever), one could quickly see the negative reviews as lashing out because they didn't get their way. If the reviews are balanced, look at the area surrounding the restaurant and identify the pattern of crime (if any). There's usually an easy explanation.

I am amazed at the current actions of our society and those willing to go out of their way to post negative comments about every location. Are there any perfect locations? No! Perfect means they make everyone happy and that cannot exist. There will always be those people who knowingly enter the restaurant with the name: "ONLY SOUP" and get angry and offended when their request for a rack of lamb is denied.

They exist and are, unfortunately, easy to find online. This is why there will never be a perfect location that appeases everyone.

It doesn't matter if you are visiting an establishment in your neighborhood, home town, next county over or in a different state altogether, remaining aware can save you and your loved ones from harm. It is wise to understand that not everyone within the establishments you visit are aware on any level. The majority of the population doesn't have the mindset of it being possible (not probable) for a gunman to step inside the restaurant they are visiting and execute everyone inside. Most are invested in their present situation, their life and the drama they are dealing with, and not thinking about an outside source of drama forcing their way into their present.

Those that refuse to be aware of their surroundings will be surprised if/when a threat was to enter the establishment where they are enjoying a nice meal, and begins causing harm onto others. Will it be a shooting? Not always, but it doesn't matter if it is a shooting, a stabbing or someone swinging a bat at people, it is still a dangerous situation. A person who is unaware and suddenly faced with a dramatic/traumatic situation where others are being hurt/killed, is more likely to freeze in their seats because their brain is experiencing a 'data-overload' situation. The brain is trying to make sense of what is happening around them.

Those that remain aware are more likely to initiate what I call their 'PLAN B' (will explain shortly) and already moving from the scene. Notice the difference? One freezes in place as their brain(s) try to make sense of what they are witnessing, while the other is already moving and escaping the situation. Survival is the desired result, right? Then why not implement your awareness techniques and enjoy your excursions, rather than take the chance that you 'might' think up a plan if something were to happen. Think about how hard it would be to think up an exit strategy in a location you have never previously visited?

Years ago, there was a shooting in a Florida nightclub. Too many people were shot and killed, with an abundance of those killed located in the bathroom. Those people were killed inside a bathroom that had zero exits, other than the entrance door. Why would there be an abundance of people killed inside a bathroom that didn't have a window or exit option? What would compel people to rush into a bathroom that was an immediate dead-end? These are important questions (especially to drive my point home)!

LEMMING MENTALITY

The lemming mentality is sort of like follow the leader. When a situation occurs that escalates the flight desire of people, those who are unsure of the area, visitors, and/or those with no defensive plan at all, will follow those they believe will lead them to safety. This occurs over and over again in our history, and with a short search online, you can easily read those stories. I will give an example.

NIGHTCLUB DEATHS

The Florida nightclub that was the scene of a horrific event where the occupants were mowed down by a gunman, was an example of people having fun, but not prepared for such an event to occur to them. As a caveat to that, I understand why they were not expecting a gunman to come in and open fire on all of them. We all have that mindset wherever we go because we live in a civil society (for the most part) where it is frowned upon and against the law to cause harm to others. I get it, but I also believe that if these people were aware of their surroundings, some would have lived through that horrible experience.

WHAT HAPPENED?

A gunman walks into the club and opens fire. The occupants freak out, with some freezing in place (quickly shot by the gunman) and others following those they think had a plan. Unfortunately, those that fled into the bathroom were followed by many of the club occupants because they had to have thought the leader had a plan and/or knew that location well enough to escape harm. They were wrong. That bathroom was their final stop because it was a dead-end, with no windows, no doors and no defensive tools (other than their hands and feet) to use against the gunman.

The police found a stack of bodies inside that bathroom when they investigated the shooting. There was an excessive number of bodies, which told the police someone was running away from the gunman and had a bunch of people following, because they believed they were following someone with a plan. Instead, those people were sitting ducks for the gunman, who opened the door and fired into the crowd until they were all dead. How do I know they were unprepared and/or unaware?

If you re-read the previous chapter on DEFENSIVE OPTIONS, you would identify where I state you have your hands, your feet, your knees, your shoes and other items at your disposal, to use as a defensive tool. Once inside that bathroom, anyone prepared would be scared, just like everyone else, but would also realize they were in a dead-end situation. Once that was identified, they could have taken off a shoe, or instructed others to take off their shoes, and direct them to throw their shoes at the gunman if he enters the bathroom. At that point in time, that person could then position themselves close to the door.

Why get closer to the door?

It does you no good to remain at the far wall of the bathroom with no exits. If the gunman were to enter the bathroom (as he did), he would then be faced with multiple pairs of shoes being rocketed towards his face. Instinctively, the threat would move his face away and/or cover his face, because his brain is activating the 'save the brain' action. That moment is the moment to strike. The person close to the door can immediately jump on the gunman, and once the gunman is dealing with someone attacking them, the others could jump on the gunman also.

If inside a dead-end situation, where there is no safe exit, or exit at all, it leaves only one action left: Attack the attacker. If you don't attack in this scenario, you will surely die if the gunman were to enter the bathroom (which he did). Had someone been aware of their surroundings and the situation, they could have had a chance at survival, but they did not. No one fought back, no one was successful in being proactive about their safety and no one survived. Can you see how that happened now?

Having a plan and being aware in a restaurant doesn't guarantee your survival, but it does increase those chances for you. Nothing is guaranteed, but something that is a sure bet is: those who are not prepared, not aware and not willing to think about these subjects, if/ when something bad were to happen, they will surely be targets for the criminal/threats. Threats want easy victims and the point to this is: if you were aware and prepared in this situation, you probably would have headed for one of the emergency exits you identified when you entered the club, instead of entering the bathroom.

Let that sink in, research that shooting and read the reports, then come back and reread this section. It's my mission to help people and to give everyone the tools to utilize and survive if/when an incident was to occur. It is my wish that no one will ever encounter this situation, but there is a chance that someone reading this book will, indeed, experience a situation that has deadly results for others. That's just a statistical projection.

LOCATION

With each restaurant design different, there are some aspects that remain the same. Each restaurant will have a kitchen, emergency exits, bathroom(s), tables, chairs and an entrance. In the United States, by law, each restaurant must have emergency exits (for dine-in restaurants). It's also safe to assume the restaurants have windows. It is important to embrace these facts because it allows for easier identification and assessment wherever you go.

Soon I will discuss the PLAN A, B and C, but wanted to explain what exists in most minds as PLAN A. When you enter a restaurant, you enter through the front door, and I know there are some restaurant designs where you could enter through a large opening that looks like windows, but for this discussion, we enter through the front door. In each person's subconscious lies the option of exiting through that same opening, if an emergency should happen.

Why?

Deep down, your brain understands that you did not get injured, nor were you threatened as you walked into the restaurant through the front door. Your brain noted that option as a viable exit strategy for the future (your PLAN A). You may not realize this, but this happens. The downside to that fact is: if you are not aware of your surroundings and a gunman were to enter the restaurant and begin shooting, your only true confidence is to exit through the front door (thus making you feel 'stuck'). This, however, is what creates victims, because the front door is where the gunman is standing. Does that make sense?

Without a plan, most people will freeze due to the immediate drama unfolding and their brain's inability to process everything that is happing in front of them. You freeze because it is an unexpected situation, which you were unprepared for. Your desire would be to initiate your PLAN A, even though you never thought about having a plan at all, your brain initiated that for you (unless you are frozen in fear). Same thing would occur if you were in a department store and you suddenly heard rapid (or any) gunshots. Your brain would send the signal-thought of: "You came in the front door, that's your safest exit route", but now you know why that's not a great place to choose.

I always state: "I have PLAN A, B and C, and PLAN A will most likely not work, so I concentrate on B and C!"

FACING THE DOOR

I always sit facing the entrance. I may be located in a booth in the far back of the restaurant, but I will be facing the entrance. I do this because I glance at people as they enter the restaurant and conduct a quick assessment. I've done this for so long, it's a natural action for me and one that takes a split second. Body language can tell you a lot about a person, and if that person is there to do something they know is not lawful or right. I want to see those who come to the establishment. I do not need to stare at the front door, I just want to remain aware of those who enter.

Where I sit matters, but if I do not have the choice of location, I will still sit facing towards the entrance, but I still need to identify the layout of the restaurant and think about my Plan B and C. I want to make sure I have easy egress options. For some restaurant designs I may need to hop over a divider or around a server station. I need to make sure I have options identified, because I know how others are going to react in a high-stress, traumatic situation. It will be chaos and people don't think about others when their lives are in jeopardy.

WINDOWS

I know Hollywood movies makes it look easy to bust through a window to escape a deadly encounter, but windows in any restaurant will not react as those Hollywood windows. Real windows (non-Hollywood) will not bust if you try to throw a chair through them. Busting through a window by running really fast and throwing your body-weight against it, will only result in you having to go to the hospital for a broken collarbone/shoulder, arm, head, etc. I highly advise you do not look at the windows as an option for egress.

PERIMETER WALK

Once I have been seated, I immediately identify where I am in relation to a landmark, such as the front door. I then proceed to take the 'long way' to the bathrooms. I deliberately weave throughout the restaurant for a couple of reasons:

1-To identify emergency exits

2-To identify where the kitchen is

3-To identify if there's a bar located within this restaurant

4-To identify where the bathrooms are (because that's where I'm going)

5-To identify who I believe are those people who are carrying a concealed firearm and not confident in their abilities.

Wait...What?

That's correct, I walk throughout the restaurant on my way to the bathroom, deliberately making eye contact with those who are paying attention to me. I smile and nod as if I know them and want to be cordial. Those who are carrying a firearm and not confident will show me (in most cases) by their body language: once eye contact is made, their eyes will get big and they will either look uneasy, look down to ensure their pistol is not exposed, reach down and tap the area to feel if their firearm is exposed, and/or they will turn their pistol-side away slightly. This tells me lots of important information: they are not confident in their carry, they are not confident in their skills, and they tell me which side their pistol is located.

Why does this matter?

If someone is not trained for defensive situations, what do you suppose will happen when skill, accuracy, confidence and precision under pressure is needed, but in an environment of chaos where those around him/her are screaming, running around and trying to scramble over everyone else to escape? For those with the ego that say "I got this" while in calm conditions, when chaos erupts, there is a great chance that they will frantically withdraw their pistol and continue pulling the trigger out of desperation (self-preservation). They may try to get their pistol towards the gunman who has opened fire on everyone, but their trigger discipline is non-existent, which means lots of bullets going places unintended.

Why do I worry about it? I am probably in the direct path of some of those bullets. I try to identify those who lack confidence and training, so I know where I need to be when I egress (which means: which path keeps me out of their area when they 'lay and spray'). I'm sure this may bruise some egos, but it is vital to understand that you own every bullet that comes out of your barrel, regardless where you WANTED the bullets to go. I'm positive most people who carry, do so to protect their loved ones and themselves, and I believe they may have the best of intentions, but intentions doesn't save me from getting hit by friendly fire.

By conducting a perimeter walk, I am able to think through my PLAN B and PLAN C. I look at how the tables are situated, how staff move through the areas, open aisles, booth locations and alley-ways that lead to emergency exits. Just by doing a harmless perimeter walk through the restaurant, I am able to collect the data needed to make appropriate decisions, in the event something bad were to happen. It also allows me to imbed a safe pathway through the restaurant as a mental 'push-pin', if the restaurant was to fill with smoke. This is also why you do the practice I recommend at home: familiarity of the area, in case the lights were to go out or the location were to fill with smoke.

PLAN A, B and C

I've already stated that PLAN A is the front door, and probably not a viable exit if criminals decided to enter the location and create havoc. PLAN B and C are the options I think more about.

NOTE: Just because I stated that PLAN A is probably not a viable solution, I do not disregard it completely. If the entrance is open and safe, I will absolutely get my spouse and I out through that door.

I may decide (depending on the layout of the restaurant) that the emergency exits are my PLAN B. Since every restaurant has a kitchen, that will probably be my PLAN C. I know the kitchen has an exit in the back, but also contains a lot of items to use for defensive purposes, if needed. I also recognize that my PLAN B and C may need to remain dynamic because of the occupants and/or threat situation. Remain dynamic in thought, so you can change your pathways on the 'fly'.

AVOID!!!

Many, many years ago (before my time), bathrooms had windows. For some, those windows were an option to escape a bad date. You would excuse yourself from the table to use the bathroom, then open the window and slip out through the alley without ever being noticed. Those days are gone. I haven't seen a window in a bathroom in decades, which means the bathroom is a dead-end. Dead-ends should not be considered in your plan because it contains YOU without options! Avoid bathrooms (unless you need to use the bathroom, of course).

Could you block the door of the bathroom?

You could block the door to keep the threat on the other side, however, what if the threat decided to torch that location? What if the fire is engulfing outside the bathroom and the smoke is coming in? You could be thinking the threat(s) are trying to smoke you out, so you decide to stay inside the bathroom...and then you pass out from smoke inhalation. It's best to avoid the bathrooms and continue to identify working options for egress.

DEFENSIVE OBJECTS

There are numerous options in a restaurant for one to use as a defensive tool against a dangerous attack(er). Think about what is usually available on your table:

-Salt and Pepper shaker

-Silverware

-Menu

-Ketchup/mustard

-Napkin

-Glass(es)

Those items could be used to jab, poke and throw at the attacker, to get a moment to further egress from the area. Again, throwing an object, even a crunched-up napkin, at the face of an attacker could cause them to stop, turn their head away from the incoming object, thus providing a pocket of time for you to egress the area.

If there is a bar in the restaurant:

If there is a bar in the restaurant, there are objects at/behind the bar that can be used against a threat:

-Knives

-Ice

-Glasses/mugs

-Napkins

-Fruit

-Hot coffee/carafes

-Bottles of alcohol

All of those items can be used as a defensive tool and/or a projectile. The kitchen has defensive tools, also:

-Pots, pans, skillets

-Knives, cleavers

-Water, hot grease

-Containers

Again, items that could be used against an attacker, if necessary. When it comes to defensive options, you are only hindered by your imagination and abilities. If you can pick it up, it can probably be used to defend yourself. Don't forget, if you're in the kitchen, you should be trying to locate the exit to egress from the location. If a threat is behind you, you may need to quickly assess to identify a defensive tool, only if you cannot successfully exit the area quick enough. Situations change and this is why your plan(s) should remain dynamic.

PAY ATTENTION

What is it I look for as people enter the restaurant? I am looking for those who are dressed unseasonably. If it is 100 degrees outside and they enter the restaurant in a winter ski-jacket, or a long, wool trench coat, they have my attention. If it's winter outside and the enter wearing shorts and flip-flops, that will raise some flags. Unseasonal or out of place catches attention. Yes, I understand fashion changes, and I am the furthest from fashion-savvy you will ever find, but if it looks suspicious (regardless of fashion trends), I am paying attention.

Someone wearing a long coat may be appropriate in colder weather, would I pay attention to that? If the person is 'twitchy' or looking around nervously, yes I would be paying attention. What I am looking for is that person proceeding in an unnatural way.

What does that mean?

When you walk, you naturally swing your arms. For some, the swinging is quite apparent and fluid, for others it is minute, but they still swing. Someone walking without their arms naturally moving, or only one arm is swaying back and forth (as it naturally should), will alert me to that inaction. If someone is holding their arm to their side, not allowing it to sway naturally, it's usually an indication that they are holding something in place. Longer jackets can conceal longer weapons (rifle, shotgun, etc.). Add this odd inaction with an unseasonal jacket and they have my full attention (and my Color code moves up in color).

If I happen to see someone holding their arm tight to themselves, I will also begin looking around to see if anyone else is posturing at a different location. My rule is: If there is one threat, there are three. I am going to assume there are more than one threat in this location, and that is when I begin scanning the area for an accomplice. At this point I am plotting my defense, and/or egress actions. My actions are dictated by my current situation and if I am alone or not. I, by no means, rush judgement or make any dangerous actions prematurely.

REMEMBER

If you do carry a firearm for defensive purposes, whether you are trained or not, if you withdraw your firearm you have to know you have become the person with the gun, by those around you. People who are itching for a gunfight could very well believe you to be the threat, and now you have a situation where you are looked at as another threat. This is why training is important, along with being aware and having your PLAN A, B and C! Oh, let me also add practicing at home to that list!

BE PREPARED FOR ACTION

You cannot save everyone. Let that sink in, embrace it and get comfortable with that reality. You. Cannot. Save. Everyone. Does this mean not to try? Of course not, but you definitely need to understand the reality of the situation and how it will unfold to the folks around you. If a gunman were to enter the restaurant you are occupying and begins to fire their weapon at the occupants, some people will freeze (data overload), and some people will scramble in a chaotic manner (trying to get over/around/through whoever is between them and an exit or safe place away from the threat) and have zero regard for you.

Having a plan in your brain means you have thought about the paths you could/would take if an emergency were to take place, but those around you may not (it is a safe bet that most, if not all around you do not have a plan nor thought about making one) and their only thought is to get as far away from the danger as possible. Some people will crawl over their own family to get to a safer place. Do they not like their family? Do they cherish their survival over their children's? Of course not.

It is natural to escape danger to survive a dangerous encounter. It doesn't mean that person hates their spouse, or their children, but it does mean their brain is signaling a flight response for survival. It is natural. You need to know this because these people will not care who is in their way, they will be frantic for the sake of their survival. Once you embrace that thought (reality), you will have a much better time creating your PLAN A, B & C. Again, it is natural for people to do what is necessary to avoid danger and to survive the encounter.

Now let's talk about some of the other people. The people who freeze out of fear may remain seated, or stand and freeze in position because of the events unfolding in front of them. Some of these people may slink down a little, thinking they are hiding away from the threats. These are the people I am speaking of. My term of: "You can't save everyone" is referring to these people (and the frantic ones, which I will explain in a second).

Sensory overload, mixed with fear and adrenaline, can cause these people to become almost zombie-like. Some will close their eyes, because in their mind if they cannot see the threat, the threat cannot/will not see them. These people are at risk from a threat who wants to cause destruction to those who are the easiest to attack. This makes these people easy targets for a deranged gunman, who only wants to execute as many people as possible before the police arrive (or before they take their own life). For these zombie-like people, their brains are trying to block out the situation in hopes of surviving. This would become a bad situation for these people, but can be avoided with your help.

My mindset is as follows: If an event were to kick off in the restaurant I am occupying, I would be implementing my Plan B/C, and along the way, I will be trying to coax my fellow patrons to come with me. I will do my best to be aggressive enough to wake them from their frozen state, to get them to follow me to safety. If the location breaks out in chaos, the elderly are at risk, and you cannot just snatch up an elderly couple and drag them out of harms way. The elderly are a bit more brittle than those of us younger than 65.

If, after quickly assessing the zombie-like folks around me, I conclude some to be elderly and unable to move, or too frozen to snap out of it, I will quickly force them underneath their table. This can hide them from the gunman, thus making them safer than those exposed. Again, I will do my best to coax those around me towards a safer exit, but if they won't move, I will try to stuff them underneath their tables.

For those that refuse to snap out of it, or will not get under the table, I am no longer invested in trying to convince them to egress towards a safer location. If I try to spend more time convincing these people to move towards safety, I become more at risk to the violence. That is what gets more people killed. Again, I embrace the fact that I cannot save everyone. I will do my best to convince you to come with me, but if you fight it or refuse to follow, I shall wish you good luck and hope you survive. I then proceed on with my plan.

For the people who are frantic and find themselves stuffed into a broom closet, or a bathroom, if I know they are there, or I watched them scramble into those locations (and it is on my path to the exit I identified), I will give it my best college try to convince them to come with me. Some will pull back and scream about having a safe place to hide, others will shut down mentally once they are behind a door as the mayhem continues. I am not beyond dragging someone out of a death-box, if it means they will survive, but I am one person and I cannot drag out a bunch of people.

If you remain on station (in a bathroom or office) trying to convince someone (or a group of people) to follow you when those people believe they are safer where they are at, you will become a casualty also. This is what you want to avoid. If you enter a dead-end location to convince people to leave that location, you too have become a resident of that dead end. It does not make you a bad person if you have to escape a traumatic/deadly situation. Embrace that and lock that deep inside your soul. Regret is a beast that eats up many people.

CARRY ITEMS FOR DEFENSE

While implementing your egress plan, it is wise to grab something to use for defense as you egress from the area. As I initiate movement from my seat, I will grab whatever is closest to me as I move. This may be my glass, knife, fork, spoon, salt/pepper shaker, whatever, but I will grab something to use as a defensive tool. I do carry a firearm, but since I am trying to keep this book about awareness, my tactics will be better served in a defensive handgun book, and not here.

As I am weaving through the people running from the mayhem, I am going to keep an eye in the direction of the threat(s), just in case others are involved and I may not have spotted them. If I happen to move towards someone who is working with the threat(s), that is what the object is for. Action beats reaction, remember? Before this person has a chance to act on my advance, I will quickly throw the object towards the face of the threat as I advance as quickly as possible. As they go to block the object, my feet/fist/body will be moving quickly to impact their body.

My goal would be to neutralize the threat. My mission is not to subdue the threat, because I don't know if the other threat(s) is behind me, coming to the aid of the other threat. If I were to grab this threat and hold him/her in position while the other threat approaches, I would be taken out by the threat relatively quick. This is not a position anyone would want to be in. I would, however, throw my body weight at this threat I'm approaching, in the hopes of knocking him/her down and away from my pathway to safety.

Situation dictates actions. It's easy to say "I'd punch him/her in the face and take their gun" or "I'd drop-kick the threat and then take out the other threat", but when in a chaotic situation where lives are being lost, it is a different story. Think realistically and not Hollywood. Your fear levels will be elevated, you're going to be desperate to survive just like those around you, but if you have a plan in mind, you have direction and purpose. Those without a plan are more likely to spot your determination and follow you to safety, with or without your coercion.

Remember, always be prepared to defend as you move through your plans and be prepared to remain flexible throughout your plan, because pathways can change in an instant and you need to adjust your plan accordingly. By practicing your movement in each restaurant you visit, you will become proficient in dynamic planning wherever you go. The title of this section is RESTAURANTS, but this information can be applied wherever you go.

CREDIT CARD RECEIPT

Always get a copy of your receipt and keep it until the charge clears your account. The reason for this is important (if you want to avoid losing money). Most credit card charges will show up as 'pending' in your account, when the charge initially occurs. The total will be what was charged, but not necessarily the tip (in most cases). This is important because you could be taken advantage of by the server, which occurs more than most know.

As an example, lets say you were to go out to eat and your bill was $100. If you had good service, you may tip 20% and think no more about that bill. You could check your account that evening and see the charge for $100 and be confident that it was charged correctly. Then, as time goes on and you check your account, you see that another $200 was taken from your account and don't know why. The $100 was for your bill, but instead of charging the $20 for the 20% tip you gave your server, they changed the $20 to $200.

Now you have the hassle of contacting your bank to dispute the charge. You would notice an extra $200 coming out of your account (I hope), and many people cannot afford to have that happen to them. If you save the receipt, you then have proof of your tip, the charge, and the date/timestamp on the receipt. You will also have the server's name or employee ID number, depending how that restaurant handles that part of their employment. This is proof of where you were and when, and can save you a small portion of the hassle you stand to face.

PIZZA DELIVERY

I had a pizza delivery guy deliver my pizza one Friday evening in Virginia. I signed the credit card slip and grabbed my pizza, I wasn't thinking about keeping the receipt. The deliveryman quickly insisted I take the receipt. This got my attention, so we had a discussion:

Deliveryman: Sir, you want to keep your receipt.

Me: No, I'm good, thanks (I really wanted my pizza).

D: No, sir, really, you really want to keep the receipt.

Me: Okay, why do I want to keep this receipt?

D: How close do you watch your account? Normally.

Me: What do you mean?

D: So, I deliver pizza on a daily basis and so many of the houses I deliver to just want their pizza and don't care about the paperwork.

Me: Okay?

D: Well, since I visit so many houses each day, let's say 30 deliveries, and each house pays with a credit card and don't care to keep a copy of the paperwork. If they didn't tip anything and I wrote in a tip, not a big one, would they even catch on that I had done that?

Me: Go on.

D: Well, it has been my experience that many people don't pay really close attention to their accounts. They may check every now and again to make sure they still have money in there, but they aren't paying too close of attention. I could add a dollar here/dollar there to their bill and there is a great chance they would never notice.

Me: I see where you are going with this.

D: Well, if I did that for 30 deliveries, that's an extra $30 dollars each night that goes into my pocket. If I work 5 days a week, I make an extra $150 dollars in tips. All because no one wanted to keep the receipt.

Me: That's very insightful and I'm embarrassed I didn't take my receipt initially. I teach situational awareness seminars almost weekly and this was not on my radar, but should have been.

D: Well sir, this has happened to people. It wasn't in Virginia, but it was with a food delivery person and they got caught.

Me: Really?

D: The guy got greedy and the people noticed an extra $10, $20 and even $50 dollar tip on an order that was already costly. It didn't take the company long to find out who the driver was and he was arrested at work, but not before he made a lot of money adding tips to the receipt.

Me: That's craziness and I thank you for giving me that information. (I hand him $5)

D: You already tipped me on the receipt, sir.

Me: I did and now I'm giving you another $5 for the information. This will become a story I tell for many years to come and will help out a lot of people who need to hear it.

D: Well, thank you sir.

Me: Thank you.

That simple interaction can save you from losing money. They might only increase the tip by a dollar or two, something you may not even notice, but it's still considered stealing and it is still a crime. Plus, ethically, it's wrong to take advantage of others like that. So, always take your receipt and watch your account(s). It's your money, after all, and I'm sure you want to keep as much of it as possible, right? Check your bill/receipt before you give up your credit card, but then keep the receipt and watch your account to ensure the proper amount has been charged. If it's wrong, or something is off, dispute the charge, call your credit card company and give them the information. They may require a copy of the receipt, which you have in your wallet/purse, which you can easily take a picture of it with your phone and immediately send it to the credit card representative.

RFID [Radio Frequency Identification]

RFID sleeves are sleeves that you can place your credit cards in, to avoid having your card skimmed. There are machines called skimmers (and readers), that criminals use to gain the data on your card without needing to touch, or see your card. Their machine can retrieve the data from a distance (the readers, where skimmers are usually attached), but with an RFID sleeve, the reader doesn't work. The sleeves are inexpensive and worth their weight in gold, if you want to avoid having your data stolen. An online search will allow for easy ordering.

Note: Search/read "How Do Thieves Scan Credit Cards in Your Purse", by Andra Picincu

These sleeves block any signal from accessing your card data. The RFID technology also comes in tablet size, phone size and laptop size. RFID protection also comes in purse and pocketbook designs. These are items that can block signals from getting your credit card information and is an inexpensive way to reduce the chance of a skimmer/reader gaining your card information. Search: RFID Sleeves.

The RFID technology for phones is marketed towards family, where the family can place their phones inside the bag and no one can receive calls or text messages. Some families use these sleeves when they sit down for dinner. This technology is great because it drops the phone off of the grid while it sits inside the bag/sleeve. The bag does the same job that the RFID sleeves do for your card: it blocks signals from getting in/out. Some bookstores have the 'game night phone bags' (which a student found and purchased, just to bring me one as a thank you for teaching them about situational awareness), some department stores may carry them, but they can be found online through some popular ordering sites.

This is an inexpensive way to protect your phone, your data and your location.

Note: I mentioned these bags previously and are the same search topics used to locate them (i.e. faraday bags). These bags accomplish the same protection as the RFID sleeves.

SCENARIO EXAMPLE

The 'what if' scenarios are endless, but I wanted to include some scenarios that could occur, to give an idea how I approach my planning and awareness situations.

DEPARTMENT STORE

I enter through the large, inviting entrance, which is well-lit and easy to access. I know my brain 'pins' this entrance as my exit (or PLAN A) option, so I grab a cart and proceed through the store. I slowly walk through the store, boxing it out by strolling through the outside perimeter, to identify the warehouse location (where I know there will be a loading dock/exit), the bathrooms, and the emergency exits. I glance around to identify the entrance, so I have a reference point to the emergency exits. Lastly, as I shop, I glance at possible hiding locations, just in case I am unable to egress to an emergency-exit immediately.

Gunshots are heard towards the front of the store and people begin screaming. I happened to forget my firearm (which rarely happens) and am stuck close to the bathrooms. Being the furthest away from the shots, I listen intently to the screams and any other shots fired so I can identify how many shooters there are and what they are shooting (i.e. pistol, rifle, shotgun), while I make my way through the aisles to get to the warehouse door.

I get to the door and give one last look around to see if any threats were headed towards my location. I listen at the warehouse door for any noises (voices, scurrying of people, sounds of a vehicle) before I crack it open slowly. The last thing I would want at this point is to open the door to see accomplices of the threat waiting on the other side of the door. If no voices are heard or chance of threats present, I would then proceed to exit.

My PLAN A was the entrance, where the shots were heard, so Plan A was a no-go. PLAN B was the emergency exits, but I was too far away from accessing those location, but close to the warehouse door, which would have been my Plan C. Had I heard voices behind the door I was standing next to, I would have to be flexible enough in my planning to proceed to an emergency exit, despite it being further away. If this was the case, I would have picked up something to use as a defensive device, as I proceeded towards the exit.

REMEMBER: If/when you pick up a defensive tool and try to egress from the mayhem, there may be some who see you with the 'tool' and believe you to be the threat. Just keep this in mind because when fear-induced situations occur in a location where multiple patrons are occupying and scared, they can easily confuse a 'good guy' with a 'bad guy'.

RESTAURANT EXAMPLE

My spouse and I arrived at a big-name steakhouse and enter through its large, sturdy wooden doors. We are greeted by a smiling hostess, who is pleasant and greets us well. As she leads us to our table, I glance around and notice the restaurant has a large seating area around the bar and smaller aisles of seating on the sides. As I follow my spouse down the aisle towards our booth, I notice where the servers have stations, where the kitchen door is, and where the bathrooms are located. My spouse takes the seat opposite of mine, so I can visually see the door. I sit and wait for the hostess to depart.

I stand and excuse myself, saying I have to visit the restroom. I then proceed through the restaurant to identify the emergency exits, but to also make eye contact with patrons who are watching me. I nod and smile, almost like I know them, but not quite, and proceed to the bathroom. I wash my hands, dry them and then exit the bathroom, where I stand for a moment to identify the access points to the bar. I then proceed through the restaurant and back to my seat, where I join my spouse for a great meal.

In my head, I identified my Plan A (out the front door), my Plan B (rush to the kitchen) and Plan C (behind the bar and to an emergency exit). From where we are sitting, my plan to get to these locations involved jumping over the partial-wall next to the table, to get to my egress location. I was able to quickly decide where I would need to move if a threat were to appear in the kitchen as I approached. At the table, I moved the salt/pepper shakers around on the table, so I could mentally identify what I could grab as I moved from the table.

This planning session took less than 10 minutes and most was inside my brain. I make it a point to not linger or creep around places in public, because then I would be identified as a creep myself. I prefer to remain low-key and quiet, as I stand out as it is. If something were to occur, I had a working plan that I knew would change on the fly, because that is how circumstances occur. When I was in the military and conducting various missions around the world, I used to say: "If the plan went perfect, without a hiccup or drama, then it wasn't our mission". This means that something would always happen that we didn't plan for. This is why we plan and plan for contingencies.

It is important to close this section out with the following words of guidance: We can train and plan incessantly, sometimes too much, and still never be truly ready for a deadly encounter. We hope bad things don't happen to us, around us, or to the people we know and love, but the reality is that bad things do happen. If you are prepared for 'something' to happen, then you are better off than most of the people around you, because too many people live in denial that evil exists (or could exist in the areas they visit).

Will this book save you from everything? No. Will it give you a better chance at surviving a dangerous encounter? It will and the reason it will is because you can slowly adapt the suggestions in this book into your daily lives. You will realize that it takes very little effort to incorporate these techniques and by doing so, it becomes second-nature (you don't realize that you automatically do the awareness techniques). I have real-world stories of students who, after attending my seminar on situational awareness, survived a deadly encounter because of what they learned (and the questions they asked during the seminar).

Just by knowing what could cause you to become a victim (or statistic), educates you higher than most. By almost-experiencing bad situations, it allows you to spread the word about how it was you were able to avoid becoming a victim. When you speak about what you did to avoid the threat, the situation, whatever it was, others will listen and the first thing that will go through their mind is: "I don't know what I would have done in that situation". This gives you a chance to give the gift of knowledge to those who desperately need it.

This is why I wrote this book and created the seminar. I wanted to provide people with information that they didn't know they needed. After the seminar I would hear all of the "I didn't know about any of that stuff before this class" and "I feel so stupid that I didn't think about this before" and I would immediately reassure them that they were not stupid, they were comfortably ignorant to the possibilities that surround us everywhere we go. I then praise them for doing the hardest thing: coming to a class. I would support them by explaining how now they will go home and look at their home in a different light. They will think about how they leave the house, how they set up their curtains, their front porch and their lighting.

This is why I would market my seminars with the following information:

Please bring a notebook or paper to take notes, a pen or pencil to write with and an open mind. Please avoid using such terms when you are asking a question: "This is a stupid question..." or "I know this may sound dumb...", because if the question or statement enters your brain, it was important enough to prompt you to ask a question. There are no dumb questions, so please be prepared to ask as many questions as you need to, and not be judged for them.

By adding that information to my seminar description, it allowed people to feel confident that they were in a safe location to ask any question they want or need. On the entrance door to the classroom, I had posted a sign that read: "If you laugh at another student for asking a question, you will be escorted out of the building. If you tell someone to shut up because it was a stupid question they asked, you will be escorted out of the building". I only had to escort a couple people out of my classroom for being rude/disrespectful to another student.

Bottom line (and I've taught well over 100k students): If someone has a question, any question, there is a very good chance that someone else in that classroom also had that question on their mind. Don't be quick to judge the questions of others, we all learn differently.

7

VEHICLE SAFETY and
AWARENESS

You may not have realized this yet, but when you first enter your vehicle, you are at your most vulnerable for that moment in time. At the moment you are inside your vehicle and seated, a threat has the best chance to gain the advantage by rushing in and attacking quickly. This action takes you (the occupant) by surprise, because the threat has the element of surprise. The threat would then have complete control. By invading your space and creating a surge of fear, the threat could easily cause the greatest amount of damage and/or harm to you. This is not a good thing, obviously.

Why are you so vulnerable once you enter your vehicle? Once you are inside YOUR vehicle, it is your property (such as when you enter your home) and where you feel is the most secure. You feel this way because it is yours, and you know that no one has the right to invade your property for any reason. An immediate action of shock and fear would overcome you if a threat were to whip open your door and assault you, because in your mind you know that is not right (or lawful). Does this mean it won't/can't happen? Nope! Threats know they have that control and as long as they maintain control, they maintain the power.

This is why this section of the book is necessary and important to read over and over again, then hand it off to your children to read. Awareness is not just when you are eating at a restaurant or shopping at the mall. Awareness is at all times and is what can keep you away from hazardous situations and serious harm. Fact is, you won't figure out solutions on-the-spot if a threat suddenly whips open your door and starts assaulting you. You will then be in defense mode, which means you will be trying to limit the assault, to save yourself from further harm by any means possible.

DEFENSIVE ITEMS

You probably have defensive items in your vehicle at this very moment and don't even realize it. There are many items that can be used for defensive purposes, but you need to identify those items, otherwise you won't be clear-minded enough to think about it while you are being assaulted. Again, I am not promoting violence, nor am I recommending violent actions towards anyone else, but I am going to provide information that could become options for anyone placed into harm's way, who does not have any other choice.

FLASHLIGHT

I carry a flashlight on my person at all times. All times! A flashlight is a great defensive tool because it can accomplish many things:
-It provides light during the darkness (I expect many to say "ah duh!" at that).
-It can also constrict pupils quickly, when flashed, to create 'snow-blindness' for a couple of seconds.
-It allows me to grip it tightly, to strengthen my fist (in case I need to strike).
-It can be used to 'punch' into areas of opportunity, to force an attacker to cease their assault.

Since my flashlight is always on my person (on/in my pocket) and I cannot access it if my seatbelt was on, I could only access that as an option if I withdrew it from my pocket as I entered my vehicle (which I wouldn't do). Most times, as I approach my vehicle, my keys are in my dominant hand and my flashlight is gripped in the other. This allows me multiple options for defense against an attacker, if it were to happen. Once my door is open, I could put my flashlight back on/ into my pocket and sit in my seat, but that would leave me without my flashlight.

With any problem identified, a little thought and preparation increases options. I happen to keep a larger flashlight in my vehicle. This flashlight is specifically for my vehicle, in the event I break down and need a longer-lasting light. It is too large to carry on my person, which is why I keep it mounted inside my vehicle. It remains close enough to grab, yet out of the way to not obstruct my movement or view. This flashlight becomes an option, if I needed something during an ambush attack (and has many D-sized batteries inside).

CHOPSTICKS

I also maintain a set of chopsticks in my vehicle. When ordering Asian food, I prefer to eat it with chopsticks and I usually get more than one pair when I order. I keep these chopsticks tucked away, out of sight but within grasp if I needed something to use for defense inside my vehicle. Chopsticks are a great set of tools to have in my luggage if I am flying or driving on vacation. It doesn't matter if I am going out of the state or out of the country and does not raise any eyebrows. They are lightweight and easy to handle.

BATON

Batons and expandable batons are an option. They come in various sizes and expand quickly with a flick of the wrist. They are usually steel and have a rubberized grip for easier handling for full control. I can attest to the fact that a baton strike hurts a lot! It is a quick hurt, sort of like being hit by a lightning bolt, and took my legs out from underneath me. I had a coworker show me its effectiveness and he barely tapped me.

That 'light' tap to my shin hurt so bad, it quickly dropped me to the ground (where I was grateful it was just a tap).

NOTE: It is vital to check the laws in your state to determine if having a baton in your vehicle (or at all) is legal. If it is not legal, do not carry/house a baton in your vehicle or on your person. Some states may consider it a concealed weapon and you may need to have a CCW permit for that item. Again, do not break the law.

PEN/PENCIL/TIRE GAUGE

Many people have a pen, or a pencil (or both) somewhere within their vehicle. For some who get their greatest inspiration while inside their vehicle, they may have a small notepad and pen/pencil above their head, wedged over their visor. Some keep a pen and notepad next to them in or on their console. Vehicles today have many storage locations. There are even storage options in the doors, where someone could place their water bottle, napkins, or notepad next to them. Unfortunately for many, more options equate to storing more junk inside their vehicle, which I have been guilty of myself.

Having a pen or pencil handy may not be your option. You may prefer to maintain a notepad and pen inside your glove compartment. What about a tire gauge? A tire gauge is not costly at all and is recommended for all vehicle owners. A tire gauge allows you to check the air pressure in your tires, without having to go to a gas station or dealership to check. The average tire gauge is approximately the size of a regular pen and/or pencil and easy to store within a vehicle. If it is within arms reach during an emergency situation, it could become a tool to use.

KEYS

Your keys are a useful tool, but only if you need to use them prior to starting your vehicle. Many people have keyless vehicles, which allows the owner to open the door and start their vehicle with a push of a button (if their FOB is inside the vehicle). Few will only have the controller on a keyring, whereas most others may have their house or apartment keys on the same ring. Some people carry an excessive number of keys on their keyring, while others keep few.

If there are other keys on the keyring, other than the FOB/controller, they could be useful for defensive purposes, to break free/away from an attacker. These keys are sharp and create instant pain, which can be enough to deter the threat from continuing their attack. If you do not have keys on the keyring, the FOB can be useful as a defensive tool, but not as effective against an attacker. The FOB/controller for the vehicle usually has an alarm option for the vehicle and if it does, the owner could activate the alarm as the attacker attempts their assault. The alarm gains attention of others and criminals do not like attention. Attention equals witnesses and possible capture.

Once you are inside your vehicle, if it starts by key, the keyring and keys attached would not do any good against an attacker. A FOB-started vehicle could still be used because the FOB does not attach to anything for the vehicle to start. This could provide a defensive tool if it was needed. Anything is better than nothing at all, especially when the discussion is about being attacked. If I needed to use my actual keys for a defensive purpose, it would become a jabbing and slashing implement, where I target any area of opportunity where I could attempt to 'start' up the attacker!

IMMEDIATE ACTIONS

When you approach your vehicle, I suggest approaching from the opposite side of the parking lot lane (if I park on the left side of the aisle, I approach from the right side and cross over when I get closer). This allows you to see underneath vehicles as you approach, and if you spot someone crouched down next to, or near your vehicle, you are warned early to leave and contact the police. When you close in on your vehicle, look inside at the backseat of your vehicle as you arrive.

As I approach the vehicle, I glance around the area to ensure no one is watching my vehicle or myself. If someone is loitering around the area or keeps checking in my direction, I will look for others who may be with this person, but I will avoid going directly to my vehicle. If I sense something is off, I will turn around and go back to the store I left, where I will call the police and report the behavior. This is important to mention because so many people keep their attention to their phone screen and do not lift their eyes up to maintain awareness. This is what creates victims.

At my vehicle, as I slowly walk alongside, I am going to check the backseat. If anything is disrupted, or if something seems out of place, I will stop and inspect closer while glancing around the area. There are many 'tricks' criminals use to divert the vehicle owner's attention, to allow the threat(s) to rush in and assault the person, and/or steal their vehicle. If things are 'normal', I then open the door and conduct one last check around. I then enter my vehicle.

The following is what I recommend for action: Once you get into your vehicle, immediately lock your door(s), start your vehicle and place it in gear. Once your vehicle is in gear, then put on your seatbelt. After those steps are accomplished, do whatever you feel you need to, such as: answer a text, blow your nose, whatever. The reason for these steps, especially since technology advances so quickly, is to avoid being ambushed and surprised by a threat. If a threat were to attack at this point, they wouldn't be able to open your door. Their actions attempting to gain entry into your vehicle would alert you and you could immediately depart the area.

Remember, threats like to maintain the element of surprise to gain the control they need. Some people have vehicles that automatically lock all doors once the vehicle has begun to move forward. The downside to that technology and the occupants' reliance on that action, is it initially leaves the driver/occupants vulnerable. The threat, if able to attack after the owner enters the vehicle, would be able to assault the driver and gain control of the vehicle and occupants. Carjackings are still occurring throughout the world, more-so in other countries than the U.S., but it still occurs.

Think about it: if you entered your vehicle and suddenly your door flies open, what would be your response? Surprise? Fear? Your action would be to look in the direction of the open door, where the threat is standing. Why? It's because you haven't taken the time to think through possible scenarios and work through them to find where you are the weakest. If you had prepared, if/when a threat attempts to open your door, you may glance in that direction, but you are more focused on a quick exit. See the difference? Do you think this is important, especially as we get older?

If you can, I would suggest you back into a parking spot, rather than pulling straight in. The reason for this is simple: a forward escape is much easier to initiate than a reverse attempt. You can see what is in front of you, whereas you would have to look behind you as you back out to ensure you do not hit or injure an innocent bystander.

If you make it a point to complete these steps (and teach your children to also): Enter the vehicle, close and lock the door, start the vehicle and place it into gear, and then do whatever else you need to do, your chances of being successfully ambushed reduces exponentially. If a threat were to attempt entry at your locked door, they would quickly realize they were rejected and at that point they would either run away, or they would attempt to break your window to gain entry. Either way, your response would be immediate, thus keeping control.

PARKING GARAGE

Some parking garages are scary as they are. Some are dark, with lights that only blink intermittently like in a horror movie and smell pretty bad. Some appear to have cameras, but that does not solidify that the cameras are operational, or monitored. In some locations, their cameras were inoperable and their cables were cut. You cannot rely on these locations to solidify your safety (or even respond to you if you needed help).

What you do have in parking garages, is the ability to hear the surrounding area better, because everything echoes (or is enhanced) inside a parking garage. Smells, other than exhaust, can be distinctly identified (enough to alert you to the smell), and sounds seem better isolated. Some parking garages have elevators and stairs, while some only stairs. Parking garages can seem daunting, and for some really scary, but if you remain aware, you can gain more confidence in that environment.

When parking, it's wise to choose a location that has working lights around it. This allows you to maintain illumination around your vehicle, which can also identify the shadows of anyone who may try to hide next to your vehicle. If you are able, park in an open area, which allows you to maintain space around your vehicle. If there are cameras, try to park in a location that is not sheltered from the closest camera (even if you believe that camera to be inoperable). If I park in a parking garage, I take a picture of my surrounding area, to include the markings on the stanchions (tells me which floor/level I am on), the cameras and vehicles around where I park.

As I approach my vehicle, I approach it in the same manner as I do in a regular, open parking lot: from the opposite side of the aisle. With some parking garages, it is difficult to do this when they only have vehicles parked on one side. I do this to see underneath the vehicles around my own, to identify if anyone is crouched down, out of sight. My ears are always straining to hear 'natural' noises around me, but especially the shuffling of feet on concrete, or adjusting weight. Those sounds tend to amplify in parking garages. I also breathe through my nose, to try and detect any 'off' smells. Such smells include: fresh cigarette smoke (with no one in view), body odor, cologne, etc. This alerts me to someone being close (or had just been in the same area I am currently in).

If someone seems to be loitering nearby, close to my vehicle, there are a couple options.

-Keep on walking by my vehicle so I can get a better look at the person.

-Turn around and go back to whatever location I just came from.

-Initiate my FOB alarm.

Note: If someone is innocently doing something in, or around their vehicle, they may not think about being viewed as a threat. If you initiate your FOB, you would/should be able to tell from their body language that they did not mean to appear as a threat. If they are there innocently, their body language would be such that quickly tells you they are not there for nefarious reasons. They may throw their hands up and apologize, then get into their vehicle and depart. They may apologize and quickly scurry away. If they are there for nefarious reasons and you initiate the alarm, their action may be to run away to avoid getting caught or identified.

-Give identifying information over the phone: This one would work in a parking garage and/or a regular parking lot, a store, anywhere. Holding the phone up to your mouth as if you are on speaker phone and identify what the person looks like and what they are wearing. Upon getting their attention and realizing you just identified them, body language (as mentioned above) will alert you to whether or not they were there innocently or if they were up to something.

As I approach my vehicle, as mentioned, my key is always in my hand. If I have to hold onto my phone, that becomes a defensive option. If I don't need to hold my phone, my flashlight is in my hand. If a threat were to 'pop' out from behind a vehicle, catching me by surprise, I could hold the flashlight up. Once I bring the flashlight up, the threat will immediately look straight at the object in my hand and that is when I initiate the light. That burst of bright light will 'snow-blind' them for about 4-5 seconds, which is enough time for me to get away.

It is wise to pay attention to any vehicles that are running in your area. Paying closer attention to the occupants of the vehicle(s) alerts you to the number of people, what they are driving and if they are trying to glance at you as you pass by. Be especially cautious of vehicles that are idling with no one inside. Approach cautiously and keep your senses piqued! The same applies to parking in a shopping plaza. Your approach, your awareness and the steps to take (your Plan A, B, or C) if an ambush where to occur, remain the same. Remain flexible, because the one thing you can count on, is that you CANNOT count on your plan being flawless.

THREAT TACTICS & APPROACH

There are some tactics that occur, where threats will place something on your windshield, which you won't see until you get into your vehicle. This forces you to exit the vehicle to retrieve that object (such as a brochure) and that is when they attack. The pamphlet is the same as the brochure tactic and threats will place them under your windshield wipers on your windshield or on your back window. Another tactic is a zip-tie on your windshield wiper or on your door handle. There were a couple reports of cologne/perfume brochures that contained some chemical that would cause the person to feel lightheaded or pass out, if they inhaled it.

If you enter your vehicle and you suddenly notice something on your wiper or back window, drive away until you get to an open area before you stop to remove it. Be mindful that no one is following you to this new location. Be cautious about touching the items also, there are chemicals that can be absorbed quickly through your skin, which could cause nausea, lightheadedness or cause you to pass out. Unfortunately, these are real concerns.

Other tactics that threats have attempted include: A crying woman who runs up to other women saying her boyfriend/husband hit her. Women have become victims of this ploy because they automatically feel for this woman and want to help. By the time they realize it was a con, it was too late. Another ploy is for a young, attractive woman who approaches middle-aged men, asking for help with their car. This, too, has caused men to fall victim. Once the women have their 'mark', they keep their attention as their partner moves in and completes the crime (assault, robbery, vehicular theft, etc.).

There have been some neighborhood ploys that include a car seat in the middle of the street, which has sounds like a baby was abandoned inside. The person stops to rescue the baby, they rush up to the car seat and when they arrive, they notice it's a tape recorder in the seat behind a doll, playing the sounds of a baby crying. By the time they turn around, their car is driving away.

STOP LIGHTS

When pulling up to a red light, if there is a car in front of you, leave a couple of feet between your front bumper and their rear bumper. Once you come to a stop, glance around the area for anyone loitering. Pay attention to movement in your side-view and rearview mirrors for anyone trying to approach your vehicle and be prepared to quickly egress from the area. If someone were to attempt to open your door (which is NOW always locked once you enter), you will be alerted to the attempt and can quickly drive away. This is why you identify your escape options. Those who bury their faces into their phones at lights are identified quickly as easy prey.

Note: Checking mirrors does not mean to constantly stare from mirror to mirror, to look for an attack to happen. It means to keep your view upwards and casually glance at your mirrors. If there were to be any action, you could catch it in your periphery and plan accordingly. If your focus is on your phone, there's a good chance you're going to miss the person approaching.

As you are driving, pay attention to vehicles that seem to be behind you the longest. If you feel that there is a vehicle behind you and they've been there for a long time, make it a point to turn into a gas station or plaza parking lot. Pay attention if they followed you. In some locations, such as in the Midwest, there are roads that are many miles long and have very few roads/streets to turn on (and those streets/roads are for those that live there) and do not offer refueling stations. In that case, continue driving until you get to a more populated area.

If you are suspicious of a vehicle and are in a populated area, turn into a location that has some traffic (such as a service road that has fast food restaurants or coffee houses) and watch to see if that vehicle followed. If it did, make another deliberate turn and watch if they continue to follow. The chance of someone turning at the same location you turned is pretty high, even a second turn where you turned is not unbelievable, but a third follow at a turn is highly suspect. At that point, I would look at that as a confirmation that they were following me and would prompt me to initiate a call to the police. I would not stop at that point.

POLICE

If I am driving and not breaking the law (not speeding) and suddenly I see blue lights flashing behind me, I immediately call 911 and ask for confirmation from the dispatch that I am, indeed, being pulled over. I would tell them my name and location, and finally ask if they could confirm that an officer is trying to pull me over. Once confirmed, I will pull over and comply, but if they deny an officer's presence behind me, they would then direct me to where I need to drive so one of their officers could help me out. Key is, I am not going to pull over during darkened hours, if I'm not sure it is truly a police officer trying to pull me over. There are too many stories of people being found dead, or handcuffed to their door handles by criminals who posed as a police officer.

ATMS

When approaching a drive-up ATM, pay attention to the area around the ATM. Pay close attention to shrubbery, or any growth, where someone could hide behind, even if it is a short distance from the ATM. An ATM in Virginia was prone to robberies. As the driver would pull up to the ATM, once they inserted their card and typed in their PIN, the criminal would ambush the driver. The criminal would place their body in the space between the car and the ATM. The drivers didn't want to drive away without their card, so they ended up losing the money they withdrew from the ATM. Despite it showing up in the local news, people still became victims.

When you are approaching, watch for any people loitering around the area, look for any parked vehicles in the area, where occupants are sitting, and if you do not have a good feeling about that ATM, go to a different one. ATMs are everywhere nowadays and it's smarter to go to another ATM than to risk being robbed. When you pull up, pull as close to the ATM as your mirrors would allow. This reduces the chance that someone could/would squeeze in between your vehicle and the ATM.

If a threat were to get the upper hand because they have a weapon aimed at you and they demand you withdraw money, do so. It's safer to give up the money than to risk your life. One key thing to remember is: ATMs have cameras and these cameras record your interaction with the ATM. If a threat is forcing you to withdraw money, mouth the specifics to the camera. Start mouthing the word 'HELP' and follow that up with whatever adjectives you can use to accurately describe the criminal. Once the act is over, you can call the police and inform them what you did, they can then retrieve the video feed from the ATM and lip-read the specifics (if you cannot remember because of the trauma). Warning: when you explain that you mouthed the specifics of the criminal that robbed you, you may be met with a lack of emotion or motivation to pursue the video and have your lips read, in the off chance they could get a description of the criminal.

Note: The above doesn't mean they won't try, it just means the officer(s) may not believe you were that aware enough to provide valid or accurate information, for them to catch the criminal.

If you are at an ATM and you spot someone meandering in the area and you suddenly do not have a good feeling, trust your feeling and press cancel on the ATM. This will stop the transaction and the machine will kick out your card. Then you can depart the area with card in hand. There was a rumor going around for years that if you were in trouble and were at an ATM, you could punch in your PIN backwards (i.e. if your pin was 1234, you would put in 4321) and it would alert the police that you were in trouble. This was/is an urban legend. This is not true and not something you should rely on. Ever!

If you need to walk up to an ATM, the same awareness is needed as you would you use for a drive-up ATM. Look closely at the area before you park and exit your vehicle. If another vehicle is parked and the occupants are not getting out, pull out and go to another ATM. If it seems safe and you walk up to the ATM, then a car pulls up and the driver walks up behind you, watch their actions on the monitor (reflection) or the mirror installed in the ATM. As always, cover the pin-pad when you punch in your PIN, to keep it private.

If the person behind you is fidgety and you do not feel good about it, withdraw your money from the ATM, place it into your pocket and retrieve your vehicle keys. Next, pull out your phone and start talking as if you received a call. This way, if the person was going to try and beg for money, or con you into stopping for whatever reason, you can keep chatting loudly on your phone and walk by this person. If they still try to stop you, immediately begin describing the person to your 'friend' on the phone, and that should prompt the person to stop what they are doing and walk away.

Remember, especially if you are approached by someone trying to beg for money or are acting fidgety around you after you withdraw your money, you NEED to remain aware of your surroundings AND your checklist once you enter your vehicle: GET IN, LOCK THE DOOR, start the car and place into gear, then you can take a breath. Threats/criminals attack when they know you are the most vulnerable (and when they can get away with it). Having an encounter with a stranger that boosts your anxiety is something that can impede clear-thinking, which gives the criminals that edge they want.

Remember: Get in your vehicle, LOCK THE DOOR, start the vehicle and place it into gear. Then worry about your seatbelt and whatever else you need to fiddle with.

GETTING FUEL

If you drive, you eventually need to refuel and there are many things to be aware of when you refuel your vehicle. Think about it, if you are refueling, you cannot just jump in and take off quickly if you were suddenly attacked. But there are more concerns as you refuel your vehicle. The gas station could be a cesspool for criminals of all types and you could become their next victim.

SCAN AREA

Before you pull up to a pump, slowly scan the area for any possible threats in the surrounding area. Pay attention to any cars that are idling off to the side, with or without someone sitting inside of it, and make the determination to get out to refuel once you've deemed it safe. Once you are outside the vehicle, you are at your most vulnerable. This is why choosing a well-lit gas station is a wise idea.

When you stop and get out to refuel, make it a point to lock your doors before you fuel up. There are numerous examples online of customers refueling, standing by the side of their vehicles with one hand on the pump, and a criminal sneaks in from the passenger side and takes a purse, steals a wallet and even steals the vehicle (as the person was refueling). If you lock your doors upon exiting the vehicle, that lessens the chance of allowing a criminal into your vehicle as you pay attention to the fuel pump.

Watch incoming vehicles as they enter and pay close attention to the people in the vehicle(s) and if they are watching you. Recently, there has been a video going around of a man refueling his vehicle. As soon as he stuffed the nozzle into his gas tank and began fueling, a van quickly pulled up alongside. The van stopped and 3-4 men scrambled out and towards the man. The man was quick-witted though, he pulled the nozzle out of his tank and squeezed the lever to shoot fuel towards the threats. The threats quickly scrambled back to their van and departed. Smart move.

Note: No, I am NOT suggesting you do this...but if I was attacked and outside my vehicle refueling, I will use whatever I can to ensure I am not going to become the victim.

Criminals look for specific things on a vehicle to determine if that is worth going after. If you have out-of-state license plates and are refueling, criminals may target you because they know you are not a local. It used to be 'popular' for threats to go after rental cars, because those vehicles had a sticker on the back window (and usually a plate holder over the license plate of the rental company), which was an advertisement for the criminals to hit that vehicle. Today, rental vehicles no longer have identifying stickers on the back windows, but they do have vehicles that have plates from other states.

If you are refueling in a location and your plates are not for that state, be extra mindful of the vehicular traffic around you, especially if they are paying close attention to you. Have an exit plan when you pull up to the pump. If there is a vehicle in front of you, either wait until they leave to refuel (which can give you an easier exit) or leave room between vehicles. I usually have my keys in hand when I refuel, which allows me to have a jabbing device if need-be, to defend myself. Criminals may think that your out of state plates also equate to you passing through the area, which means you wouldn't want to hang out in that location any longer than you have to.

CREDIT CARD SLOT

As I have spoken about previously regarding skimmers and readers, gas stations have been identified as a location where portable skimmers have been installed. These skimmers are located where you would insert your credit card, but look like they are purposely installed. An easy way to check to ensure the card reader is legitimate (until the criminals find a way around this) is to press on the outer frame. If the part of the skimmer that extends further than the rest of the pump moves, report it to the attendant at the station and DO NOT insert your card into that slot.

These attached frames look the part, are authentic-looking and have fooled many people, but inside the outer frame was a chip reader. That chip reader/skimmer was reading the data off of that card and immediately allowing whomever installed the fake frame, full access to your credit card. Most readers today have a security tape-seal on the seam of the device, but even if it doesn't, the card reader is one solid piece. Again, if it moves do not insert your card. It's much safer to go into the station and use your card there, or pay in cash. That will save you a lot of hassle and time in the long run.

FOB USE

When pulling into a gas station or rest area, be extra mindful of vehicles and people around you, especially if you are using a FOB to lock your doors. Technology exists that can capture the frequency of your FOB as you activate it, and if there is someone close by with that technology, they can get into your vehicle. You may think: "They might be able to get in, but what then? They can't drive it away!", which is a somewhat-true thought to have. What the criminal could do, is hunker down in your backseat and wait for you to re-enter the vehicle, then they could ambush you and have the control they need.

Note: The same awareness is needed for your remote garage door opener. It uses a signal to reach the door unit on the inside of the garage. If someone was close by, they could use their device to capture the signal and use that signal in the future. Once they have the frequency, they could open your garage door and access your home while you are away (or worse, while you are sleeping).

FLAT TIRE

There are tactics that occur in waves, which means that there's a time when a tactic is popular and used a lot, and then a time when that tactic is not used much (if at all). One of those tactics is letting the air out of a tire. When the owner of the vehicle arrives and spots a flat tire, they will not think the tire is flat because someone let the air out, they will believe it to be a flat tire due to running over something sharp. They won't be happy about it, but will either call for assistance or change it themselves. If they change it themselves, they will open their tailgate/trunk to retrieve the jack and spare tire, and there is a high probability that their doors are unlocked as well.

As the owner proceeds to break out their gear to change the tire, the criminal(s) can swoop in and either ambush the owner (to rob/assault/whatever them), or could play the role of good Samaritan and offer to help them change their tire. If they opt to act as the good Samaritan, they will get their hands on the lug-wrench, which can then be used as a weapon, but also has succeeded in getting the owner to drop their guard (because they think the criminal is an actual good Samaritan). Once the job is done and the owner shows their gratitude, the criminal could coerce the owner to 'drop them off' at a specified location. From there, things could get quite ugly.

If you walk out of a store (or wherever) and you notice your tire is flat, turn around and go back into the store. This way you can call for assistance, or if you believe there to be some people loitering around the area, or sitting in vehicles around your vehicle, you could ask the store security to escort you to your vehicle, so you can change your tire. It is better to call for assistance and have someone else deal with your tire, than it is to take the chance that those loitering around the area are innocently hanging out...next to your vehicle.

If you actually get a flat tire and have to pull over, there may be some good Samaritans that offer to help you out. Remember, you are not obligated to take their help. Do not assume anything, especially in our society today, because there are people that look for the 'wounded' just to appear as a good Samaritan so they can assault/attack etc. the person(s). Sadly, this is factual information and I am not happy about it, but you have to know how it is. If someone approaches and asks you if you need help, roll your window down enough to call out to them to thank them, and then inform them you have help coming. Do not unlock your doors or roll your windows down further than you have to.

Have defensive objects in your vehicle, but make sure they are legal objects for the state you live in and any state you may visit. Ignorance is not a defense and you cannot cry "I didn't know" or "I don't live in your state, why would I know your laws", because they will smile as they give you your pricey ticket/summons. There are objects, which I have mentioned previously, that you can innocently store within your vehicle. I store chopsticks, my flashlight, a comb and have my keys handy when I'm not driving. There are other items that could be used if I needed them as a last resort, such as my tire gauge or my pen, which I keep close by.

Note: If you happen to break down at night and you are unsure of the area you are in, or you are fearful of stopping (but you are not sure how far the nearest help is), you can call 911 and inform dispatch that you are broken down and need assistance. Many towns/cities/counties have roadside assistance available to help those broken down.

NOTE: Another helpful piece of advice is to keep a can or two of 'fix-a-flat' in your vehicle. I keep 2 cans inside my vehicle for just such occasions, along with my can of wasp spray (just in case a bee or wasp were to get into my vehicle). The can(s) of fix-a-flat can inflate the tire long enough for me to get to a service station (or safer location). Fix-a-flat (or other brand names of the same product) are temporary solutions to get you further, but are not to be used as a final solution.

RENTAL VEHICLES

I have previously mentioned that most, if not all rental companies have removed identifying stickers/license plate borders, but there may be other ways they can visually identify the vehicles. If rentals are obtained close to, or at an airport, there is a good chance the plates are for the state it is rented in. There may be some vehicles that have out-of-state plates, but those are usually the drop-off rentals. When I rent a vehicle, it is from a national organization and the plates are out-of-state every time.

If you are in a rental vehicle with out-of-state plates, know that someone could easily identify you as someone on vacation, on business, or passing through. These are the vehicles targeted by criminals for a couple of reasons:

-If visiting from out of state, there is a chance you have 'extra' vacation money, and if passing through the state, you are not going to delay your trip towards your intended destination.

-If there for business, you are not local and may not know the area. You may also have extra technology (laptop, tablet, etc.) and you are not there for a lengthy amount of time, which means you are less likely to remain once business is concluded.

You would want to avoid having anything that can identify your purpose for being in that state, visible to anyone that can walk by and look in the windows. Leaving identifying objects on the seat or the floorboards could gain the attention of a criminal. It would not take long for that criminal to smash the window and remove any/all objects from the vehicle. This is why you bring valuables into the hotel with you and store them in the hotel safe or the safe located within your room.

I have also mentioned this previously, and will touch on it once more: have defensive options close to where you will be seated. Personally, I carry chopsticks with me when I travel. I place them into the passenger-side sun visor, where I could easily reach them if necessary. I also carry my flashlight, comb, pen, notepad and tire gauge. All of these items serve a purpose, but can also be used if I needed to defend myself against an attacker. All of these things can also reside in my luggage, if I were to fly to a location where I will rent a vehicle, without cause for concern. They break no laws.

Note: If I was worried about bees and/or wasps in whatever location I was flying to, once landed I could easily stop at a hardware or department store to pick up a can or two of wasp/bee spray. A can is relatively inexpensive and can be thrown away prior to dropping off the rental vehicle.

If/when you rent a vehicle, before you leave the parking lot of the rental location, adjust all of your mirrors and get familiar with the options inside the vehicle. Know where the gas tank cover/access is located. Usually, there is a 'gas tank' icon on the dashboard, with an arrow (which looks like a triangle on its side). The triangle/arrow will point either to the left or to the right. Where that arrow points is where the access cover is located. Figure out how to initiate the windshield wipers, windows, headlights, etc. before you depart the lot.

UBER/LYFT/TAXI

There are many items to discuss when talking about safety and awareness, specifically when discussing calling a ride-service, such as UBER, LYFT and/or a taxi company. First thing to embrace is the fact that you won't/don't know the driver that is coming to pick you up. That, in itself, should raise your awareness levels. As time moves forward, I am sure more transportation companies will be created, so this section applies to any/all ride organizations that provide the service up picking up strangers and driving them to their desired destination.

When you call for a ride, through whomever you choose, it is wise to ask the driver a way to identify them when they arrive. Some, if not all applications, now include a picture and name of the driver coming to pick you up. That can give you an immediate clue as to who is picking you up. That's a great security feature that had been implemented. Another great feature in many of these vehicles, is an installed camera, which records the entire cabin of the vehicle. This is good for the driver, but also for the occupants of the vehicle.

When the vehicle arrives at your location for pick-up, initiate your camera on your phone and begin recording. Hold the phone up and approach the vehicle in a wide fashion, making sure you capture the license plate. As you enter the vehicle, capture the driver on your phone and maintain your video recording until you arrive at your destination.

This allows you to maintain a video log of specific events and participants and can be saved on the cloud.

Note: Before I get into any taxi, or transportation vehicle, I roll down the window and shut the door. I then reopen the door from the inside by reaching my hand/arm inside the open window to open the door. This tells me the inside door handle works. This is to make sure a problem doesn't exist when I attempt to exit the vehicle.

Before you enter the vehicle, match the driver up with the photo you received on your phone application. If it doesn't match and you were not notified of the change, get this driver on camera for your own safety and do not get into that vehicle. For taxi cabs, the driver has a displayed license on their front dashboard-area. Match the driver with the picture on the license and capture them on video. You want to make sure you feel safe before you get into the vehicle, because if something were to go wrong while you are inside, you have limited options for freedom.

There are numerous horror stories throughout the previous years concerning the passengers, but also concerning the drivers. There were a couple stories regarding a 'fake' Uber-type vehicle arriving close to closing time of a drinking establishment, who stopped and called out a name. An inebriated young lady took the opportunity to claim it was her, as soon as she realized no one answered to the name being called. That young lady was killed by the driver of that vehicle, which was not from that company. There are horror stories about passengers attacking the drivers also. The criminal story goes both ways.

As much as I would like to tell people to not drink too much because it can warp judgement (when it comes to identifying a threat) and to make sure the driver is actually taking you towards your destination, I cannot because people will do what people do. So, I will say this: TRY to be sober enough to be aware of your surroundings and focus on where the driver is taking you. If you are not paying attention, it would not take too much effort for the driver to 'suddenly' get ambushed at a stoplight. Criminals also work in teams (especially overseas). Know the route you need to go and be watchful/mindful as you head that way.

If you call for an UBER or LYFT, the transportation will be done through that person's vehicle. This is different than with a taxi service, since most taxi vehicles have a plastic partition separating the passengers from the driver. On these vehicles (taxis), I definitely make sure the doors work from the inside before I enter, but if it is just me riding in that type of vehicle, I sit in the front passenger seat. I do this to maintain a level of control, in the event this driver decided to drive me off of the intended route.

If I were in an UBER or LYFT type vehicle, sitting in the back-seat allows me to have the control I need, if the driver were to become dangerous. I have had numerous experiences overseas where the driver acted like they didn't speak English and thought we did not know the area well enough to see the driver take 'extra' turns. Once I got loud and insisted that he drive correctly, his English-understanding skills became better. I knew the directions to our destination, as I have had to take it daily for that week. The driver expected to scam us as vacationers, but he learned quickly that that was a big mistake.

NOTE: If you are a female, or are with females who carry purses/pocketbooks, ensure the purse/pocketbook is clutched in their hand, opposite of any open window. In some locations the route taken could be very populated and it wouldn't take much for someone to run up, reach in and snatch that purse and run into the crowd (and disappear). In some locations the drivers are working with the purse-snatchers, to deliver vacationers to these specific 'hit points' and then claim their innocence as 'just' the driver (while getting their percentage of your money, once the criminals regroup).

The awareness and safety aspects within and around your vehicle is important, because most people gain a false sense of security and comfort when entering their vehicle. The reason for this is because they know that vehicle is their property and they also know that no one has the right to invade their property. It is because of this fact, that when/

if some criminals were to assault/ambush the driver as they enter their vehicle, the owner of the vehicle is frozen in surprise because the brain says: "wait! That's not right!".

Being aware and following the guidance of: Enter the vehicle, lock the door immediately, start the vehicle and place it into gear, can greatly increase your chance of appropriately responding to a surprise attack. You will still be surprised, but within an instant of identifying that a stranger just attempted to open your door, you can take your foot off of the break, apply it to the accelerator and away you go. You have that control, but only if you are prepared for it. Making it your standard operating procedure (SOP) to, again: Get into the vehicle, shut and lock the door, start the vehicle and place it into gear, then deal with anything/everything else, could save your life one day.

It is better to implement that as your SOP and never need it, than to need it but never applied it! Sound familiar: It's better to have it and not need it, than to need it and not have it! I changed it slightly to drive the point home that if you implement this safety and awareness protocol and you ever need it, at least you implemented it and keep control of the situation.

NOTE: I truly hope none of my readers ever need this information.

8

WALK-UP ATM or BANK

Sometimes we do not have the option to use a drive-thru ATM and we need to withdraw cash. Since many convenience stores (and some department stores) now carry ATMs, there are more options for this action. That is a positive thing, because criminals capitalize at walk-up ATMs because of how vulnerable and exposed the person using it is/was. The ATM-availability was varied: some were attached to a bank, some out in the middle of a parking lot and some fully enclosed (some in the middle of parking lots, others attached to a bank). That brought with it its own levels of danger.

ENCLOSED ATM
If you must utilize an ATM that is enclosed, check the area thoroughly before entering the enclosure. Make sure there are no people loitering in the area, no approaching vehicles and no one standing inside the enclosure, doing nothing. Some enclosures have dual ATMs, which makes it a bit more threatening, if someone you don't know is inside the enclosure with you. With the enclosed ATM, there is only one way in and one way out. Not having another way to escape the area increases the anxiety of the action. Some of these ATMs require the user to use their card to gain access to the space, while others did not.

Maintain a visual awareness around you as you use the ATM. Glance around to maintain updated awareness on anyone approaching, vehicles, etc. By doing this, you are giving yourself a timeframe to escape the area/situation, before it becomes dangerous. If you are in an enclosed ATM that requires your bank card for access, and someone attempts to knock on the door to have you let them in, that quickly becomes a sticky, and possibly dangerous situation. With only one exit/entrance, you eventually need to leave that space.

If a stranger were to knock on the glass door, to try and get you to open it, think about it logically: if the person had a bank card, which would be the same card to withdraw money from the ATMs, they would have the needed access into that space. Manners and courtesy mean anyone that needs to use the ATM, would wait until the current user is done and has exited the space, before they entered and conducted their business. It should be obvious that this person wants entry into the enclosure to get to you. There is no other reason for their attempts.

If the person remains at the door, finish your withdrawal but call 911 and inform them of the stranger attempting access to the enclosure. While you are finishing your business with that ATM, a police officer should arrive to handle the situation. It is wise to maintain a grip on your vehicle keys, just in case the person somehow gains access to the enclosure. It is a scary situation and many people have become victims because they did not think the actions through. The person on the outside of the enclosure deliberately caused fear for the people inside the enclosure and held that control firmly. Had the people/person on the inside had this information, chances are the end result would've been different.

ATMs have cameras installed. I mentioned this previously but it is worth mentioning again. If a person were to beat on the exterior of the enclosure, demanding you open the door and let them in, take a good look at them and mouth the specifics to the ATM camera. Be precise in your descriptions to ensure the police can read what you are mouthing, in the event the person runs away as the police arrive. The police may not have a need to pursue the person, because that person never gained entry, but if that person did gain entry and something happened to you, they would have that information on the ATM video.

WALK UP ATM

If needing to use an ATM result in you choosing a walk-up ATM, there are awareness steps needed to reduce your chances of being targeted. Some walk-up ATMs are stand-alone and usually set away from a building or mall. Other walk-up ATMs are inside gas stations, malls, department stores, etc. Regardless where you choose, be mindful of those meandering around the area. Criminals evolve and learn tactics that reduces their chances at getting caught.

One of the ways criminals get away with preying on innocent people at ATMs is the chip reader/skimmer tactic, which I've explained previously (but will touch on again). If the area is 'shady' at best, a location that is better fit for a Halloween-type movie set, the person using the ATM is more likely going to pay more attention to their surrounding area, rather than the ATM itself. This is a perfect location for a chip reader/skimmer to be installed. The solution is the same as described at the fuel pump: try to move the outer 'casing' of the card slot to see if it moves. If it moves, there's a good chance it is a chip reader/skimmer and you should choose another ATM.

You always want to check the area for people loitering for no reason, cars that have occupants in the vicinity, but do not move and repetition of a vehicle (or vehicles) that seem to pass by the area. Even if you feel the ATM is in a safe location (and determined the card insert-location is not a reader/skimmer), you want to stand close enough to the ATM to obstruct any eyes from seeing your PIN. Cover the number pad, make finger motions without touching the actual numbers and pay attention to anyone that gets closer as you type in your PIN. Making finger motions around the keypad masks your actual PIN depressions.

Choose a PIN that is not easily figured out because if a criminal were to get your ATM card, chances are they will attempt a PIN or two. The simple choices are the ones that gives the criminals money from your account. Avoid using 1234 as a PIN. Avoid using your street address, your social security number (any variation), your phone number and avoid using birthdays of your children. Now, you may ask: "How could/would a criminal know the birthdays of my children" and my reply is: "Have you thought about how many criminals are also family"? This scenario exists and a stolen card could cause havoc to your life, especially if/when you find out it was a family member who took and used your card.

Note: Today, with debit cards providing an option that simplifies the need to carry cash, ATM visits are much lower than they were years ago. If your ATM card were to be 'lifted' by a family member, how much time would pass before you caught onto that loss? When would you realize money has been withdrawn from your account? Things to think about.

Some ATMs are doubled up in the same area. This means, some locations have two ATMs side-by-side, which causes people to be very close when they withdraw their money. This could provide a criminal a view of your pin, could allow a criminal to use a chip reader/skimmer on your card as you hold it (without you knowing about it), and could give a criminal the chance to snatch your cash as it is dispensed, leaving you baffled and shocked.

Should you avoid withdrawing money from an ATM that has another next to it? Not necessarily, but you should be cautious. Chances are, if you are using an ATM and there's another next to it, you are probably at gas station/convenience/department store. The thing to understand is, you may not realize the person that steps up next to you to use the ATM, is actually someone who has been standing between the aisles, far enough away to avoid being noticed. The criminal spots you stepping up to the ATM and they make their way over.

If someone attempts to step next to you and you do not feel confident that they are there to withdraw money and not become a threat to you, hit cancel on the keypad, grab your card and step away. If the person was there innocently, they will continue with their transaction(s) and when finished, will walk away. You could easily walk away and peruse the shelves elsewhere in the store and revisit the ATM after a couple of minutes. If the person was a threat/criminal, you have reduced their chances of robbing you, or gaining your PIN information.

Simply by stepping away, walking around the store and returning, you impeded the criminal's chance of succeeding in their mission. There is a chance they would return as you step up to the ATM, but that would be a stupid decision on behalf of the criminal. Smart criminals know they lost their chance the first time as you walked away. Remember, threats want easy targets and don't want to get caught. They know there are cameras around, regardless where you withdraw money, there are cameras around. If they attempted to step to the ATM again, there is a better chance the camera(s) will catch a better glimpse of them, thus putting them at risk of getting nabbed.

ATMs sometimes provide a receipt, even if you do not ask/request one. Once you complete your transaction and after you have counted your cash (always count your cash), remain in front of the ATM until the monitor changes/clears. There are ATMs that will put your balances on the monitor-screen. Stand at the ATM until the screen defaults back to its original 'welcome' screen and your balance is no longer present, but also you want to remain standing there long enough to get the receipt, if one prints. Do not leave your receipt in the ATM and do not crumple it up and toss it into the trash. Put it in your pocket (if the ATM prints it) and bring it home to throw away.

It is worth repeating again that a reverse ATM PIN will not alert the police to your situation at an ATM. This is a myth and is worth repeating. If under duress and do not want the criminal to get your card, punch in your PIN incorrectly multiple times. Usually, if you incorrectly input the wrong PIN three times, the card will not be returned. You would, however, have to call your bank and get a new card after that, but the criminal/threat would not get your card nor your money. I would only do this in a dire situation where I ran out of options.

Again, awareness can help you avoid situations that are dangerous, especially when dealing with money, but you need to be proactive about your awareness levels wherever you go. Knowing your awareness weakens if the location is shady and causes you to spend awareness-energy checking your area constantly, should make you more aware of the ATM itself and a possible chip reader/skimmer. You have to increase your awareness enough to be able to quickly pick up on a dangerous situation and/or dangerous person, who others may ignore.

Worst case scenario, if you are unable to escape a situation, give the criminal the money you withdrew. I know it is your money and you are not going to want to hand it over, but you can make more money. Why risk having the criminal hurt you? Plus, chances are the criminal only wants your money and will run away after you hand it to them. If you don't give them your money, they may injure you (or worse) to get your money anyway, but could also leave with your vehicle and everything inside it.

If you are a good actor/actress and can act frantic and 'sloppy' with your body movements, you may be able to punch in the wrong pin enough times for the machine to eat your card. If you do this, you need to commit to the scene. The criminal is not going to be happy they were not successful, but if you act frantic and upset at the machine eating your card and not being able to get cash to get groceries to feed your 70 hungry kids at home, it could be confusing enough for the criminal that they quickly depart the area (or hand you $20 because they feel bad for you). Each situation is different, but control needs to remain in your hands. If you practice awareness, you can maintain that control.

9

WALKING OUT & ABOUT

What sort of awareness do you need when you are out and about, walking through shops, grabbing a bite to eat, and doing weekly shopping? What are most people doing currently? If you take a moment to look around at the other people who are out in public doing their running around, what you will notice is: rare eye contact with others, focus deeply invested into phones, lack of physical awareness, and little safety and personal awareness. There are too many reports (you can find online) of people walking onto railroad tracks and getting hit by a train, walk into and fall in water fountains in the mall because focus was on phone, and people getting hit by cars/trucks/buses because they were busy on their phone.

PAY ATTENTION TO SURROUNDINGS
You may have noticed by now that I've hammered the idea of paying attention wherever you go, into the theme of each chapter. Sadly, if I didn't hammer that thought into each reader, it places you at risk for a surprise ambush or attack. The internet is full of reports that somehow do not make the mainstream media outlets. Technology seems to have engulfed society and personal safety has taken a back seat. This reality is what will create too many victims, but I am here to tell you that there are solutions and this book contains them.

There is a 'game' I teach to my students, used/practiced to increase identification specifics. The following can be used to increase your ability to absorb details that could become very important if you are ever in a life-threatening situation. This 'game' also increases your chances at avoiding threatening situations, because it is all about awareness and paying attention to the details. You can fine tune your skills each time you go to a store, restaurant, mall, park, wherever. Main point here is: you will have accuracy on your side and that matters.

GAME

When you go into a store (or go to a park) or to a location where other people will be, do the following:

-Enter the store/park (wherever)

-Pick out a person visually

-Look at that person for 5 seconds

-Turn and walk the other way

-Try to name everything you can remember about that person

This drill/practice works well if you have someone else with you who can play along. This way, once you turn and walk away, you each try and state as many facts as you can about that person. Then, turn around and subtly find that person and see how many 'facts' you got right. If you are with someone else, make it competitive with a reward for the one who has the most facts correctly identified. You can conduct this game as you shop, also.

The goal to this drill/practice is to work your way up to memorizing as many accurate facts as you can, up to 3 people. I have found that trying to remember anything over 3 people could mix-and-match 'facts' between the people, thus reducing accuracy considerably. Accuracy is important, especially if your life is at risk.

Example: You are practicing your memorization at a store using a person who was standing at the front of the store looking around. You depart the area and go down an aisle as you suddenly hear gunshots at the front of the store. You whip down another aisle to go towards an emergency exit when you spot the person you noticed at the front of the store, as he waves a pistol in the air and screams loudly. You escape the area and call 911. You are able to provide accurate details about the threat in the store, which can give police a much better chance at catching the criminal.

How accurate do you think the people are at the front of the store, who are quickly surprised at the actions of this threat, when the police arrive? What do you think they would pay attention to the most? The gun? The screaming? The sweatshirt the criminal wore? When traumatic events occur, people tend to go into a tunnel-vision mindset where they focus on something minute as they try to make sense of the situation. Most will have survival as their main thought/priority and not really 'see' the criminal/threat.

Which do you think is a better description scenario:

1-Police question the people at the front of the store and the consensus was: it was a male with a big gun.

OR

2-The threat was a male, approximately 6 feet tall (using my own height as a reference when I walked into the store), he was right-handed (because I noticed his watch was on his left wrist), he was wearing a dark hooded sweatshirt, navy blue or black, he had blonde hair, wore glasses, goatee facial hair, blue jeans with rips at the knees and white Adidas sneakers with a red, clay stain around the soles.

Obviously the second description would be more helpful for the police to properly identify the threat, correct? By knowing the descriptions accurately, you are also able to avoid running straight into this threat, if he were to be outside running away from the scene. Just by knowing the specifics, you can quickly act to better save yourself. Otherwise, you could run into this threat, which has occurred to people in the past. The criminal runs into the break room where staff were hiding and the staff pulled him down and away from the door, while informing him there was a threat in the store. They learned quickly that their efforts weren't as good as it should have been.

By improving your ability to identify specifics, you will be able get quick 'snapshots' of the people around you, wherever you go. How does this help you? If someone were to follow you, you could pick up on it sooner and make your defensive plan. As you are out and about, don't just pay attention to what is in front of you, look around more and take in your surroundings. You will be amazed at what you will see.

SUBCONSCIOUS

Your subconscious is a wonderful thing...if you pay attention to what it tells you. Example: Have you ever gone into a location and the hairs on your neck go up? Your nerves tingle? You feel as though something is 'off'? That is your subconsciousness trying to tell you that something is wrong and that something is in that location. Deep inside you, you have an early warning system that could keep you much safer, if you paid attention to it. It may not be dangerous to you, but your subconscious is identifying something that you would consider to be 'off'.

You get to make the decision to acknowledge that feeling/warning, or not. If you recall correctly, those who survive the Boston bombings, who were close enough to see the two males drop their backpacks and run off, had a bad feeling about the situation. Then the backpacks blew up. Some of these people who had the bad feeling only spotted the backpacks and never saw the males running off. Had they identified that feeling and egressed quickly from the area, they wouldn't have been directly impacted by those bombs. If they had acknowledged the warnings and screamed about the situation as they ran away, it could have saved some lives.

Not all tingles or subconscious warnings are threatening, it could be someone staring oddly, but not at you, but your senses may pick up on it. Now, if you are tingling because your subconscious is warning you, you have a decision to make:

-Should I stay and get my coffee

-Should I leave and find another coffee shop

What you decide is what you decide, but know that, again, there are many articles online from reputable sources that describe the situations that people thought where threatening, but they didn't leave and succumbed to an explosive device or threat(s). Lots of articles exist on this subject. In some occurrences, the surviving witnesses stated they watched the vehicle screech to a halt in a parking spot next to the eatery, watched the driver rush out of the vehicle and sprint away and then the car blew up. Shrapnel spread outwards quickly and impacted many people, all who witnessed this action, but didn't act on what they witnessed.

If I go into a location and the hairs on my neck go up, I immediately look around the area. I make eye contact with anyone that is watching me and I continue scanning the area until I identify what may be off. If I cannot identify anything, I will leave the area and go to another store. I consider my subconscious an early warning system, one that could save me from something I consciously didn't catch onto at the moment. Remember, criminals evolve and some criminals do not have a desired result, aside from causing mass trauma. That is a dangerous evolution.

IF FOLLOWED (while on foot)

While you are out and about, if you feel you are being followed, immediately enter the closest store. Once you enter the store, immediately find a location you can step behind and peer outwards. You want to see if that person is going to follow you into that store, or if that person walks on by. If the person walks by the store, did they look into the store? Did they glance through the windows as they passed by? These are tell-tale signs that they may have been following you. Body language provides a lot of information, if you pay attention.

Once inside the store, immediately identify exits, offices, break rooms, warehouse and exit signs. You may not need them, but if you do suddenly need an exit strategy, by identifying an exit as you enter the store, you are well ahead of everyone else in that location when things begin to happen. Since you are inside the store, look around, plan on spending a couple of minutes meandering around in the store, while you glance at the entrance. If you feel as though the situation has cleared, prepare to depart the store.

As you exit the store, take a step outside and stop. You stop so you can quickly glance around the surrounding area, to ensure the area is safe. If you identified someone following you, you retain the information you memorized. This is helpful to, once again, identify that same person if they step out from an unknown location and begin to follow you again. If you cannot spot that person, step out and proceed towards wherever you planned on going. As you progress, make it a point to glance around now and again.

NOTE: Another helpful technique is to turn and face the windows of a store, as if you were window shopping. The window provides a reflection of whatever is around you and could quickly help identify someone who is paying attention to you, but doesn't think you can see them.

Go to the store you planned on visiting and before you enter, take a look around to see if you can spot that person who you identified earlier. If so, act normal and enter the store. As you enter, identify your exits quickly, but find a location that can provide you concealment from on-coming pedestrians. Pay attention to the people that pass by and again, see if the person that was following you comes into view. If so, that is an indicator that they are, in fact, following you. Now you need to decide what your next action is going to be.

As you exit the store, do the same action you completed at the previous store: step outside and stop. Look around and try to identify the person that you spotted earlier. If you spot that person, again, you need to decide what your next action is going to be. If someone is following you, you may be safer to get to your vehicle and quickly leave the area, or you may want to call a friend and ask them to come to your location to help you out. The main point to this scenario is to keep you safe and not this person's next victim.

If you don't spot them, but deep down you still feel like you are being followed, as you glance around your area, you are absorbing the specifics of those in that area. Colors are quickly identified and some ages, such as: elderly couples and teenagers wearing bright clothing. The goal is to identify if you are still being followed and another way to check your area without looking around, is to use your phone. Your phone can be a great asset in situations such as this.

As you walk down the sidewalk, take out your phone, initiate the camera and tap the option to turn the camera onto you (selfie mode). This way, as you bring the camera up to your face, you are now seeing you...but you can also see what or who is behind you. You could easily step forward while holding the phone high up (as if you are trying to take a selfie) and the entire time you can see who is behind you. If you spot the person, you could initiate your camera into video mode and record the person. Now, you would not only have the mental specifics of the person who is following you, but you also catch them on video. This gives you a file which you can share with the police.

DEFENSIVE TOOLS

If you find yourself in a situation where you are being followed and you enter a store, not only are you quick to identify exit options, but you should also be identifying possible defensive tools. Remember, it doesn't have to be a gun or knife to use as a defensive tool. You can find a defensive tool in any location you enter. As an example:

If I were to identify that I was being followed, I could quickly enter the closest store and it happens to be a store where females can buy bras. I could easily grab a bra off of a rack to sling at a threat entering the store. I could use a hanger as a projectile and/or a handheld device. I could use most anything found on the counters of the store. It doesn't matter the store, if I can throw it or use it against an attacker, it becomes my go-to device for that situation. I am not concerned about breaking it when my survival is at stake.

Sure, it would be convenient to have items such as a rake, shovel, dowel, spade, etc. at my disposal, but you have to embrace the fact that anything and everything is a possible defensive device when your life depends on it. Do not be concerned with "what happens if it breaks" or "I don't want to get in trouble for grabbing a (insert item here)". My main concern is survival and escape and if I can help others along the way, then that is a bonus. What I am not concerned with is if I break the item.

ASK SECURITY

If you enter a store because you feel you are being followed, even if you cannot confirm the following, ask a security guard at that store to escort you to your vehicle. If the store doesn't have its own security guard, ask them to contact the contractor that patrols the area. Some plazas have a security contractor that patrols the storefronts, but doesn't go into the store(s) unless they have to.

In locations that do not have an on-site security guard currently patrolling, and they do not have one in the store, you could ask if one of the employees would be willing to escort you to your vehicle. Having someone else with you can boost your courage and make you feel safer in your pursuit to get away from the area. If someone is nice enough to escort you safely to your vehicle, you may want to repay that favor by driving slowly next to that person as they go back to their store.

As much as I would like to say: "If the store employee was nice enough to escort you to your vehicle when you were concerned about your personal safety, you should offer them a ride back to the store", I cannot recommend that. Why? Do you know this person? So, again, it comes down to awareness and personal decisions. Would you be safe if you had that stranger enter your vehicle so you could bring them back to the store? You do not know that person and if you don't know that person, even though you are a caring, giving person who appreciates the effort, you still need to think about your personal safety. One mistake is all it takes and you cannot come back from some mistakes.

When you are on foot, you are slower to get places when compared to traveling in your vehicle. This fact is the reason why you should be more aware of your surroundings and finite your ability to retain specifics. Since you go outside your home to shop for groceries, that is a perfect place for you to practice memorizing specifics about people. Remember, the goal is to be highly accurate about specifics of the people around you, up to 3 people. Don't rush progress, playing the identification game can take time and effort, and for some people it could take months to fine-tune the memorization of one person. Do not rush it, let it advance naturally.

If you feel you are being followed, identify a store you can step into to verify if that person is following you. Find a concealment location where you can still see the door, but always check for an exit first. Always have an exit strategy wherever you go. As you are glancing towards the entrance for confirmation of the person following you, identify what you have close by to use as a defensive tool. If it can be picked up, held and/or tossed at a threat, it is a defensive tool and most things qualify.

As kind hearted as you might be, if you ask a stranger to escort you to your vehicle because you feel someone may be following you, you still do not know that stranger personally, so avoid offering them access into your vehicle. You can always tell them you will follow them back to the store in your vehicle, but since you don't know them, you wouldn't let a stranger into your vehicle. If there are no security guards in the store or who patrol the plaza, ask a store employee if they could contact the security guard contractor, and ask them if they would escort you to your vehicle. If no guards, you could always contact 911 and ask the police to assist.

10

VISITING STORES

This chapter is specifically designed to interweave information from other chapters, to better deliver how interconnected these awareness techniques are and their importance to your safety. If you have a family, including small children, awareness should be a priority in your lives, especially today. It doesn't take much time, effort, or money to increase your safety and awareness throughout your daily living. I can tell you this, if you do not apply awareness into your lives and something were to happen to you, you will forever regret not having this information.

NOTE: It is better to have the information and never need it, than to need it but not have it.

PARKING

When visiting a store, for whatever reason, you may not expect to be inside that store very long initially. What I mean by this is, there are times we go into a store (or mall) to pursue an item or two, only to exit hours later. At the time of exiting the store, the sun could have set and the surrounding area quite dark. This is why it is important to park wisely as you arrive and think about the 'what ifs' that exist.

If possible, park close to the store you intend on visiting. This allows you a shorter distance to walk if the weather were to turn bad and a shorter distance to carry your items/bags. Parking closer to the store is a benefit, but do not sacrifice close for illumination. Park close to, or underneath the lights in the parking lot. This way, if the sun happens to set while you are inside the store, you'll have some level of illumination over and around your vehicle when you exit. Overhead illumination allows for quickly identification of shadows around your vehicle, if a threat were to crouch down next to your vehicle, prepared to ambush you.

Be mindful when you park and identify landmarks in the vicinity to better locate where you parked when you exit. Those of us with bad memories tend to do this everywhere we go, to better find our vehicles within the larger parking lots. Know that it is easy to confuse landmarks if you happen to visit numerous stores within a day. An option is to take pictures of the areas, or drop a pin on the map in your phone, to better locate your vehicle.

Since threats are opportunists, it is important to be extra mindful as you approach your vehicle, especially if you have small children in tow. You would not have a quick egress opportunity if you have small children in hand. To ensure their safety, along with your own, it is important to have a plan as you approach your vehicle. As mentioned previously, I approach my vehicle from the opposite side of the lane, to clearly see underneath the vehicles, to identify anyone possibly kneeling/crouching down in preparation to attack.

You are also vulnerable as you place your purchases into your vehicle. This is another chance for a criminal/threat to attack. The criminal wants the element of surprise because they know they can control the situation. If you are prepared (with a plan and training) and a threat were to attempt an ambush, your action could beat the threat's reaction, thus giving you the control. Keep your children close and involve them in your training, that way they respond to your orders and remain away from the threat(s).

FOLLOWED IN THE STORE

If you feel you are being followed inside the store, make it a point to change locations within the store to verify your suspicions. As you move from area to area, if that person continues to follow you, you solidify your suspicions and can initiate your action plan. Meander your way towards an employee and get close enough to speak low, to not tip off the stalker that you know they are following you. Inform the employee of the situation and ask him/her to call their manager over to their location.

Once the manager arrives, inform them of the situation and ask them to have their security look at their monitors where the security cameras are, to verify the suspicion that you are being followed. Using the camera system, they can easily gain footage of the stalker and possible close-up-stills from the video. Once confirmed, the manager could call the police and have them arrive at the store to question the person. Since that person hasn't broken the law, they may ask that person to leave. The manager could also ask that person to leave, but that now leaves you still needing to safely get to your vehicle.

If you cannot identify an employee or manager for some reason, make sure you have identified the exits within the store, in case you need a quick egress from the area. As you move through the store, identify the objects you could use as a defensive tool. This will obviously change as you change locations within the store. Avoid going into a bathroom while you are in a store (if you are being followed), because bathrooms do not have another exit apart from the entrance.

Have your phone in hand as you navigate through the store and if the stalker continues to follow you throughout the store, turn on your camera, place it on video and capture that person. At this point you are now in a confrontation and it's wise to gain as much attention to your situation as possible. This gives you witnesses and hopefully gains the attention of staff and management, who could provide assistance. Taking a video also provides you with a file that you can provide the police, if necessary. Your phone can also be used as a defensive tool, if needed.

Remember, during traumatic situations many people get tunnel vision and the specifics suffer. Play your 'specifics' game (identification) wherever you go, to keep your skills of identification strong. Maintain eye contact towards others and watch body language. If someone is up to something they know to be wrong, their body language will show you. Upon making eye contact, if the person looking back gets 'big eyes' realizing you can see them, that will tell you something. If they suddenly stiffen, turn and flee, that is another indicator.

There are certain body actions that give away certain details. For example: Someone who is not confident in carrying a firearm, when eye contact is made, will get big eyes, may turn a side away from you (indicating that is their carry side), and may tap their side that has their gun, because they are not confident enough to be comfortable with their carry. Someone running across the street and holding their side indicates they don't want something to fall out of their pocket (or holster). Someone walking while holding one arm to their side is an indicator that they are trying to keep something concealed as they move along.

Eye contact is something that many do not embrace any longer, which is strange to me. Nowadays, if you make eye contact with someone, the other person has a tendency to look away or to look down at the floor. Pay attention to the body language and keep your attention upwards, rather than in your phone.

BIG BOX STORES

If you are shopping in a big box store and something were to occur, know your exit strategy where you are located. Escape may be difficult in the big box stores, because most are big warehouse-type buildings with shelving and pallets stacked to the ceiling/roof. You have to embrace the fact that you may not be close enough to an exit to escape. This is why we have Plan A, B and C. In these stores, if something were to occur, I am going to climb up the shelving and find a cover location up high.

Threats/criminals that enter businesses are doing so to rob them of their money, or to cause maximum damage to those inside. Threats want easy targets and if you climb the shelving there is a great chance the threat(s) will not pursue you. You would not be an easy target and if you can climb fast enough, the threats many not know you are up there. Being high allows you the luxury of the high ground, where you can remain hidden and call 911. The high point advantage gives you a birds-eye view of the action below, which also allows you to provide real-time updates to the police.

If you are unable to climb up the shelving, you could hide behind the pallets on the floor-level merchandise. Again, these threats/criminals want easy targets and are not necessarily going to hunt around and search behind objects, just to get more victims. Behind the pallets of merchandise on the floor is probably the only location where the elderly would be able to hide, same for children. Rather than spend more time attempting to get people up, you can concentrate on finding a lower concealment location, where you can keep yourself and your children safe and away from the action.

ZIP-TIES

Carry a zip-tie with you, if you are able. I carry a small zip-tie in my pocket for emergency purpose. Mostly, I keep it for my firearm, but I also keep it for the hydraulic arms on doors within the stores. Office and breakroom doors usually have a hydraulic closer attached. This allows the door to slowly open or close. Just by using my zip-tie around those arms, a threat would be unable to enter that space. If you cannot carry a zip-tie on your person, you could do the same thing around the hydraulic arms with a belt, or a purse strap. The main goal is to stop the hydraulic arms from uncrossing, which allows it to open the door. This is used when you are stuck in a dead-end location and there is an active threat-situation occurring on the other side of that door.

OFFICE/BREAKROOM

Most stores have at least one office and a breakroom. If your only egress option includes those locations, you have to be prepared, mentally and physically, to defend yourself. If you cannot escape and cannot hide (because the threat is trying to break into the room you are in), then you must be prepared to fight for your life. First thing to do is try to secure the door from the threat, and if you do not have a zip-tie, a belt could hold the hydraulic arms closed. If you don't have a belt or purse strap, then try and find something to block the door from opening.

As you prepare for the oncoming attack, call 911 and place them on speaker (if the threats already know you are inside that space). Provide 911 with every bit of information you can, because what you describe is what the police will go off of when they arrive. Try to provide: number of threats, what they look like (what they are dressed in, facial hair, tattoos) and what weapons they have (guns, knives, bats, chains). Then give your location within the store and the location of the threats. As you do this, pursue finding a defensive tool.

If it is a breakroom, there are objects inside the room that could provide defense: fire extinguisher (pull pin and blast CO2 in their faces or hit the threat with the extinguisher), microwave oven, eating utensils, napkin holder, chairs, etc. Be prepared to swing something or throw something at the threat, if they are able to breach the entrance door. There are no rules to survival other than to survive. If the threat breaches that entry point, be prepared to fight for your survival.

Throwing an object into the face of a threat will cause that threat to turn their head and try to protect their face/head. It's a natural brain response and everyone has that response. Use that knowledge to throw something at the face of the threat, to cause them to flinch for a moment as you close the distance between you and the threat, to further defend yourself. If you don't and this threat has been shooting up the store before getting to your location, the chance that the threat is going to let you survive is slim. Most threats go into their actions knowing if the police show up, they are either going to give up and go to jail or get shot dead, and many have already decided they are not going to get caught alive.

If you must defend yourself, you must commit to that defensive action. Tossing a napkin dispenser at the threat and remain in place is not going to bode well for your safety. Be prepared to follow up one thing with another, and remain active until you escape or the threat is neutralized. Pulling the pin on the extinguisher (very important to activate the spray of CO_2) allows you to blast the threat in their face as you race towards them. The threat will cover up to avoid getting a face-full of CO_2, which allows you to the use the extinguisher as a blunt tool, to neutralize the threat.

AGAIN, the goal is to survive.

Do not rationalize the situation and humanize the threat. If you do so, the threat has the control over your situation. The threat knowingly went into this location and harmed innocent people. The threat is going to do the same to you, if they gain access to your location. Given the chance, the threat is going to do to you what they did to those outside the room you are located. Commit to the fact that you may need to be violent to survive the encounter and that doesn't make you a bad person. It makes you a survivor. Keep in mind, if you must defend yourself in a violent manner to survive, pursue counseling once the event is over, to help you mentally. It is important that you sort through the emotions connected with whatever actions you needed to pursue, to survive the encounter.

If/when the police arrive and you are still located on the inside of the room, do not open the door until 911 verifies the officer on the other side. Ask the 911 dispatch officer to give you the name and badge number (first and last name) of the officer on the other side of the door. Once you have that information, ask the officer to give you their name and badge number. If the information matches, then you know for certain it is the officer on the other side of the door. If they answer incorrectly, you know it was a ruse to get you to open the door.

If you are inside the room and the threat is trying to gain access, but unsuccessful, as they continue to try to gain entry, work through possible scenarios in your brain on how things can play out. Identify the objects you intend to throw. Look at the microwave you are going to hurl at the threat. Point at the table you are going to push at the threat. Run through the scenarios and ensure each scenario ends with you being victorious. Try and identify possible failure points to each scenario so you can come up with a solution that eradicates that possibility of failure.

If you must get physical, it is important to understand each person has pain receptors and your goal is to find which spot is going to get you to freedom. Whatever you can grab, twist, pull, jab and/or scrape, that is your mission. If you are too close where movement is limited, you could use your phone to slam against the threat's nose (blurring the eyes), or behind the ear, under the jaw, into the throat. You could stick your thumb into their eye, as far as you can get into their skull, to force the threat to break contact. If you can only grab a hold of an ear, grab that ear and yank down with as much force as you have to, to force the threat to release you so you can escape.

The overall mission of defense is to survive and escape. I do not advocate violence against another, but do advocate for appropriate defensive measures to survive a deadly encounter. Know this: you should only apply the appropriate level of violence needed until the threat is neutralized and nothing further. If the threat lets you go and you can escape, you cannot continue to battle or harm the attacker, because they are no longer a threat. Your mission is to escape from the dangerous situation, anything above the action that provides escape, could be considered excessive and you could go to jail for that.

IF YOU CARRY A GUN

This is not a firearm book, so this is for those who do carry and haven't read my book on defensive shooting. Find a reputable instructor and take classes. Learn from everyone that teaches you. Practice excessively and practice at home (dry fire, no ammo). You own every bullet that comes out of that gun and ignorance is not a defense. If you pull your firearm, you are the person with the firearm and those nearby may think you are the threat. If you have not thought of this fact prior to reading this, then you need to attend classes and need to train with those who have the knowledge, skills and experience to teach you well!

Police do not know you. If you have to use your gun, the police are showing up to a shooting location, which means they could mistake you for that shooter. Be wise on how you approach this situation.

HIDING SPOTS

Always try to identify locations within the store that you could use as a hiding location. This does not include the bathrooms. If you are in a department store, you could use any opportunity to hide from a threat. A rack of clothing may provide an empty center location, where you could remain without being seen or heard. Anything that you could identify as a viable location to fit in and hide away from a chaotic situation, is game. This is why I have mentioned climbing the shelves at the big box stores and/or hiding behind the merchandise on the floor-level pallets.

You are only limited by your imagination when it comes to your safety and being aware opens your eyes to opportunities. These opportunities exist and hopefully you'll never need to use them, but if you ever do, you now have the tools available to embrace that as an option. You have a decision to make: grow your awareness and be prepared if a bad situation were to present itself, or be surprised and leave your existence up to fate.

The choice is yours. I hope you choose to invest in yourself and your family.